The Smart Guide to

Access

2000

Further Skills

A Progressive Course

for More Experienced Users

Also available from Continuum:

Morris: *The Smart Guide to Word 2000 Basic Skills*
Morris: *The Smart Guide to Word 2000 Further Skills*
Muir: *The Smart Guide To Windows 2000 Professional*
Weale: *The Smart Guide to Excel 2000 Basic Skills*
Weale: *The Smart Guide to Excel 2000 Further Skills*
Coles and Rowley: *Access 97 Basic Skills*
Coles and Rowley: *Access 97 Further Skills*

The Smart Guide to

Access 2000

Further Skills

**A Progressive Course
for More Experienced Users**

Nat McBride

CONTINUUM

London · New York

Continuum
The Tower Building, 11 York Road, London SE1 7NX
370 Lexington Avenue, New York, NY 10017-6550

First published 2001

© Continuum International Publishing Group, 2001

British Library Cataloguing-in-Publication Data
A catalogue record for this book is available from the British Library

ISBN: 0-8264-5648-0

Typeset by PK and Elle McBride, Southampton
Printed and bound in Great Britain by Creative Print Design, Wales

Contents

About this book

About Access 2000

Access is the industry-standard database management system for Windows, combining the power to handle the most demanding data processing tasks with an easy to use graphical interface. Professional on-screen forms and report printouts are easily designed using a range of colours and fonts, and further sophistication can be added using macros to perform tasks such as non-standard data validation.

Access is one of Microsoft Office 2000 applications and as such can interface with the other applications, such as Word and Excel. Access will also import data in a variety of formats so existing databases may easily be upgraded.

Aims

Although this book is aimed at students on a wide variety of business studies and other courses, it is suitable for anyone who needs to learn about databases and their application through the use of Microsoft Access. The book assumes no prior experience of other database packages. While the theme of this book is oriented towards business studies students, it will be equally applicable to students on a variety of further and higher education courses as well as to the independent learner.

Structure

This book introduces the reader to the basics of databases and database design through a series of application-oriented tasks. The basics are then developed further through basing the tasks on the operations of one organisation, Chelmer Leisure and Recreation Centre. A series of self-contained but interrelated units takes the reader through the design of a database for Chelmer Leisure and Recreation Centre. Each unit comprises a series of tasks. As each new function is introduced, the book explains both why the function is useful and how to use it.

The approach does not assume any previous knowledge of databases or the Windows environment. However, readers who are familiar with Windows (whether 95, 98, Me, NT or 2000) and Microsoft Office products such as Word, Excel, PowerPoint and previous versions of Access, will find their road into Access 2000 to be much more intuitive than those who are not familiar with these related products. Equally, readers who have some familiarity with other database products may find the database concepts introduced in this book easier to grasp.

The approach is designed not only to introduce readers to Access but also to offer them a conceptual framework for the use and design of databases that will encourage the development of skills transferable to other applications.

The units will give readers the confidence to perform and understand the central tasks concerned with database design, creation and maintenance:

❑ designing and defining a database

❑ designing and using queries, screen forms and printed reports

❑ using multiple tables

❑ importing and exporting data

❑ creating and using macros.

Getting started

Readers who have not used a Windows program before should first read through Quick Reference 1, *Basic Windows operations*, which summarises the key features of the Windows environment, and then turn to Unit 1, *An overview of Access*.

Each unit opens with a summary of its objectives and the skills to be gained, and is divided into a number of activities. Each activity includes instructions on how to perform operations, and tasks that ask you to perform those operations. You will also find integrative exercises that offer you the opportunity to practise your newly acquired skills. These exercises have minimal instructions.

This book may be used as a basis for independent study or for class activities. In either instance it is important to:

❑ work methodically through the exercises in the order they are presented

❑ take time for rest and reflection and break learning into manageable sessions

❑ think about what you are doing

❑ expect to make mistakes; think about the consequences of any mistakes and learn from them

❑ use the integrative exercises to test your understanding of the earlier concepts and exercises.

A note to lecturers and students

The learning material requires little, if any, input by lecturers, and can therefore be used in programmes based on independent learning. Students and independent learners learn by practising the commands and techniques.

The text is selective and does not deal with all of the features in detail. However, it does take students step-by-step to a level at which they can happily use the help provided by the Office Assistant to master further features.

Lecturers' disk

A 3 *1/2"* disk is available (free of charge to lecturers recommending the book as a course text) containing files of data for completing the exercises, plus the reports and queries produced via the tasks in the text. It can be used as a shortcut to avoid lengthy keying in of data and as a means of checking the outcomes of the tasks. The disk, or selected files from it, can be made available to students to allow them to check their own work.

Conventions

The following conventions have been adopted to distinguish between the various objects on the screen:

❑ Dialog box names, menu items and commands are shown as **File–Exit**, which means choose the **File** menu and select the **Exit** option from that menu.

❑ Buttons, tabs and icons are shown in bold, e.g. **Design**

❑ Keys on the keyboard are shown in underlined italics e.g. _Ctrl_

❑ Filenames, names of databases, fields, tables, forms, queries, reports and other items created by the user are shown in italics, e.g. *Membership*

❑ Text that you type in is shown in bold italics e.g. ***Aerobics.***

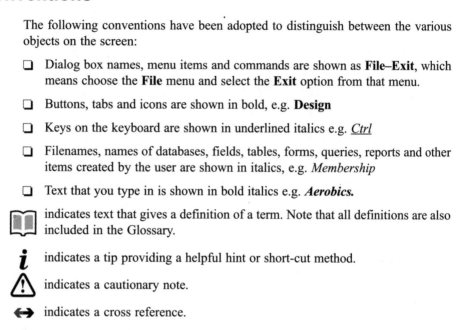 indicates text that gives a definition of a term. Note that all definitions are also included in the Glossary.

indicates a tip providing a helpful hint or short-cut method.

indicates a cautionary note.

indicates a cross reference.

An overview of Access

All students, except those who have some experience of Access, should read this module. *Quick reference 2* (page 236) reviews the basic features of Windows for the benefit of inexperienced users or as a ready reference. It also introduces mouse techniques and gives a summary of the terminology used throughout these units.

A tour of the Access window and the Database window

It is worthwhile studying the two basic windows in Access - the Access window and the Database window – for a few moments before trying to use the program. This section can be used as a ready reference and returned to later as necessary.

The Access window

When you first start Access, the Access window shown in Figure 1.1 is displayed.

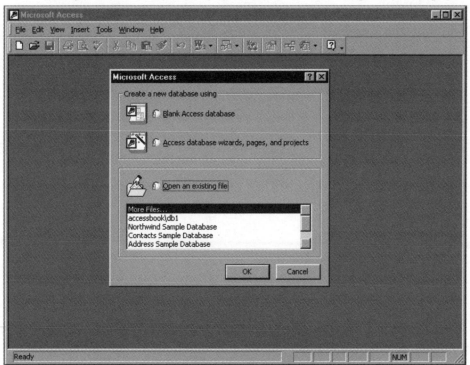

Figure 1.1

When this window first opens, you will see the Access dialog box, from where you can create a new database or open an existing one. We will return to this later. First, let's have a look at the other features of this window.

The window has the following components:

Component	Description
Title bar	Shows that you are in Microsoft Access
Access control menu (top left hand corner)	You can click on the Access icon, to open a menu commands for sizing and moving the **Access** window, and for closing Access
Access menu bar	Shows the pull-down menus
Toolbar	Shows the standard set of buttons
Status bar (bottom of the screen)	Shows the status of the system, and whether switches such as NUM for Number Lock are on or off

The Database window

Once you have opened a database, a window like the one in Figure 1.2 is displayed. This window allows you to access any *object* in the database by opening one of the sets of objects and selecting from there. The objects are automatically organised by type (table, query, form, report, etc.), and you can set up your own *groups* of objects. Initially the **Table** set is selected and the window displays all tables in the database.

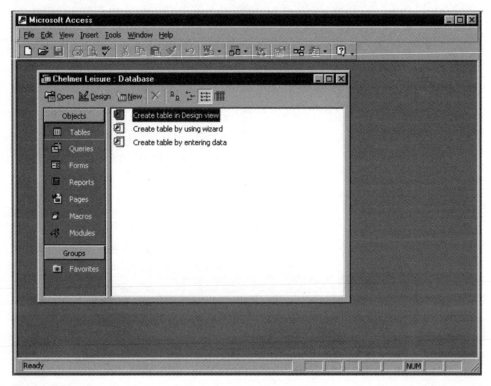

Figure 1.2

The Database window has the following components:

Component	Description
Title bar	Shows the name of the current database
Toolbar	Shows the buttons for working with objects. The buttons vary depending on the type of objects that are being displayed. For example, when looking at table objects, there are toolbar options for opening or designing existing tables, or for creating a new one. The four buttons on the right set the display style, and are always present. All toolbar choices have equivalent menu selections.

Help and the Office Assistant

When you start using Access for the first time the Office Assistant will appear to guide you. This is an animated graphic, with accompanying sounds.

To show or hide the Office Assistant, select the approriate option on the Help menu.

When you have a question about how to do something you can ask the Office Assistant, for example, 'How do I create a query?'

1   If the **What would you like to do** box is not visible, click on the Assistant image to open it.

2   Type in your question – using natural language, e.g. 'how do I print a report?'

3   Click on the **Search** button.

4   The Assistant will offer several possible answers. Click on one to read the Help page.

You can choose the appearance of the Assistant, and as this is shared by rest of the Office suite, it will be a familiar guide when you are working with other applications. To change it, right-click on the Assistant and select **Choose Assistant...** Be prepared to install new images from the Office CD-ROM.

You can get into the Help system directly, without using the Assistant. If you want to do this, turn the Assistant off in the Options panel. To access the Help system then, use any of these methods:

❑   Pull down the **Help** menu and select **Microsoft Access Help**.

❑   Press the function key _F1_.

❑   Click on the **Office Assistant** button 🔲.

Click on a blue phrase for a definition

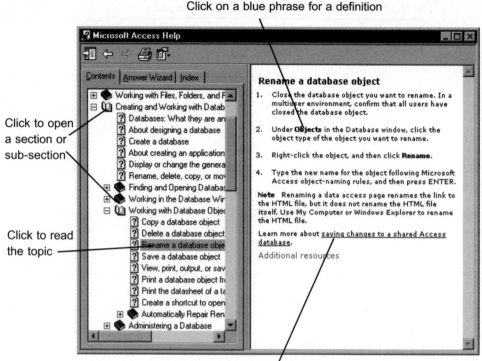

Click to open
a section or
sub-section

Click to read
the topic

Figure 1.3   Click on an underlined phrase to read the linked topic

These all take you to the Access Help panel (Figure 1.3). Here you can can browse through the Contents or Index, or ask a question through the Answer Wizard.

In the Contents section you may select any of the topics to find information about that topic. The Answer Wizard section enables you to type in a question, as you can through the Office Assistant. In the Index section you may type in a word that is matched by the index about which you can display information.

Other sources of Help

❑ Pull down the **Help** menu and select **What's this?** or press _Shift_+_F1_. The pointer will then have a question mark after it ▷**?**. Point and click on any object to read a brief description of it. When you click a second time, the pop-up description box will close and the pointer revert to normal.

❑ Most dialog boxes have a ? Help button on the title bar. Click on this to activate the **What's this?** pointer, then click on the item in the dialog box to find out what it does.

What is an Access database?

Access is a database management system and provides a means of storing and managing data or information. Microsoft refers to Access as a 'relational database product', meaning that it allows you to relate data from several different sets or tables.

An Access database comprises all of the tables of data and associated objects, such as screen forms and reports, macros and program modules and queries.

Tables

Access stores data in tables that are organised by rows and columns. A database must have at least one table.

Columns represent *fields* of information, or one particular piece of information that can be stored for each entity in the table. For example, in a client database, there might be one column for surname, another for telephone number.

Rows contain *records*. A record contains one of each field in the database. In a client database, there would be a record for each client.

Generally a table represents each major set of information in a database. There might, for instance, be a Supplier table, a Client table and an Employee table.

We will return later to the issue of how data might be organised in tables, and how relationships can be defined between tables so that they can be used together, so that, for instance, data from more than one table can be shown in a report.

Queries

Queries are used to select records from a database. Access has three different types:

Select queries are the standard type. They are questions that you may wish to ask about entries in fields. They choose records from a table and store them in a new table called a *dynaset*. Queries are specified by completing entries in the Query by Example (QBE) window. You can define complex combinations of criteria if you need to select a specific set of records.

Action queries update values in a database table. They can be used to change an entire group of records, as in, for example, the removal of all records for former employees.

Parameter queries allow you to change the criteria for a query each time you use it. Access prompts for criteria entries with the QBE (Query by Example) grid. They can be used to create an environment for end users who can then work with dialog boxes instead of a QBE grid (see *Access 2000 Further Skills* for more on QBE).

Reports

Reports are used to print information from a number of records. They can show the data from either a table or a query. In addition to records, they may show summary information relating to the records displayed. Graphs created using Microsoft Graph may be added to reports.

Forms

Forms can be used to customise the way in which records from tables or queries are presented on screen. They help provide a user-friendly interface for adding new records or editing existing ones. Subforms allow you to display related records from another table at the same time.

Controls are placed on a form to display fields or text. Text on the form acts as labels to controls and headings. Changing the font or adding bold or italic emphasis can change the appearance of text on a form. Text can also be shown as raised or sunken or displayed in a specific colour, and lines and rectangles can be added to give the form a pleasing appearance. Controls, attached labels, form sections and the form itself all have properties that can be changed.

Charts

Charts can be added to forms or reports for quick visual access to data. They can be used to illustrate a single record or to summarise data from all the records or a selection of the records in a database.

Macros

Macros are a series of steps or keystrokes that you have recorded, and which can then be repeated by running the macro. Examples of the potential uses of macros are:

❑ to add a button to a form so that it will open a second form

❑ to create custom menus and pop-up forms for data collection.

Modules

Modules are programs or sets of instructions designed to perform a specific task or series of tasks. Modules are written in Visual Basic script, the programming language provided with Office 2000.

Task 1: Questions

1 What is the difference between a report and a screen form?

2 What types of queries may be used in Access?

3 What is a table? What is the relationship between a table and a database?

4 Give an example of when you might use a macro.

Unit 2

Defining a new database

What you will learn in this unit

This unit focuses on the creation of an Access database file. This file is used to store all the components of an Access database, which you will be building as you work through these units.

By the end of this unit you will:

❑ appreciate the reasons for analysing data before creating a database

❑ be able to define a new database

❑ be able to retrieve this database

❑ understand that data is kept in tables and there is usually more than one table in a database

❑ understand that the tables in a database can be related or linked together.

Before a database can be created, careful thought needs to be given to the data that should be held, and in planning the way in which the data is to be organised. This process is known as data analysis and you will be introduced to its basic concepts in this unit.

Data analysis

A database is used for storing data that can be used by a system. A 'system' is not easily defined, though they abound in society and nature. In society there are legal systems, political systems, educational systems, tax systems, etc. Organisations may have order systems, management-information systems, product information systems, personnel-data systems, sales-marketing systems, etc. Libraries have cataloguing systems and information retrieval systems. In general terms, systems can be viewed as being concerned with taking inputs or resources, executing some form of regulated change and achieving results or outputs. Systems often need access to data to act upon their inputs; if this data information is easily accessible, i.e. via a well-designed database, then the system will perform well.

Data or systems analysts are highly trained individuals who design information systems of which databases usually form a major part. They use their skills to determine how to organise the data in the tables in the system's databases. It is not the intention of this book to teach analysis skills but it will give you a practical insight into the building of a database.

We shall be considering the database needs of a small leisure centre. Data is recorded about various aspects, such as membership details, court and course bookings and financial information. The information about these different things may be kept in tables in the database. If data from more than one table needs to be retrieved then the tables can be linked or related together.

A table generally holds data about one thing or entity. There are usually several or many instances of this particular thing, for example, the members of the leisure centre. A members' table would hold details about each member.

Records and fields

For each member there is a separate *record* in the table. Each record is composed of data about the member, such as name, address and so on. Each piece of data within the record is known as a *field*. In this first set of units we will see how the fields of the database must be defined – setting the size and the type of data each will contain — before data can be entered into the records. Fields are given names to describe the kind of data they will hold; for example, the field named *Lastname* will hold people's last names such as 'Harris'.

The field names can be considered to be the column headings in the table and each row in the table is a separate record. Each record in the table will have fields with the same name but containing different data.

Defining a new database

A database is used to store all the tables, queries, forms and reports that belong to the system. To begin with, a database will hold the tables of data needed for the system. Note that Access stores all of its tables, forms, reports, queries, macros, etc. in a single file, and that this file must be created on disk at the start.

Task 1: Defining the Chelmer Leisure database

1   Start Access by clicking on the **Start** button, selecting **Programs,** then **Microsoft Access**. If you have a Desktop shortcut icon for Access then you may double-click on it to start the program.
Shortcut to
Msaccess

2   In the **Create a New Database using** area, choose **Blank Access database** and click on the **OK** button.

If Access is already running, choose **File–New...** and double-click on the Database icon.
Database

3   In the **File New Database** dialog box select the drive and folder in which to store your database. If you do not change the folder then your database is likely to be stored in the *My Documents* folder provided by Windows.

4   In the **File name** box enter the file name *Chelmer Leisure*. Access will add the extension of *.mdb*. (You will not see this extension on screen)

5   Click on the **Create** button.

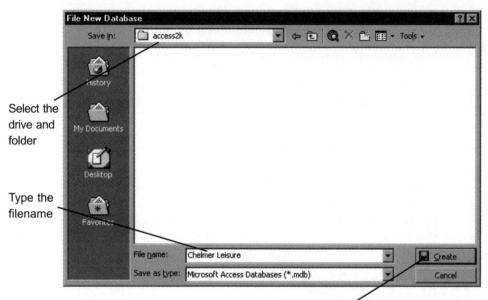

Select the
drive and
folder

Type the
filename

Figure 2.1   Click the Create button

Access, like other Windows applications, allows you to use long descriptive file
names. The complete path to the file including drive letter, folder path name and
file name can contain up to 255 characters. Any characters may be used except the
following: * ? ; \ / : " < >. You cannot use a period (full stop) except to separate the
file name from the extension.

Closing and opening a database

When you have finished working with the database you can close it using **File-
Close**. If you have made changes that you have not saved then Access will prompt
you to save them.

To open an existing database use **File-Open** or click the **Open Database** button
. Select the drive and folder in which the database is stored, select the filename
and click on the **Open** button.

When you have finished working with Access you can close it using **File-Exit**.
Next time you start Access you will see the database listed in the **Open an existing
file** section of the Access dialog box. Simply click on it to open the database.

Task 2: Closing and opening the Chelmer database

1   To close the database choose **File-Close**.

2   To open the database choose **File-Open**. In the **Look in** drop-down display select
     the drive in which your database is stored.

3   Select the folder and then the file *Chelmer Leisure* from the main display.

4   Click on the **Open** button.

5   To close Access choose **File-Exit**.

6   To open Access and choose an existing database, start Access by clicking on its icon or using **Start-Programs-Microsoft Access**.

7   Select *Chelmer Leisure* from the list in the **Open an existing file** area and click OK.

Understanding relationships between tables

Having created the database, the next step is to create the tables that go into it. How do you decide what constitutes a table and the sort of data it should contain?

First consider the nature of the Chelmer Leisure and Recreation Centre. A leisure centre basically needs a building, staff and people that use it. Usage charges are often cheaper for members and some centres only allow you to use the facilities if you are a member. When someone joins the centre details about that person are obtained. Details about the staff that work at the centre will also be needed so that they can be paid correctly. Details about the bookings of various rooms, halls and courts in the centre will be required so that the building is used efficiently. If the centre sells fitness equipment then details about items kept in stock would need to be kept as well as sales records.

Let's look at the membership data in more detail. What sort of information will the centre be asking for on the membership form? Apart from name and address, date of birth is useful for targeting advertising to specific groups, e.g. senior citizens. Knowing something about the sporting interests of the member would also be useful. The information that Chelmer Leisure and Recreation Centre requires about each new member is shown here.

Last Name	Occupation
First Name	Date of birth
Title	Date of joining
Street	Date of last renewal
Town	Sporting Interests
County	Smoker
Post Code	Sex
Telephone No	

Before issuing a membership card the centre will allocate a unique membership number, and will charge a fee. The centre offers different categories of membership for which different fees are charged. Therefore it is necessary to have two additional fields, *membership number* and *membership category*.

The centre will need to hold data about the current fees for each category of membership. This forms another table in our system, the *Membership category* table.

Category No
Category Type
Membership Fee

To discover the fee that a member has paid by matching his or her membership category with category number in the membership category table, the information in the two tables can be linked. This is known as *relating* the tables.

One advantage of using more than one table is that less storage space is required. Consider the situation where there wasn't a membership category table and the information about category type and membership fee was stored in the table containing the member's information. Say there are 500 members: 500 membership category descriptions and 500 membership fee details will need to be stored: 1000 pieces of information, which may be a couple of words each. If, on the other hand, there are two tables, then there will be 500 category identification numbers, which need only be one digit. If there are six categories, then the membership category table needs only hold six category identification numbers, six descriptions and six fee details, a total of only 518 pieces of information. Another advantage is that the six fees can be amended in one table and the new data is available throughout the database simultaneously, without having to amend 500 records individually – and when a new member joins or membership is renewed the correct fee details are used.

Two other tables that will form part of our Chelmer Leisure and Recreation Centre system are concerned with bookings of the rooms, halls and courts, and the classes that are held. The centre will need to keep track of room use to prevent double booking and to schedule classes. Rooms can be booked either by members or by a class so there is a link between a member and a room booking and there is a link between a class and a room booking. The bookings and classes tables are shown below.

Bookings	Classes
Booking No	Class No
Room/Hall/Court	Class Day
Member/Class	Class Time
Member No	Class Tutor
Date	Female/Male/Mixed
Time	

Figure 2.1 (overleaf) shows the relational database used by our system for Chelmer Leisure and Recreation Centre. It shows the four tables: *Membership*, *Categories of membership*, *Classes* and *Bookings*, and how they are linked. Each table is composed of records and the fields in each table are listed in the boxes.

The fields in bold italics are known as *primary key fields*. You will be introduced to these in the next unit.

Task 3: Creating and linking tables

The centre will need to have details of the class tutors that it employs. Design a tutors' table on paper by considering the fields that will comprise the records in this table. How could this table be linked in with the tables in Figure 2.1?

Choosing data types

The first stage in building the database is to define the tables. To do this we must define the fields that the tables will contain, giving a name, setting the size and selecting the data type for each field. No data has yet been entered but before it can

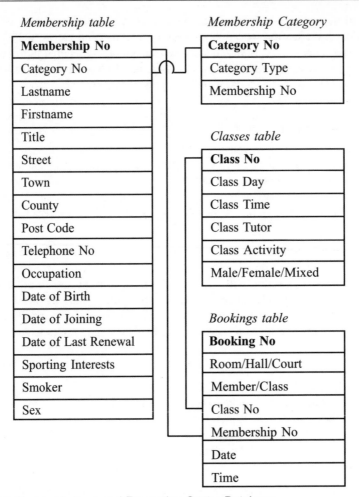

Membership table

Membership No
Category No
Lastname
Firstname
Title
Street
Town
County
Post Code
Telephone No
Occupation
Date of Birth
Date of Joining
Date of Last Renewal
Sporting Interests
Smoker
Sex

Membership Category

Category No
Category Type
Membership No

Classes table

Class No
Class Day
Class Time
Class Tutor
Class Activity
Male/Female/Mixed

Bookings table

Booking No
Room/Hall/Court
Member/Class
Class No
Membership No
Date
Time

Figure 2.2 Chelmer Leisure and Recreation Centre Database

This is just one database structure that could be used for part of the system at Chelmer Leisure and Recreation Centre. The total system would be more complex and a number of alternative database structures are also possible. The best database structure for a given application depends upon the way in which the database is to be used.

be, Access needs to know what sort of data to expect. Take the member's last name. You need to tell Access the field name, i.e. *Lastname*, and whether the data is text, numeric, date/time, etc. before you can actually start entering people's names.

Every field in your table will be of a particular data type; for example a name is *alphanumeric text*, a price would be *currency* and a date would have a *date* data type. The data type that you choose for a field determines the kind and range of values that can be entered into it and the amount of space available in the field.

You will probably define most fields in a table of names and addresses as Text fields. There are likely to be instances where a Text field should be used when the data is actually numbers. Fields such as telephone numbers or employee works numbers that contain only digits should be defined as Text fields. One reason is that there is no need to do calculations with such numbers. Also telephone area codes often start with a zero, and employee works numbers may also start with one or more zeros (known as leading zeros), which is not allowed in a true number. So, reserve the Number data type for fields on which you want to perform calculations.

The table below lists the data types available in Access and their uses.

Data type	Use for...
Text	Text and numbers. A Text field can contain up to 255 characters. Examples, names and addresses, class activity.
Memo	Lengthy text and numbers. A Memo field can contain up to 64,000 characters. For example, comments about a hotel in a travel company's database.
Number	Numerical data on which you intend to perform mathematical calculations, except those involving money. Set the FieldSize property to define the specific Number data type. Example, number of items in stock.
Date/Time	Dates and times. A variety of display formats are available and you can create your own. Example, date of joining.
Currency	Money. The Currency data type maintains a fixed number of digits to the right of the decimal point. Example, membership fee. Don't use the Number data type for currency because numbers to the right of the decimal point may be rounded during calculations.
AutoNumber	Sequential numbers automatically inserted by Access, beginning with one. Makes a good primary key field. Example, membership number. The AutoNumber data type is compatible with the Number data type with the FieldSize property set to Long Integer.
Yes/No	Yes/No, True/False, On/Off. Example, smoker/non-smoker. These are normally displayed as a checkbox, with a tick indicating Yes, True or On.
OLE Object	Document, image or other file created in another application. It can be linked into the database – in which case if its original file is updated, the changes will be reflected automatically in the database. Alternatively, an object can be embedded, putting a separate copy into the database, from where it can be edited directly. OLE objects can be up to 1 gigabyte in size.
Hyperlink	Clickable link to another file within the PC, the local network or the World Wide Web.
Lookup Wizard	Creates a link to another table, allowing you to choose a value.

Task 3: Choosing date types

Think about the following questions.

1 What would be the effect of rounding on currency (money) data?

2 What data type do you think you would choose for the following fields?
Category No
Lastname
Street
Telephone No
Date of Birth
Sporting Interests

3 Later we suggest that you use a Yes/No field for *Sex*. Explain this!

4 Why would you use a text field for a postcode?

Defining a new table

What you will learn in this unit

This unit focuses on the creation of a table. This requires the definition of its fields, giving each a unique name and specifying the type of data to be stored in it.

By the end of this unit you will be able to:

❑ name the component parts of a table

❑ create a table

❑ define data types for fields.

Defining a new table

In this activity you will define the membership table, setting up the fields so that they correspond to the type of data that will be stored in them.

Task 1: Creating a new table

1   The Database window should be active (indicated by a blue title bar if you are using the standard Windows colours). The **Tables** set should be selected as shown in Figure 3.1. If it is not, then click on the **Tables** button in the left-hand pane.

2   Click the **Create table in Design view** shortcut.

Or   Click on the **New** button in the table window to display the **New Table** dialog box, then select **Design view** and click on the **OK** button (Figure 3.2).

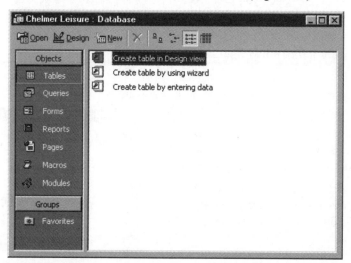

Figure 3.1

Figure 3.3

The **Table Design** window will open. This is where you define the table's structure.

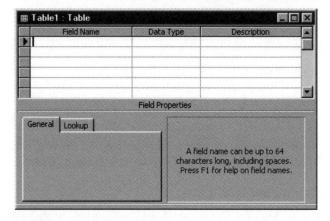

Figure 3.3

Task 2: Defining the fields in a table

In this task the fields for the membership table will be defined, by filling in the Field Name, Data Type and Description, and by setting Field Properties in the Table Design window. You should be able to complete this by following the immediate instructions, but additional notes are given in the activities described in the next few pages, which you may wish to consult. The table is defined as illustrated in Table 3.1.

Fields are defined like this:

1 Enter *Membership No* for the first field name.

Do not type a full stop after *No* as these are not allowed in field names (see the section on '*Naming Fields*', below).

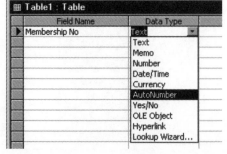

2 Press *Enter* to move to the **Data Type** column and click the drop-down button, to display this list box.

3 Click on the data type **AutoNumber**. Press *Enter* to move to the Description field. Key in the description as shown in Table 3.1.

Field Name	Data Type	Description
Membership No	AutoNumber	Automatic membership numbering
Category No	Number	Categories are 1-Senior, 2-Senior Club, 3-Junior, 4-Junior Club, 5-Concessionary, 6-Youth Club
Lastname	Text	
Firstname	Text	
Title	Text	
Street	Text	
Town	Text	
County	Text	
Post Code	Text	
Telephone No	Text	
Occupation	Text	
Date of Birth	Date/Time	
Date of Joining	Date/Time	
Date of Renewal	Date/Time	
Sporting Interests	Memo	
Smoker	Yes/No	
Sex	Yes/No	

Table 3.1 Membership fields

4 Press *Enter* to move to the next field.

See below for details of moving around the Table Design window.

5 Continue to enter the definitions for the fields as detailed in the table. Where there is no description press *Enter* to take you to the next field name.

The table will be revisited later to set individual field properties.

6 The next stage is to define the primary key. Click on the row selector (see below) for *Membership No* and click on the **Primary Key** button in the toolbar.

i Primary keys will be discussed in more detail later.

You will save this table definition in Task 4.

Moving around the Table Design window

Through the Table Design window you can enter the field name, the data type and a description of each field (the description is optional) into the grid in the upper part of the window. To move between cells you have a choice of pressing either *Enter*, *Tab*, or the *right arrow key*, or clicking in the required cell in the grid.

Row selector symbols

Along the left-hand edge of the grid you will see the row selector symbols. By clicking in the row selector box you can select an entire row.

Naming fields

Fields need names, lengths and data types to be defined. Access allows field names to be up to 64 characters long with spaces. Field names should be meaningful so that the data is easier to work with. Some characters are not allowed in field names: these are full stops (.), exclamation marks (!), and square brackets ([]) and you should note that you cannot start a field name with a space. You cannot give the same name to more than one field. Why not?

The length of a field (amount of storage space allocated to it) may be pre-determined according to the data type of that particular field. If the field is of a date type then it will have a standard length. Other data types such as text and number can have their lengths defined. If a text field is being used to hold the title of a song, for example, then you need to estimate the length of the longest song title and set the size of the field accordingly.

Adding a field description

You can add a description for any field in the description cell in the table's Design view. The maximum length allowed is 255 characters. It is not necessary to enter a description but it can be useful to provide additional information about a field.

Correcting mistakes in field name or description

Point and click in the cell containing the mistake. Correct the mistake in a normal fashion by inserting or deleting text at the insertion point. Click back in the current cell to continue working.

Correcting mistakes in the data type

Click on the cell with the mistake. Open the drop-down list by clicking the down arrow and select the correct data type.

Creating a primary key

The primary key is a field or combination of fields that uniquely identifies each record in a table. As the main index for the table, it is used to associate data between tables. Though not required, a primary key is highly recommended. All the tables used in our system will have a primary key defined. It speeds data retrieval and enables you to define default relationships between tables. In Figure 2.2 in Unit 2 the primary field key is shown in bold italics. If the membership table is considered then the membership number is the primary key; each record has a different number as every member's number will be different.

If the table does not include an obvious primary key field, you can have Access set up a field that assigns a unique number to each record. This automatically numbers each record uniquely. See Unit 5 for more discussion of primary keys.

Task 3: Setting or changing the primary key

This is an optional task that you may find useful to try on tables that you create later.

To set or change the primary key

1   In the Table Design view, select the field(s) you want to define as the primary key.

   ❑   To select one field, click the row selector.

   ❑   To select multiple fields, hold down the *Ctrl* key, and click the row selectors for each field.

Click on the **Primary Key** button ⛨ on the toolbar, or choose **Edit-Primary Key**.

Access places the primary key icon in the row selector column.

To have Access define the primary key

1   With the Table Design view displayed, save the table (see below) without specifying a primary key.

2   Access asks if you want it to create a primary key field. Choose **Yes**. Access creates a field in your table called *ID* with the AutoNumber data type.

Saving the table definition

Once the structure of the table has been designed it needs to be saved. Access uses this information to set up templates through which you enter data into the table.

The table is saved as part of the database file. There may be more than one table in a database file, each with its own unique name. Access allows the same freedom for naming tables – and queries, forms, reports and macros – as it does for files. A name may be 255 characters long and contain any alphanumeric text. Give your tables meaningful names so that they can be easily recognised later.

Task 4: Saving the table definition

Continuing from Task 2.

1   Choose **File-Save**.

2   In the **Save As** dialog box, type *Membership* in the **Table Name** box and click **OK**.

3   Close the table using **File-Close** (shortcut key *Ctrl+W*).

Closing the table

1   Double-click on the table's control menu button.

Or Choose **File-Close**.

Opening a table

You can open an existing table in either Design view or Datasheet view. So far we have only considered the Design view of a table.

To open a table in Design view

1   In the **Database** window, click on the **Table** tab.

2   Select the table you want to open, and then click on the **Design** button.

Figure 3.4

Defining field properties

What you will learn in this unit

Once the fields of a table have been defined, further refinements may be made to them by setting field properties.

By the end of this unit you will be able to:

❏ define field properties

❏ create data validation rules

❏ define custom display formats

Defining field properties

You may have noticed that once you start to enter the field definitions, field name, data type and description, then the Field Properties are displayed in the lower left hand section of the design window (Figure 4.1). You have defined the basic data type for each field and by setting the field properties you can specify the data type in more detail. For example, you can define the length of a Text field.

Field Properties		
General Lookup		
Field Size	10	
Format		
Input Mask		
Caption		The maximum number of
Default Value		characters you can enter in the
Validation Rule		field. The largest maximum you
Validation Text		can set is 255. Press F1 for
Required	Yes	help on field size.
Allow Zero Length	No	
Indexed	No	
Unicode Compression	Yes	

Figure 4.1

In the Field Properties section, in the bottom part of the window, you can set properties for individual fields to specify how you want data stored, handled, and displayed. The available options depend on the field's data type, and some will have default values set. When you click into a property definition slot, a description of the property is displayed to the right.

Setting a field property

To set a field's properties first select the field, then in the Field Properties section, click on the property you wish to define. Setting the options is described over the rest of this unit.

The table below lists all the field properties, and the following sections describe some of these in more detail. Remember that you will not always see all of these properties as they do not apply to all data types.

Property	Description
Field Size	Maximum length of the text field or type of number
Format	How data is displayed; use predefined formats or customise your own (see page 25)
Input Mask	Data entry pattern (see page 26)
Caption	Default field label in a form or report
Default Value	Value entered in a field when records are created
Validation Rule	Expression that defines data entry rules
Validation Text	The message displayed when invalid data is entered
Required	Whether or not an entry must be made
Allow Zero length	Allows you to store a zero length string ("") to indicate data that exists but is unknown
Indexed	Single-field indexes to speed searches

Field size

This property sets the maximum size of data that can be stored in a field. If the data type is Text, enter a number less than 255. This number should be chosen by considering the length of the longest text that is to be entered into the field. The default setting is 50. For fields containing more than 255 characters, set the type to Memo instead of Text.

If the data type is Number, the Field Size property settings and their values are related in the following way.

Setting	Description
Byte	Whole numbers with values between 0 to 255. Occupies 1 byte.
Integer	Whole numbers with values between -32,768 and 32,767. Occupies 2 bytes.
Long Integer	Whole numbers from -2,147,483,648 to 2,147,483,647. Occupies 4 bytes.
Single	Numbers with six digits of precision, from -3.402823E38 to 3.402823E38. Occupies 4 bytes.
Double	Numbers with 10 digits of precision, from -1.79769313486232E308 to 1.9769313486232E308. Occupies 8 bytes.

Default Value

 Access will assign a default value to each of the fields in your table, which is automatically entered when a new record is created. These are values that are usually appropriate for the addition of new records to a table. The default value for Number, Currency and Yes/No fields is zero (in the case of Yes/No fields, zero means No). Text, Memo and Date fields are empty by default. You can save time by specifying your own default values for fields.

You can specify a default using text or an expression. For example, in an address table you might set the default for the Town field to London, if the majority of records are London addresses. When users add records to the table, they can either accept this value or enter the name of a different town or city.

Expressions produce calculated values. For example, the expression =*Date()* produces the current date and might be used in the *Date of Joining* field.

Validation

 The data entered into tables must be accurate if the database is to have any value. However, even the most experienced data entry operators can make mistakes. To try to detect mistakes you can test the data entered by creating validation rules. These are simple tests, which are entered as short expressions into the **Validation Text** box, and are performed on data whenever a record is added or edited.

Examples of expressions that can be used often relate to numeric fields, e.g. a credit limit that cannot be greater than a certain value. Fields with other data types may also be validated, e.g. a date may only be entered in a certain time period.

If the data entered does not conform to your validation rule, a message box will be displayed to inform the operator that the data is incorrect. The message is defined by the text that you put in the Validation Text box. The maximum length for both the Validation Rule and the Validation Text boxes is 255 characters.

Required entry

If the Required property is set to *Yes*, you will need to make an entry in that field for every record. Where it is not necessary to have an entry then this property can be left as its default value. In the *Membership* table the *Category No* field has been defined as required, as a member cannot be enrolled without being given a category of membership. When you create the *Membership* table in the following exercise, consider which fields in this table are required and set this property accordingly.

Task 1: Defining field properties

So far we have not changed any of the field properties. In this task the field properties of the *Membership* table will be defined. You should be able to complete this by following the immediate instructions, but additional notes are also given in the activities described in the next few pages.

1   First open the *Membership* table in Design view.

2   From the Database window click on *Membership* and click on the **Design** button.

3   Select the field *Category No.*

This field has a data type of Number and the Field Properties are preset as Field Size = Long Integer, Decimal Places = Auto, Default Value = 0, Required = No and Indexed = No. The data that will be entered here is a number between 1 and 6 inclusive, as there are 6 categories. The **Byte** number type allows whole numbers up to 255 so is a good choice for the number property of the *Category No* field.

4   Click in the **Field Size** box, open its associated list and select **Byte**.

There are only six categories so a validation rule can be created.

5   Click in the **Validation Rule** box and key in *<=6* and type the text *'Please enter a category number between 1 and 6'* into the **Validation Text** box.

6   To prevent a number less than 1 being entered, modify the rule to read *<=6 And >0*.

7   Open the **Required** list box and select **Yes**. It is necessary for an entry to be made in this field.

8   Select the field *Lastname*.

9   Click in the **Field Size** box, delete the default size of 50 and replace it with *25*.

10 Alter the sizes of the other text fields as follows:

Firstname	*30*
Title	*10*
Street	*30*
Town	*25*
County	*20*
Post Code	*10*
Telephone No	*12*

11 Select the *Town* field again and in the **Default Value** box type *Chelmer.*

12 Select the *County* field and put *Cheshire* into its **Default Value** box. Why do you think these defaults are set? Refer to the section on defaults, above.

13 Select the *Date of Birth* field and in the **Format** box select the *Short Date* style from the drop-down list. Repeat this for the two other date fields.

14 Select the *Smoker* field and in the **Format** box replace 'Yes/No' with the expression *;"Smoker";"Non-Smoker"*. This should display *Smoker* and *Non-Smoker* in place of the normal checkbox. Note it is important to type both semi-colons.

15 Click on the **Lookup** tab and then click on the **Display Control** down arrow. Select **Text Box**. Click on the **General** tab. This is so the defined formats (Smoker/Non-Smoker) will be displayed instead of the defaults (Yes/No).

16 Select the *Sex* field and in the **Format** box replace Yes/No with the format *;"Male";"Female"* which will display Male and Female instead of the checkbox. Set the **Display Control** to **Text Box** as for the **Smoker** field.

16 Save the changes using **File-Save**, and close the table using **File-Close**.

Creating custom display formats

Custom formats will display the data in the format that is specified regardless of the format in which it is entered. For example a display format can be created which will show all telephone numbers using a particular format e.g. (01777) 565656 or 01777-565656. A custom format is created from an image of the format. To design the image a special set of characters, known as *placeholders* are used. Here are some examples of custom formats.

Numeric format

\# indicates a place for a digit, to be left blank if no digit is entered.

0 indicates a place for a digit; if the place is not used leading/trailing 0s are shown.

, (comma) may be used as a thousands separator.

Examples:

##,###.00	56.98 or	6.90	or	5,890.07	or	100.00
#0.000	12.456 or	0.020				

Date

d is the days placeholder. **d** displays 1, **dd** 01, **ddd** Mon, **dddd** Monday.

m is the months placeholder. **m** displays 1, **mm** 01, **mmm** Jan, **mmmm** January.

y is the years placeholder. **yy** displays 01, **yyyy** 2001.

/ or – separates the day, month and year.

Examples:

dddd d mmmm yyyy	Thursday 26 March 2001
dd/mm/yy	26/06/01
d-m-yy	2-5-01 (this format does not display leading zeros).

Time

h is the hours placeholder. **h** displays 3, **hh** 03.

m is the minutes placeholder. **m** displays 6, **mm** 06.

s is the seconds placeholder. **s** displays 7, **ss** 07.

: (colon) separates hours, minutes and seconds.

AM/PM or **am/pm** displays time in 12 instead of 24 hour format.

Examples:

h:mm AM/PM	6:34 PM
hh:mm:ss	11:09:57

Text

@	indicates that a character is required in the particular place.
>	Changes all text in the field to uppercase.
<	Changes all text in the field to lowercase.
(@@@@@) @@@@@@	(01777)565656

Yes/No

;"Male";"Female" Displays Male for true and Female for false.

Task 2: Customising a field format

1   Open the *Chelmer* database and open the *Membership* table in Design view.

2   Select the **Post Code** field and put > in the **Format** property.

3   Save and close the table using **File-Save** followed by **File-Close**.

Creating input masks

Data entry can be made simpler by creating an input mask, which is a particular format or pattern in which the data is entered. An input mask is only suitable where all the data for that particular field has the same pattern, for example, stock numbers like ABM-372-4590-C.

A mask is created using special mask symbols and these are described in the following table.

Mask character	indicates
0	a number (digit) must be entered
9	a digit may be entered
#	a digit, + or – sign or space may be entered
L	a letter must be entered
?	a letter may be entered
A	a letter or digit must be entered
a	a letter or digit may be entered
&	any character or space must be entered
C	any character or space may be entered
. , : ; – /	decimal point, thousands, date and time separators
<	characters to right are converted to lower case
>	characters to right are converted to upper case
\	the character following is not to be interpreted as a mask character
!	Causes the input mask to display from right to left, rather than from left to right. Characters typed into the mask always fill it from left to right. You can include the exclamation point anywhere in the input mask.

If the mask includes characters other than these special ones, it specifies that they must be entered. Let's work through the first example below, \ABM-000-0000-L:

\A   'A' must be entered – the \ overrides the special character meaning of 'A'

BM-   'BM-' must be entered – these are normal characters

000-   enter three digits followed by '-'

0000-   enter four digits followed by '-'

>L   a letter must be entered; it will be converted to upper case

When you try to enter data in this field, the first part, ABM- is already entered, and cannot be changed. Only numbers can be typed into the next two sections, and only letters are accepted for the last character. Try typing it in and experimenting with entering data to see for yourself. You may prefer to come back to this after we have dealt with data entry in Unit 6.

Other examples:

Input Mask	Sample Values
\ABM-000-0000->L	ABM-372-4590-C
0000-0000000	0777-567890
>L<????????	Jackson

Task 3: Setting an input mask

Revisit the properties of the *Lastname* field and set the mask using the third example illustrated above. Check that you use the correct number of question marks, i.e. 24, one less than the field width of 25.

Unit 5

Creating table indexes

What you will learn in this unit

Fields in a database table may be indexed, which can speed up retrieval of records. This unit explains the function of indexes and how to select them. Note that the speed-up in retrieval will not really be noticeable on this small sample database – but in a commercial context where you may well have thousands of records, it can make a substantial difference.

It is important for long-term database maintenance to keep documentation concerning the fields and the properties chosen for them. A quick way to do this is by printing a 'table definition' using the Documentation facility.

By the end of this unit you will be able to:

❑ create table indexes

❑ print a table definition

Creating table indexes

What is an index? You are probably familiar with the index at the back of a book, which helps you to find a particular topic quickly. A table index works in a similar fashion, enabling Access to locate a particular record without having to search through every single record to locate the one you want. When you enter data into a table the records are stored in the order in which you entered them – in other words, in no particular order!

A useful order for the table is that of the primary key because this uniquely defines each record. If the records are not physically in primary key order then Access does not actually rearrange them, it just creates an index, which it uses to locate the records in that order.

When a primary key is defined the indexed property is automatically set to *Yes (No duplicates)*. 'No Duplicates' means that Access expects this field to be unique in each record, which it should be if it is a primary key field.

i Indexes on other fields may also be defined to help Access find records faster. For example, an index could be set on the *Date of Renewal* field, useful when the table is used to provide projected cash flow of membership fees. Do not index every field in your table as this will slow record updating: each time a record is added, the indexes need to be modified to account for the new record. The fields you choose for indexing should be those used frequently to search for data.

You can create indexes based on a single field or on multiple fields. For example, you can index just on a *Lastname* name field or on both the *Lastname* and the

Firstname fields, if you think you'll often search or sort by these fields. An index on *Lastname* will not distinguish between Liam Locker and Alison Locker, but an index on the multiple fields *Lastname* and *Firstname* will. Another example is a date and time in the *Booking* table. Multiple-field indexes enable you to distinguish records in which the first field may have the same value. Instead of finding nine booking records for Monday, you can find one record for Monday at 14:00 and Access will do this more quickly if an index on date *and* time has been set. Of course, the time saving will be most noticeable if there are thousands of records to be searched or sorted.

Creating a single-field index

In the table's Design view, select the field. In the **Indexed** property box at the bottom of the window, choose **Yes (Duplicates OK)** or **Yes (No Duplicates)**.

Choose the **Yes (No Duplicates)** option to ensure that no two records have the same data in this field.

Creating a multiple-field index

In the design view of the table, choose **View-Indexes** or click on the **Indexes** icon in the toolbar.

Access displays the **Indexes** dialog box. In the **Index Name** column enter the name of the index. In the **Name Field** column open the list box, select the field you require, and set the sort order in the **Sort Order** column.

In the next row select the next field name of the multiple index and set its sort order. By leaving the index name blank, up to nine subsequent rows may be used to create a multiple field index, with each field having its own sort order defined.

Note: fields should be listed in order of priority.

Task 1: Setting indexes

1 Open the *Membership* table in Design view.

2 Select the *Category No* field and set **Yes (Duplicates OK)** as the **Indexed** property.

3 Repeat for *Date of Birth* and *Date of joining* choosing **Yes (Duplicates OK)** for **Indexed** property. Why can't **Yes (No Duplicates)** be chosen?

4 Save these table design modifications using **File -Save**.

5 Display the **Indexes** dialog box. In the **Index Name** column enter the name *Member*. List the fields **Last Name** and **First Name** as illustrated in Figure 5.1

6 Close the **Indexes** dialog box and the table.

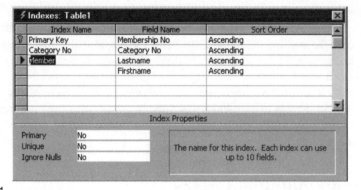

Figure 5.1

Making a printed copy of the table design

Access allows you to view and print the design characteristics (definition) of your tables, forms, queries and reports. To make a printed copy of the table design

1   Choose **Tools-Analyse** and then click **Documenter**.

Note: you may need to install Access' analysing tools.

2   Click on the tab corresponding to the type of database object you want to document and view or print. In this case choose the **Table** tab.

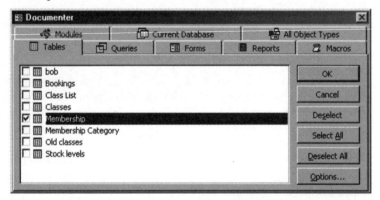

3   Click in the check box of each table for which definitions are required.

4   Click **Options** to specify which features of the selected object or objects you want to print, and then click on **OK**.

5   You might want to check the length of your definitions in the **Print Preview** window, because some definitions, particularly those for forms and reports, can be many pages long.

6   To print the definition, click on the **Print** button 🖨 in the toolbar.

 Before such tools were available, database designers created another table as a means of storing table definitions, called a 'data dictionary'. This required more work but gave a complete perspective and a chance to revise the work already done. Each data element in the database system had an entry in a dictionary table.

Task s: Printing the Membership table definition

1. Display the Database window and follow steps 1 to 3 on page 30. Choose the *Membership* table.

2. Click **Options...** and set the following options:

   Include for Table: *Properties*

   Include for Fields: *Names, Data Types and Sizes*

   Include for Indexes: *Nothing*

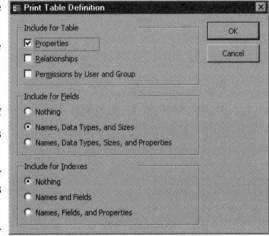

3. Click **OK** to close the Options dialog box.

4. Click **OK** at the Documenter dialog box, and wait for Access to analyse the table.

5. Preview and print the definition.

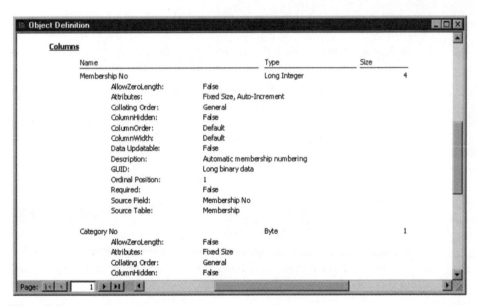

Figure 5.2

Unit 6

Entering and editing data

What you will learn in this unit

By the end of this unit you will be able to:

❑ display a table's datasheet and use it to enter data

❑ make a backup copy of your table.

Entering data

The next stage is to enter data into the table. Up until now you have probably only opened a table in Design view. To enter data it must be opened in the Datasheet view.

Opening a table in datasheet view

In the Database window, click the **Tables** button. Double-click the table name or select the table and choose the **Open** button. The table will open in Datasheet view.

Once a table is open it is possible to switch from the Datasheet view to the Design view and vice versa. There is a button on the toolbar for this. Click the button to switch to the alternative view, or click the down arrow and select the view from the drop-down list. If you make changes to the design you will be asked to save them when you switch back to the Datasheet view.

In Design view   In Datasheet view

Datasheet **view** ◀──   Design **view** ◀──

In the Datasheet view the headings of the columns are the field names you previously designed. Each row in the datasheet is a record and as you complete each record it is automatically saved into the table.

Task 1: Membership data

1   Open the *Membership* table in Datasheet view.

Notice that there are some fields already filled in; these are the default values. A default value can be accepted or it can be overridden.

2   Do not enter a value into the *Membership No* but press *Enter* to move to the next field. This is an *AutoNumber field* and you cannot enter data.

3   Enter the data for the *Membership* table as shown in Quick Reference 1 (page 236).

4　After entering the data for a field move to the next by pressing _Enter_, _Tab_ or the _Right Arrow_ key. When entering data for logical fields, click to set (Yes) or clear (No) the tick, or enter an appropriate word as defined by the format, e.g. **Male** or **Female**.

5　While entering the data, test the validation rules – both those that Access applies and those that have been defined. For example, try entering a _Category No_ greater than 6 to test the validation rule set up in the field properties for _Category No_.

6　When there is no data to be entered for a field, skip it (see below).

 If you make a mistake, or if something unexpected happens, always try **Edit-Undo** _or click the_ **Undo** _button before doing anything else._

When you press _Enter_ after entering data into the last field of the first record, Access saves the record. Notice what appears in the _Membership No_ field. Let Access number all these fields.

7　Save the table.

Validation

Data is validated as it is entered, and if it does not conform to the data type set for that field an error message will be generated. If validation text has been specified in the field's properties, this appears as the error message.

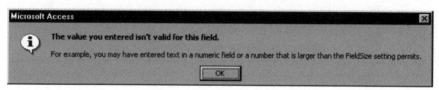

Skipping fields, null values

Sometimes not all the data for a record is available, for example, the telephone number may be missing. To skip a field, press _Enter_ or _Tab_ to take you to the next field. You can skip any field where data is not required, but not for data such as the _Membership No_. Access automatically enters a membership number, as the field was defined with an AutoNumber data type.

 Where a field is left without an entry it is said to be 'null', i.e. there is nothing there. If you perform mathematical calculations on numeric fields, then Access ignores fields containing nulls. Keep this in mind if you are doing any kind of statistical analysis. For example, you could write a query to calculate the average age of the members, using the **Average** function. If there were 21 member records, one of which had no entry in the _Date of Birth_ field (from which age is found) then the average of the 20 known ages would be calculated. This would be valid, as long as it was recognised as being based on incomplete data. If a count of members was required, basing it on the _Date of Birth_ field would give the incorrect result of 20. If you intend to use a numeric field for calculation try to ensure that each record has an entry in that field or that you are careful about how you ask Access to count the records.

Zero length strings

Nulls indicate that data may exist but is not known. To enter a null leave a field's *Required Property* as 'No' and leave the field blank. A zero length string can be used to indicate that there is no data for the field in that record, for example, a company without a fax machine doesn't have a fax number. To enter a zero length string check that the *Zero length string* property is set to Yes. In the datasheet, type two double quotation marks with no space between, i.e. "". Nulls and zero length strings may be distinguished when searching the data table.

Editing data

Once the records have been entered into a table, this data is available for use, as you will see shortly. It can also be viewed and edited to correct any mistakes. The text and figures within a cell can be edited, deleted or added to exactly as in any other Windows application. The only differences are in how you navigate between the cells and how you select data.

Moving between records

You can move between records in the datasheet using the options on the **Edit-Go To** menu, the *Up Arrow*, *Down Arrow*, *Page Up* and *Page Down* keys or the vertical scroll bar. The most efficient way to move between records in large databases is with the navigation buttons in the lower-left corner of the window.

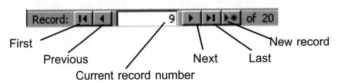

Figure 6.1

Using the navigation buttons

❑ Click on the appropriate button to leap to the first or last records in the database, or to move to the next or previous ones.

❑ To move to a specific record, click into the record number box (or press *F5*) and type its number then press *Enter.*

❑ Click on **New Record** to move to the end of the database and start to create a new record.

Selecting data

Various parts of the datasheet can be selected. When an area is selected it appears in inverse colour, so if text is normally black on white, selected text is white on black.

To select	Do This
A single field	Move the pointer to the left hand side of a cell, so that it changes shape into a white cross, and click.
A word in a field	Double-click on the word
A record	Click in the record selector at the left edge of the record, or click on any field of the desired record and choose **Edit-Select Record**
Several records	Click and drag in the record selector edge for the required records.
A column	Click on the heading (the field name at the top of the column).
Several columns	Click on the first column heading required and drag to the last.

Moving and copying fields

❑ To move data from a field, select it, use **Edit-Cut**, move to the target field and insert it with **Edit-Paste**.

❑ To copy data, select it, use **Edit-Copy**, click in the target cell and use **Edit-Paste**.

❑ If you prefer, you can use these buttons instead of the **Edit** menu options.

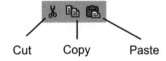

Cut   Copy   Paste

Hiding and showing columns

Columns may be hidden from view. It can be useful to do this where there are a lot of fields in a table, as is the case with the *Membership* table, and you want to be able to see certain columns more clearly. Hiding columns reduces distractions and leaves more screen space for the ones that contain the information you want to see.

To hide a column in a datasheet

1   Click on the column selector at the top of the column. More than one column may be selected for hiding.

2   Choose **Format-Hide-Columns**.

To re-show the columns

1   Choose **Format-Unhide-Columns**.

2   In the dialog box, click in the check boxes to show or hide columns.

3   Click on **Close.**

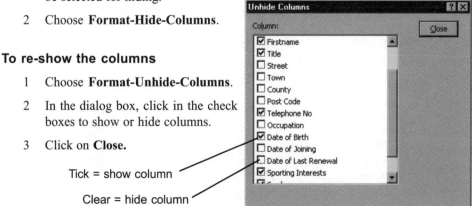

Tick = show column

Clear = hide column

Freezing and unfreezing columns

You can freeze one or more of the columns on a datasheet so that they become the leftmost columns and are visible at all times no matter where you scroll.

To freeze a column or columns:

1   Select the columns you want to freeze.

2   Choose **Format-Freeze Columns**.

To unfreeze all columns:

1   Choose **Format-Unfreeze All Columns**.

Moving and copying records

Records may be moved and copied using Edit-Cut/Copy and Edit-Paste, as explained above – though generally moving isn't an operation you would need to carry out within the same table, since records can be displayed in any order you want without affecting the underlying data. Moving and also copying can be carried out between databases providing the table structures are similar. A complete table or some records of a table can be to the clipboard. Importing and exporting data is considered in more detail in Units 35 to 38.

One instance where copying is useful is for making a backup of a table. Should you decide to revise the data types of fields in a table then it is advisable to make a backup of the table first, in case mistakes are made which could result in the loss of data.

Task 2: Backing up a table

In this task a backup of the *Membership* table will be made.

1   Click on the **Table** tab in the Database window.

2   Select the table *Membership* and choose **Edit-Copy**.

3   Create a database to hold the backup: choose **File-New Database,Database** and select the folder in which the backup file is to be stored. Type *Chelmer backup* in the **File name** box and click on **Create**. This database is now active.

4   Choose **Edit-Paste** and in the **Table Name** box of the **Paste Table As** dialog box type *Membership backup*.

5   Check that the default option **Structure and Data** is selected before clicking **OK**.

6   Use **File-Close** to close the backup database.

If this backup is needed to restore a damaged file then open the backup database, select and copy all or part of the table, then open the normal database (use **File-Open**) and paste as described above. Alternatively, you can make a backup of the entire database by closing it, switching to Explorer and copying the file to another folder, floppy disk or other back-up medium.

Managing data

What you will learn in this unit

By the end of this unit you will be able to:

❏ use the spell checker

❏ delete data

❏ use find and replace to edit data

❏ print the data in your table.

Managing records

It is very difficult to create a perfect set of data. Mistakes of transcription or keying occur despite data validation techniques. Besides this, the data itself changes – members move home, for example. Simple changes can be made using the **Find** technique described below, and old records can be deleted.

Where text fields are used to store descriptions such as occupation or sporting interests then it is useful to be able to spell check the entries.

Deleting records

Old records can be deleted when no longer needed. You can delete a record from a table using a datasheet or a form. (You will meet forms in Unit 14.)

To delete records using a datasheet:

1   Display the datasheet.

2   Select the record or records you wish to delete. Press the _Delete_ key (or choose **Edit-Delete** from the menu).

3   Access prompts you to confirm the deletion. Choose **Yes** to delete the record or **No** to restore it.

Finding and replacing

Before you can edit or delete a record, you must first locate it. In a small table, this can be done by glancing through, but in practice databases usually have thousands or even millions of records. The Find technique will help you to locate a record.

To find data in a field:

1   Make that field current by clicking on the column header.

2   Choose either **Edit-Find…** or click on the **Find** button 🔍 in the toolbar to display the **Find and Replace** dialog box.

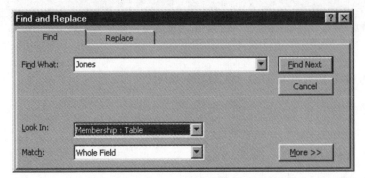

3   Type the text you want to find, such as the last name 'Jones', into the **Find What** text box.

4   In the **Look In** box, select either the current field or the whole table.

5   In the **Match** box, select whether your string should match the whole field, any part of the field or the start of it. A string is a set of characters (letters, digits and punctuation) making up the field data, e.g. a name or a telephone number.

6   Click the **More** button 🔘▓▓▓▓ if you want to set the other options.

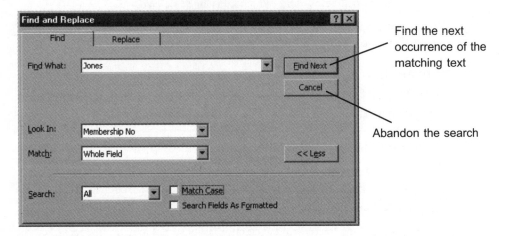

7   In the **Search** box, choose **Up**, **Down** (starting from the current record) or **All**.

8   Tick the **Match Case** option if you want to match the same combination of capital and lower case letters.

9   Tick **Search Fields As Formatted** if you want to match with the way the data is formatted, e.g. 14-Jul-01, rather than as it is stored (14/7/01).

10 To start the search click on **Find Next**, which will search from the first record, or from the current position in the direction you have chosen.

11   When a matching entry is found, its record will be highlighted. If the top or the bottom of the table is reached, you will see a message telling you that Access has finished searching.

12   When you have found the record you want, click on **Close**.

To replace an item of data:

Use this when you need to replace repeated occurrences of an item of data, e.g. when telephone codes are updated.

Follow the steps as for finding, but with these differences.

Start from **Edit-Replace.**

The dialog box has a **Replace With** text box into which you type the text that is to replace the **Find What** text, and two additional buttons.

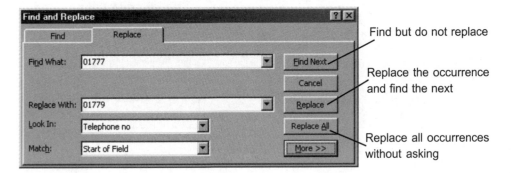

Using the spell checker

With the data displayed in the Datasheet view, you may spell check a single entry or column(s) selection by clicking on the **Spelling** button . The spell checker will prompt you to correct words that it does not recognise.

Task 1: Editing data

In this task we experiment with finding and replacing data.

1   Open the *Membership* table. Move to the end of the table.

2   Add another record. For the *Category*, enter **3**. Copy the *Lastname* field from record 9 and use **Edit-Paste** to copy it into the *Lastname* field of the new record

3   Finish the record as shown below.

Firstname	Title	Street	Town	County	Post Code
Frances	Miss	70 Meir View	Chelmer	Cheshire	CH2 7BZ

Date of Birth	Date of Joining	Date of last Renewal	Sporting interests	Smoker	Sex
5/5/82	1/3/96	1/3/00	Swimming, judo	No	Female

4   Go to the first record. Click on the *Telephone No* column header.

5   Choose **Edit-Find** or click on the **Find** button in the toolbar.

6   Key *01778* into the **Find What** box and select *Start of Field* in the **Match** list box.

7   Click on the **Find Next** button. This should highlight the first occurrence. If the **Find and Replace** dialog box is in the way, drag it to the side.

8   Click on **Find Next** to find other matches. Close the **Find and Replace** dialog box.

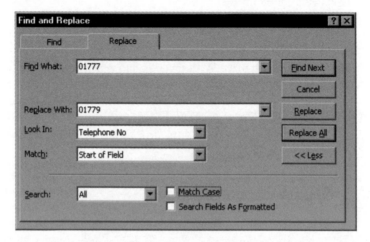

9   Move to the top of the table again and select the *Telephone No* field. Choose **Edit-Replace** and key *01777* into the **Find What** box and *01779* into the **Replace With** box. Limit the search to the current field and select *Start of Field* in the **Match** box.

10 Click on the **Replace All** button.

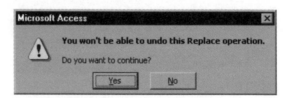

11 Click **Yes** to continue. If you have any doubts about the replacement, click **No** to abandon it.

12 While you cannot *undo* a Replace, you can reverse it by repeating the operation with the Find and Replace strings swapped over. Try it now. Replace all 01779 codes with 01777.

13 Close the **Find and Replace** dialog box.

14 Select the last record, which you have just created, and delete it.

15 Select the *Sporting Interests* column and click the **Spelling** button to spell check it.

Customising the datasheet layout

Adjusting column widths

You can adjust the column widths to make the datasheet display more readable – the default widths tend to be on the large side. Column widths are easily adjusted, especially if you are familiar with Windows applications.

To alter a column width:

1   Move the pointer to the column header.

2   Move the pointer to the dividing line between the column you wish to change and the column to the right, it should change shape to a ╬

3   Click and drag the column to the desired width.

Adjusting row heights

If you make the font larger (see below), you will need to increase the row height to match. If you make the rows deep enough to take two or more lines of text, then long entries will wrap round within cells.

To alter the row height:

1   Move the pointer to the row header.

2   Point to the dividing line between the any two rows – it doesn't matter which, as all rows are adjusted at the same time. The pointer should change shape to a ╬.

3   Click and drag the row to the desired height.

Changing the font used in the datasheet

You can change the font used in the datasheet – but only for the whole sheet, not for selected columns or cells.

1   Choose **Format-Font**.

2   At the **Font** dialog box, set the font, size and other options as desired.

3   Click **OK**.

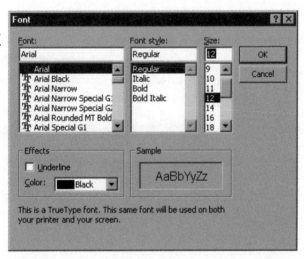

Changing field data types

 You may find it necessary to change a field data type as the design of your database develops or if you import data. (Units 35 and 36 deal with importing data.) Before you changes any field data types, make a backup copy of the table in case you accidentally lose data as a result of the changes.

Note the following considerations.

Numeric fields

Changing from one data type to another that can hold a larger number is generally safe, for example from Byte to Integer (refer back to Unit 4 for definitions of field size). If you change to a data type that holds a smaller number, for example from Double to Integer, then your data will be truncated, in this case by losing the decimal part of the number. Truncation means reducing the number of digits in a number to fit the new field size.

 Note: You cannot convert any other numeric type of field into AutoNumber.

Text fields

The field size of text fields may be altered but note that if you reduce the size, text may be truncated. Text fields may be converted to Memo fields (unlimited size), but if a Memo field is converted to a text field it will be truncated to 255 characters.

Conversion between data types

It is possible to convert a field from one data type to another, e.g. Text to Number, or Date/Time to Text, but this may result in loss of data.

Primary key or fields used in relationships

You cannot change the data type or field size property of these fields.

Moving columns

You can easily rearrange the order of fields in the datasheet, using 'drag and drop'.

1   Select the column you wish to move.

2   Click again on the column header and drag the column to a new position. A thick vertical line indicates where the field will go when the button is released.

When you close the table you can choose whether or not to make the rearrangement permanent by selecting **Yes** or **No** in the 'Save changes' message box.

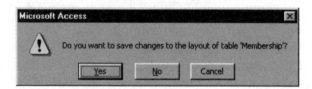

Displaying data in sorted order

Records are normally displayed in a datasheet in the order in which they were entered. This may not be the order in which you want to see them. You can control the order using the **Sort Ascending** and **Sort Descending** buttons on the toolbar ⬆⬇ .

To change the displayed order of the records using one field:

1 Click on the field name at the top of the column by which you wish to sort.

2 Click on either the **Sort Ascending** or **Sort Descending** button.

To change the displayed order of the records using more than one field:

1 Arrange the columns so that the ones that you wish to sort by are next to each other, with the highest priority one(s) to the left. Click on the field name at the top of the first and drag across to the last to select the columns.

2 Click on either the **Sort Ascending** or **Sort Descending** button.

Task 2: Customising the membership datasheet columns

1 Display the *Membership* datasheet.

2 Adjust the widths of the columns to accommodate the data displayed.

3 Select the *Sporting Interests* column and drag it to between the *Occupation* and the *Date of Birth* columns.

4 Close the table without making the rearrangement permanent by choosing **No** in the 'Save changes' message box when closing the table.

Task 3: Displaying records in sorted order

In this task the records in the *Membership* table will be viewed in different orders.

1 Open the *Membership* table in Datasheet view.

2 Select the *Lastname* column and click on the **Sort Ascending** button. Observe the result. Now click on the **Sort Descending** button and check the new order.

3 Try this for other fields in the table.

4 Select the *Category No* and *Lastname* columns together and click on the **Sort Ascending** button. Note the effect.

5 Drag the *Town* column so it is to the right of the *Category No* column, select these two columns, and click on the **Sort Ascending** button.

6 Drag the *Town* column so it is to the left of the *Category No* column, select these two columns again, and click on the **Sort Ascending** button. Note the difference between these last two sorts.

7 Close the *Membership* table without saving the layout changes.

Printing a table

You can print a table from its datasheet. Access prints a datasheet as it appears on the screen. For large datasheets, Access prints from left to right and then from top to bottom. For example, if your datasheet is three pages wide and two pages long, Access prints the top three pages first, then the bottom three pages. You should preview your datasheet before printing by choosing **File-Print-Preview** or clicking on the **Print Preview** button in the toolbar.

If you need to set up your printer, choose the **Setup** button in the **Print** dialog box.

To print a table datasheet:

1   Display the table in Datasheet view.

2   If you only want to print selected records, select them now. To print all the records, select nothing.

3   Choose **File-Print-Preview**, and if the preview is satisfactory choose **File-Print** to display the dialog box.

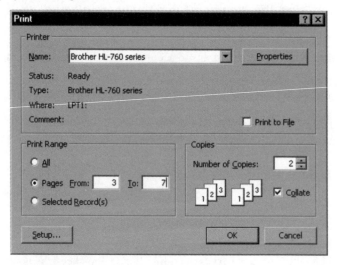

4   Under **Print Range**, choose one of the following:

•   **All**, to print all of the records in the table.

•   **Pages**, to print specific pages – you should then specify the page numbers of the first and last pages you want to print.

•   **Selected Records**, to print a previously selected set of records.

5   Set other **Print** dialog box options if necessary.

6   Click **OK**.

Task 4: Printing the membership table

1   Display the *Membership* table datasheet.

2   Choose **File-Print Preview**, and then select **File-Print...** to display the **Print** dialog box.

3   Under **Print Range**, select **All** and click on **OK**.

4   Close the table.

Unit 8

Relationships between tables

What you will learn in this unit

In this unit you will be introduced to the concept of the relationship between tables. If you wish to use only one table in your database you may omit this unit. You will find that you can still complete most of Units 10 to 31 as many tasks are based on the *Membership* table. However, in most cases you will need more than one table, and in any case you should return to this activity before moving on to Unit 32.

By the end of the unit you will be able to:

❑ define and create relationships between tables

❑ apply referential integrity

Defining relationships between tables

Relationships are made between a field in one table and a field in another table. Relationships fall into three types:

❑ one-to-one

❑ one-to-many

❑ many-to-many

A one-to-one relationship between two tables means that for a particular field in one table there is only one matching record in the other table and vice versa. A one-to-many relationship means that for one field in one table there are several matching records in the other table, but each of these records will only match one in the first table. A many-to-many relationship means that for one field in one table there are many matching records in the other table and vice versa.

One to many:

Membership Table
Membership No
1
2
3

Bookings table
Membership No
1
4
1
6
1
17
3

One to one

Membership Table

Membership No
1
2
3

Youth Club table

Membership No
1
4
6
3
12

The most common type of relationship is one-to-many, and it is the only one used in our system. Consider the relationship between a member and that member's booking. A member may make no bookings, one booking or several bookings. This implies a one-to-many relationship, i.e. there is only one record with that person's membership number in the *Membership* table, yet there can be several records with that person's membership number in the *Bookings* table.

In our database these relationships do not yet exist because they have not been defined. The relationships can be set up before data is entered into any of the tables. Before any relationships between tables can be defined the tables must be closed. It is important that when a link is made between a field in one table and a field in another table, the two fields have the same data type.

Referential integrity

When a relationship is created between two tables, Access allows the choice of whether or not to enforce 'referential integrity'. If the relationship between the *Membership* and *Bookings* tables is considered then what is to stop a membership number being entered into the *Bookings* table that does not exist in the *Membership* table? By enforcing referential integrity Access will check the membership number entered into the *Bookings* table against those in the *Membership* table and will prevent non-existent membership numbers being entered.

Task 1: Creating relationships

As yet only one table has been created in the Chelmer database. Before relationships can be defined the other tables in the database need to be defined. For this task you will need to define the *Bookings* table.

1 Click on **Create Table in Design view** in the Database window to open the table design window (see Units 3 and 4). Define the field types as shown below:

Field Name	Data Type
Booking No	Auto Number
Room/Hall/Court	Text
Member/Class	Yes/No
Membership No	Number
Class No	Number
Date	Date/Time
Time	Date/Time

2   Define *Booking No* as the primary key. Save the table as *Bookings*. Amend the field properties as shown below. Save and close the table.

Field	Property	Setting
Room/Hall/Court	Field Size	20
	Required	Yes
Member/Class	Format	;"Member";"Class"
	Required	Yes
Membership No	Field Size	Long Integer
	Default value	=Null
Class No	Field Size	Long Integer
	Default value	=Null
Date	Format	d/m/yy
	Required	Yes
Time	Format	Short time
	Required	Yes

3   Make sure that both the tables are closed, so that just the database window is left open. Now you can create the relationship between *Membership No* in the *Membership* table and *Membership No* in the *Bookings* table. The data type of the *Membership No* (*Bookings*) is a long integer number, which is compatible with the data type field of *Membership No* (*Membership*).

In one-to-many relationships the primary table in the relationship is the 'one' table, in this case the *Membership* table, and the related table is the 'many' table, i.e. the *Bookings* table.

To define a relationship between tables:

4   Choose **Tools-Relationships** and the **Relationships** dialog box appears with the **Show Table** dialog box within it. (If the Show Table dialog box does not appear click on the **Show Table** icon ⊞ on the toolbar.)

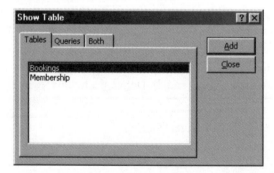

5   Select *Membership* and click on **Add**. Select *Bookings* and click on **Add**.

6   Click on **Close**. The two table windows should be displayed and you may resize them if you wish.

7   To create the relationship, click on the *Membership No* field in the *Membership* table and drag to the *Membership No* in the *Bookings* table. This displays a **Relationships** dialog box.

8   Click in the **Enforce Referential Integrity** check box and click on **Create**. The relationship between the tables will be shown by a line joining the two *Membership No* fields.

9   Use **File-Save** to save changes to the layout and close the Relationships dialog box.

Unit 9

Defining the other tables in the database

What you will learn in this unit

↔ If you wish to use only one table in your database you may omit this unit. You will find that you can still complete most of Units 10 to 31 as many tasks are based on the *Membership* table. You should then return to this unit before moving on to Unit 32. This unit revisits techniques used in Units 2 to 8 so you may wish to refer back to these.

The aim of this unit, through a series of tasks, is to

❑ reinforce techniques already introduced

Task 1: Defining the other tables in the database

Create the tables *Membership Category* and *Classes*.

1 Click on the **New** button in the database window to open the table design window.

2 Define the field types as shown.

Membership Category

Field Name	Data Type	Description
Category No	Number	A one digit identification number
Category Type	Text	Categories are Senior, Senior Club/ Junior, Junior Club, Concessionary, Youth Club
Membership Fee		Currency

3 Define *Category No* as the primary key. Save the table as *Membership Category* and close the table.

4 Now do the same for the *Classes* table:

Field Name	Data Type
Class No	Auto Number
Class Day	Text
Class Time	Date/Time
Class Tutor	Text
Class Activity	Text
Male/Female/Mixed	Text

5. Define *Class No* as the primary key. Save the table as *Classes* and close the table.

In your database window you should now see four tables listed.

Task 2: Defining field properties for the other tables

1 Open each table in turn, in design view.

2 Amend the field properties as shown below.

3 Save and close the tables.

Membership Category **table**

Field	Property	Setting
Category No	Field Size	Byte
	Required	Yes
Category Type	Field Size	15
	Required	Yes
Membership Fee	Required	Yes

Classes **table**

Field	Property	Setting
Class Day	Field Size	10
	Required	Yes
Class Time	Format	Short time (equivalent to hh:mm)
	Required	Yes
Class Tutor	Field Size	30
Class Activity	Field Size	20
	Required	Yes
Male/Female/Mixed	Field Size	10
	Validation Rule	"Male" or "Female" or "Mixed"
	Validation Text	Please enter Male, Female or Mixed

Task 3: Creating indexes

In this task, indexes for the **Classes** and **Bookings** tables are created.

1 Open the *Classes* table in design view.

2 Select the *Class Tutor* field and set **Yes (Duplicates OK)** for the indexed property.

3 Repeat for *Class Activity* choosing **Yes (Duplicates OK)** for the indexed property.

4 Close and save changes.

5 Open the *Bookings* table in design view.

6 Select the *Room/Hall/Court* field and choose **Yes (Duplicates OK)**.

7 Set a multiple field index (refer back to Unit 5) using the fields *Date* and *Time*. You may name this index *Date time*.

8 Close and save changes.

Task 4: Defining the other relationships

There are two other relationships in the database, (see Figure 1 in Unit 2). These are

❏ between the *Classes* table and the *Bookings* table

❏ between the *Membership Category* table and the *Membership* table.

Both these relationships are one-to-many relationships. Using the **Relationships** dialog box set these relationships up as follows.

1   Choose **Tools-Relationships**.

2   Add the tables *Classes* and *Membership Category* using the **Show Table** dialog box. Display this dialog box by clicking on the **Show Table** button on the toolbar.

3   To create the relationship click on the *Class No* field in the *Classes* table and drag to the *Class No* in the *Bookings* table. Note the direction of dragging is one to many, i.e. you drag from the primary ('one') table to the secondary ('many').

4   Click in the **Enforce Referential Integrity** check box and click on **Create**. The relationship between the tables will be shown.

5   Close the Relationships dialog box.

*Note: when you try to create a relationship between two new tables you may find that if you check the **Enforce Referential Integrity** check box, Access will not create the relationship. This is because if there is no data in the tables, Access has nothing to check for referential integrity. In this case however, the fields we are relating are Number fields. These have a default value, which – though zero – are sufficient to establish the relationship.*

Task 5: Documenting the table definitions

Use **Tools-Analyze-Documenter** to print the documentation for these two newly created tables, in the same way as you did for the *Membership* table in Unit 5.

Designing a basic query

What you will learn in this unit

The information stored in a database is of no use unless it can be retrieved, and only if it can be retrieved readily and in a meaningful form. If you know one piece of information in a record, you can use a query to find the rest of it, or to find all the records matching certain criteria.

In this unit you will learn how to create a basic query without using any search criteria. This will find all the records in the table, but only display those fields that you are interested in. You will learn how to add search criteria in Units 12 and 13.

By the end of this unit you will be able to:

❏ question the database by creating a query

❏ view the results

❏ save a query so that it can be retrieved for later use

❏ print out the results of your query.

Queries play a very important role in database systems. They are used for:

❏ on-line search and retrieval of specific records. For example, to find out the full details of a particular member, or to find all room bookings for a given day.

❏ creating forms and printing reports. Queries retrieve a selected set of records and fields; reports are used to print this information. A form based on a query can be used to restrict data entry to certain fields. Units 14 to 20 introduce forms and reports.

↔ Queries may be based on more than one table but here all the queries will be based on the **Membership** table. In more sophisticated databases than our examples, queries may be based on more than one table. This concept is introduced in Unit 24.

The Simple Query Wizard and Query Design window

Creating a query involves two aspects, these are:

❏ selecting the *fields* that are to be shown in the query. It is not usually necessary to retrieve all fields, for example, the names and telephone numbers may be all that is needed for a telephone survey of a group of members.

❏ selecting the *records* that are to be shown in the query. For this Access provides a method of querying by which you can describe the characteristics of the data that you are looking for. This is know as Query By Example (QBE) and it works by giving examples of the data that you are searching for.

Simple Query Wizard

The Simple Query Wizard helps you design a simple 'select' query. A select query will select fields from a table. The Wizard will ask you to select the table you wish to query and which fields you want in your query. It will create the query, which you can then modify later using the Query Design window.

1   At the Database window, click on the **Queries** tab and double-click on **Create query by using Wizard**.

If you have not yet created any queries the **Open** and **Design** buttons will not be available

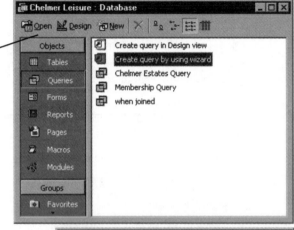

Figure 10.1

Or Click on the **New** button then select **Simple Query Wizard** in the **New Query** dialog box and click **OK**.

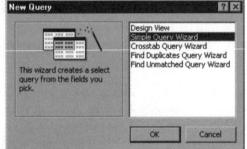

❑   The Simple Query Wizard dialog box will be displayed.

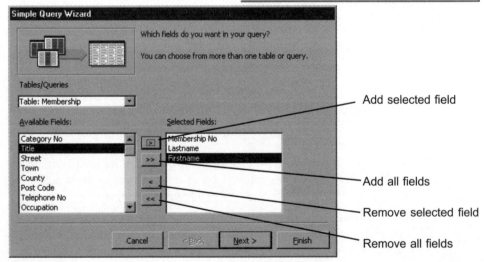

Add selected field

Add all fields

Remove selected field

Remove all fields

Figure 10.2

2   From the **Table/Queries** list, select the table on which the query is to be based.

3   Add fields as required from the **Available Fields:** list to the **Selected Fields:** list.

To add all the fields to the query, click on the ▶▶ button.

To add a selected set of fields, highlight each in turn and click the ▶ button.

If you add fields by mistake, select them and use the ◀ button or click the ◀◀ button to remove all fields and start again.

4   When the fields have been chosen click on ▶ ▓▓▓▓▓▓. Give the query a title, select **Open the query to view information**, and click on ▓ ▓▓▓▓▓▓. The result of your query will be shown in Datasheet view.

Task 1: Selecting fields for a query using Simple Query Wizard

1   From the Database window click the **Queries** button and double-click on **Create query by using Wizard**.

2   In the Simple Query Wizard dialog box, select the *Membership* table from the **Table/Queries** drop-down list.

3   Add the fields *Membership*, *Firstname*, *Lastname*, *Sex* and *Date of joining* to the query by highlighting each field in turn and clicking on the ▶ button.

4   Click on ▶ ▓▓▓▓▓▓. Give the query the title *Dates of joining* and click on ▓ ▓▓▓▓▓▓. The result of your query will be shown in Datasheet view.

Membership No	Lastname	Date of Joining	Sex
1	Walker	03/02/92	Male
2	Simpson	16/07/91	Female
3	Cartwright	12/12/96	Male
4	Forsythe	16/09/91	Female
5	Jameson	15/06/98	Female
6	Harris	03/05/94	Female
7	Shangali	16/07/99	Male
8	Barrett	24/06/92	Male
9	Weiner	04/03/00	Female
10	Ali	21/10/92	Male
11	Young	06/12/99	Male
12	Gray	24/03/94	Female
13	Swift	02/01/00	Male
14	Davies	15/11/96	Female
15	Robinson	23/07/99	Female
16	Adams	14/08/98	Female
17	Everett	12/08/94	Male
18	Locker	01/01/00	Male
19	Locker	01/01/00	Female
20	Jones	21/04/95	Male
(AutoNumber)			Female

Record: ◀◀ ◀ 1 ▶ ▶▶ ▶* of 21

Figure 10.3

5   View and close the query window; the name of the query will be listed in the Database window.

Using the Query Design window

The Query Design window (Figure 10.4) allows you to design a query that will select the required fields and records.

Before asking questions of a database you must first decide which tables in the database are required to answer them. The following activities will describe how to ask questions of the *Membership* table. You will see later, in Unit 24 how to include more than one table in a query.

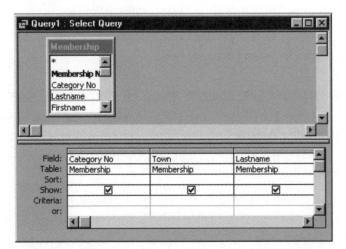

Figure 10.4

Task 2: Open the Query Design window

1 Click on the **Queries** tab in the Database window and select **Create query in Design view**.

Or Click on the **New** button then select **Design view** in the **Next Query** dialog box and click on **OK.**

2 The **Show Table** dialog box appears in front of the Query Design window. This box allows you to select all the tables needed for the query.

3 Select a table and choose **Add** to add it to the query. When the selection of table(s) is complete click on the **Close** button.

This window is in two sections. The upper section holds the table windows of the tables used in the query. In the lower section is a grid for the query design.

After choosing the table for the query it will be displayed in the upper section of the Query Design window as seen in Figure 10.3. The next step is to decide which fields in that table you wish to include in the query. Later we will explore query criteria, which allow us to select specific records.

The query is designed in the lower section of the Query Design window. The three most important rows in the grid are **Field**, **Show** and **Criteria**. Each column needs a **Field** name. You can choose as many of the table's fields as you need. The Show box should be ticked if you want the field's data to be displayed in the output. In the

Criteria row an example of the data may be given and only those records with matching data will then be selected.

As you work your way through this session you will be introduced to the function of the other rows in the grid.

Adding all the fields in the table to the query

The simplest case is where we want to include all the fields in the table.

1   Double-click on the title bar of the field list box of the table in the upper section of the window. This selects all the fields.

2   Click on any of the selected fields (not the *) and drag to the field cell in the lower section of the query window. The pointer should look like a set of record cards.

3   When you release the button all the field names will be added to the query. Use the scroll bar to move to the right as all the columns will not fit on the screen.

Adding individual fields in the table to the query

There are three alternative ways of adding the fields one by one to a query.

❑   Double-click on the name of the field required in the field list box in the upper section of the window. It will appear in the next available column in the grid below.

❑   Use the drop-down list associated with each field cell:

1   Click in the field cell in the lower section of the window.

2   An arrow button appears at the end of the cell. Click on the button to drop down a list of field names.

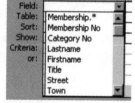

3   Click on the name of the field (if necessary scroll through the list) and it will appear in the **Field** cell.

❑   Use the *drag and drop* method:

1   Click on the name of the field required in the field list box in the upper section of the window.

2   Drag and drop this field into the field cell in the lower section. While doing this the pointer should look like one record card.

If you drop the field onto a column containing a field, then a column will be inserted to contain the new field.

Removing fields from the query

Fields may be removed singly or in blocks from the query. To remove all the fields from the query:

1   Select the first column by clicking on the bar at the top of the column, (the pointer will change shape to a down arrow) drag to select all the columns.

2   Press the *Delete* key or choose **Edit-Delete**.

To remove an individual field from the query, just select the required column for deleting and use **Edit-Delete**.

Viewing or running a query

To see the result of a query, either click on the **Datasheet** button or the **Run Query** button in the toolbar. To return to the query design click on the **Design** button next to the **Datasheet** button in the toolbar.

Design button   Datasheet button   Run Query button

 Access displays a datasheet containing the records that match the query with fields as defined in the query. This query result is what Access calls a dynaset. A dynaset is a temporary table and is not a permanent part of your database. If you modify your query the resulting dynaset will change accordingly.

Task 3: Selecting fields for a query

In this task you will query the *Membership* table; data from all records will be shown in the dynasets. Initially all fields will be shown and then you will see how to select only certain fields.

1   Starting from the Database window, click on the **Queries** button.

2   Click on **New** to open a new query and choose **Design view**

3   Select the table *Membership* from the **Show Table** dialog box and close the dialog box.

4   Add all the fields to the query, following the method described above.

5   Click on the **Datasheet** button in the toolbar; you should see the whole of the table forming the dynaset.

6   Click on the **Design** button in the toolbar to return to the Query Design window.

7   Remove all the fields from the query, following the method described above.

8   Add fields individually to the query, experimenting with the different methods described above. Add the fields *Membership No, Lastname, Sex, Date of joining*.

9   Click on the **Datasheet** or **Run Query** button in the toolbar; you should see only these fields from all the records of the table forming the dynaset.

10   Click on the **Design** button in the toolbar to return to the Query design window.

11   By adding and removing fields alter the fields in your query so that they are *Lastname, Sex, Category No, Sporting Interests*.

12   Click on the **Datasheet** button in the toolbar, or the **Run Query** button and you should see only these fields from all the records of the table forming the dynaset.

Saving a query

Sometimes you may wish to ask the same question of a database over and over again, for example, is a membership subscription due? As time passes members need to renew their membership and the Centre will want a quick way of checking whom to send reminders to. A query designed to do this would be saved so that it can be used repeatedly.

To save a query:

1   With the query window open, choose **File-Save.**

2   In the **Query Name** box of the **Save As** dialog box enter a name that will remind you what the query is about. The name can be up to 255 characters. Click on **OK.**

If you close the query window, you will see the name of your query in the Queries list of the Database window, from where it can be opened for use again later.

Task 4: Saving a query

In this task you will save the query created at the end of the previous task.

1   Choose **File-Save.**

2   Give the name *Members' Sporting Interests* to this query and click on **OK.**

3   Close the query and you should see the name of the query in the Database window.

Closing and opening a query

To close a query, either:

1   Double-click on the query's control menu button.

Or Choose **File-Close.**

To open a query in Design view:

1   In the Database window, click on the **Queries** button.

2   Select the query you want to open, and then click on the **Design** button.

To open a query in Datasheet view:

1   In the Database window, click on the **Queries** button.

2   Select the query you want to open, and then click on the **Open** button.

Printing a query

Before printing the dynaset produced by a query it is advisable to preview it first.

To preview a Queries table:

1   Open the query.

2 In the Datasheet view, click on the **Print Preview** button on the toolbar. You will be shown a miniature version of what is to be printed.

3 The pointer becomes a magnifying glass and can be use to zoom in to the page. If you use other Windows applications you will be familiar with this. Click the **Zoom** button 🔍 to toggle between zoom in and zoom out modes. When zoomed in the vertical and horizontal scroll bars can be used to scroll around the preview.

4 Click the right mouse button to get a context menu of preview and print commands.

5 You may well find that some columns are not wide enough for their contents. To adjust the column widths you must return to the Datasheet view. Click on the **Close** button to exit the preview then select Design view

6 To adjust the column widths, place the pointer between the column headers, then click and drag the dividing line.

Once you are satisfied with the preview display, you are ready to print.

1 Choose **File-Print.** The **Print** dialog box appears. If you want to print without changing anything *skip the next three steps.*

i *Note, if you know that the current print settings are what you want, then you can print directly without displaying the **Print** dialog box by clicking the **Print** button .*

2 Click on the **Setup** button and the **Page Setup** dialog box appears.

3 To change the margins click in the appropriate box and edit the default setting. You can select the orientation of the page, the printer and the paper size. The **Print Headings** check box, if not checked, will suppress the printing of the field names as headings. Click on **OK** to return to the **Print** dialog box.

4 Click on **OK** to print, then click on the **Close** button to return to the query datasheet.

Task 5: Printing

In this task the dynaset produced by the query created in Task 3 will be printed.

1 From the Database window open the query in Datasheet view.

2 Click on the **Print Preview** button on the toolbar.

3 Some columns may need widening. Change to Datasheet view and adjust as required (see *Customising the datasheet layout,* Unit 7).

4 Preview again, zooming in to check the column widths, then click on the **Print** button.

5 Click on **OK** in the Print dialog box and the dynaset shown in Figure 10.5 should be printed.

6 Click on the **Close** button to return to the Datasheet view.

Lastname	Sex	Category No	Sporting Interests
Walker	Male	2	Tennis, squash
Cartwright	Female	1	Aerobics, swimming
Perry	Male	6	Judo, Karate
Forsythe	Female	2	
Jameson	Female	1	Aerobics, squash
Harris	Female	3	Swimming, judo
Shangali	Male	5	Badminton, cricket
Barrett	Male	2	Weight training, squash
Weiner	Female	1	Judo, swimming, football
Ali	Male	1	Keep fit, aerobics, squash
Young	Male	6	
Gray	Female	2	
Swift	Male	5	Aerobics, squash, swimming
Davies	Female	5	Tennis, aerobics
Robinson	Female	1	Squash, fitness training, football
Adams	Female	1	Bowls, cricket
Everett	Male	2	
Locker	Male	4	Judo, swimming
Locker	Female	4	Judo, karate
Jones	Male	1	Weight training

Figure 10.5

Deleting a query

Some queries may only be used once, in which case it is not really worth saving them. Queries that will be used more than once should be saved but a query may have a limited usefulness or be superseded. Therefore, from time to time some queries will need to be removed.

However, care must be taken when removing a query. Later, we will see that reports and forms can be based upon queries so it is important to assign these to alternative queries or to delete them as well. At present there is nothing based on the queries we have created and they may be deleted safely.

To delete a query, from the Database window, click on the **Queries** button to display the queries. Highlight the query that is to be deleted and press *Delete*.

Task 6: Deleting a query

In this task you will delete the query created using the Simple Query Wizard.

1 Display the queries in the Database window.

2 Select the query, *Dates of joining* and press *Delete*.

3 Reply **Yes** to confirm the delete operation.

Unit 11

Sorting the dynaset

What you will learn in this unit

The dynaset or result of a query can be displayed in different orders. If no sorting order is specified then the records in the datasheet will be shown in their natural order, i.e. the order in which they were entered. Sorting is particularly useful. For example if the records are shown in date of birth order then it is easier to see an age profile; if records are shown in town order, geographical information becomes apparent. If a report is to be created from the query (see Unit 19) then the order of the records can be defined by the query.

By the end of this unit you will be able to:

❑ sort the information shown in the answer to your query.

Sorting the dynaset

The grid in the lower section of the query design window includes a sort row, used to define how the dynaset is sorted. To define the type of sorting:

1 Click in the **Sort** cell for the field in which you are interested. A list box button appears at the end of the cell.

2 Click on the list box button to reveal the sorting choices.

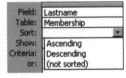

Ascending will sort from low to high (A-Z for alphabetical sorting); **Descending** sorts from high to low; **not sorted** will not apply any sorting on that column.

⚠ *Note: there is an order of priority when several fields are being sorted. This is determined by their order in the query; leftmost fields being of higher priority.*

Task 1: Sorting

This task investigates the different orders in which the query created in Task 2 of Unit 10 can be displayed.

1 Open the *Member's Sporting Interests* query in Design view.

2 Click in the **Sort** cell for the *Lastname* field. Drop down the list and pick **Ascending**.

3 Display the dynaset by clicking on the **Run Query** button. Return to Design view.

4 Change the **Sort** order of the *Lastname* field to **(not sorted)**.

5 Choose **Ascending** as the order for the *Sex* field.

6 Display the dynaset, note the difference and return to Design view.

7   Choose **Ascending** order for the *Lastname* and **Descending** order for the *Sex* fields. What order do you expect the data for the twins to be shown? View the dynaset.

8   Close the query without saving it.

Task 2: Sort order priority

For this task you will create a simple query to illustrate the effect that the order of the fields in the query has upon the priority of sort order. By choosing different priorities and viewing the resulting dynaset, the effect can be appreciated.

1   Create a new query using the *Membership* table.

2   Add the fields *Category No*, *Town* and *Lastname* to this query.

3   Set **Ascending** as the order for both the *Category No* and *Town* fields (Figure 11.1).

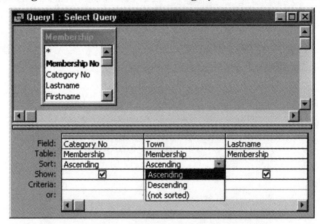

Figure 11.1

4   Run the query to view the resulting dynaset (Figure 11.2).

Category No	Town	Lastname
1	Chelmer	Ali
1	Chelmer	Jameson
1	Chelmer	Adams
1	Chelmer	Jones
1	Meriton	Cartwright
1	Meriton	Weiner
1	Meriton	Robinson
2	Branford	Gray
2	Chelmer	Everett
2	Chelmer	Walker
2	Chelmer	Barrett
2	Chelmer	Forsythe
3	Branford	Harris
4	Chelmer	Locker
4	Chelmer	Locker
5	Chelmer	Davies
5	Chelmer	Swift
5	Chelmer	Shangali
6	Chelmer	Perry
6	Chelmer	Young

Figure 11.2

Record: 1 of 20

5 Return to the query design window and select the *Category No* field by clicking at the top of the column (while the pointer looks like a down pointing arrow). With the column selected, click on the column header and drag to reposition it *after* the *Town* field. Leave the sort order of *Category No* as **Ascending** (Figure 11.3).

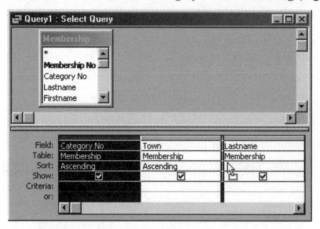

Figure 11.3

6 View the resulting dynaset, which should be in a different order from the previous one (Figure 11.4).

Town	Category No	Lastname
Branford	2	Gray
Branford	3	Harris
Chelmer	1	Jameson
Chelmer	1	Jones
Chelmer	1	Ali
Chelmer	1	Adams
Chelmer	2	Everett
Chelmer	2	Forsythe
Chelmer	2	Walker
Chelmer	2	Barrett
Chelmer	4	Locker
Chelmer	4	Locker
Chelmer	5	Davies
Chelmer	5	Shangali
Chelmer	5	Swift
Chelmer	6	Perry
Chelmer	6	Young
Meriton	1	Robinson
Meriton	1	Cartwright
Meriton	1	Weiner

Record: 1 of 20

Figure 11.4

7 Close this query without saving it.

Using query criteria

What you will learn in this unit

There are many reasons for asking questions. In business, questions are important in decision making, and to be able to question data relating to, for example, marketing or management, can be very effective using a database management system. In the case of Chelmer Leisure and Recreation Centre the answers to such questions can help with decisions regarding:

❑ where members come from and the effect of local competition

❑ introduction of no-smoking areas and new facilities for older members

❑ discount scheme for loyal members

❑ fees charged for various categories.

To ask questions, criteria need to be set and entered into the criteria cells of the **Query** design grid. Querying is done by example, so an example of the answer to the question is entered into the criteria cell.

By the end of this unit you will be able to:

❑ enter query criteria

❑ rename and hide fields in a query

❑ use logic in queries.

Entering query criteria

Query criteria allow the enquirer to frame questions that enable specific records to be retrieved from the database. We might want to find out various things using the data stored in a table. For example, some questions that might be asked about the *Membership* table are:

❑ Which members live in Chelmer?

❑ Which members smoke?

❑ Which members are over 60?

❑ Which members joined before 1/1/96?

❑ Which members are in categories 1 and 2?

Task 1: Query criteria for the membership table

In this task the questions listed above will be formulated as queries for the *Membership* table. The queries use the data types Text, Number, Date and Yes/No.

Each question will be dealt with in turn.

1 Create a new query using the *Membership* table.

2 Add all the fields to the query.

Which members live in Chelmer?

1 In the **Criteria** cell of the *Town* field type ***Chelmer***.

2 Click on the **Datasheet** or **Run Query** button.

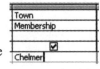

The resulting dynaset should only contain records for which the *Town* field is equal to "Chelmer".

3 Return to Design view. Note that Access puts double quotes around your criterion if it thinks it is text. Delete the criterion "Chelmer" – double-click to select the contents (including the quotes) and press *Delete* or click in the cell and use *Backspace* to delete the criterion.

 Note: If you do not delete the quotes, when you next run this query, Access will look for records with "" (i.e. nothing) in the Town *field.*

Which members smoke?

1 In the **Criteria** cell of the *Smoker* field type ***Yes***. You may need to scroll to the right to display this cell on the screen.

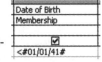

2 Click the **Datasheet** or **Run Query** button and view the resulting dynaset.

3 Return to Design view. Delete the last criterion.

Which members are over 60?

1 In the **Criteria** cell of the *Date of Birth* field type ***<1/1/41***.

2 Click the **Datasheet** or **Run Query** button and view the resulting dynaset. Return to Design view.

Notice that Access has recognised your query example as a date and has converted it to <#01/01/41#.

3 Delete this criterion.

Which members joined before 1/1/96?

1 In the **Criteria** cell of the *Date of joining* field type ***<1/1/96***.

2 Click the **Datasheet** or **Run Query** button and view the dynaset.

3 Return to Design view. Delete this criterion.

Which members are in categories 1 and 2?

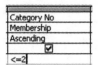

1 In the **Criteria** cell of the *Category No* field type *<=2*.

2 Click the **Datasheet** or **Run Query** button and view the dynaset.

3 Return to Design view. Close the query without saving it.

Renaming and hiding fields in a query

When queries are printed it is sometimes necessary to widen the column so that the field name at the top can be seen. As this can lead to unnecessarily wide columns, it is useful to be able to rename the field. The field header in a query can be given an alternative name, for example, *Last Renewed* instead of *Date of last Renewal*.

i *Note: Renaming the field header does not affect the name of the field in the underlying table.*

To change field header names:

1 Open a query in Design view. Click in the field header so that the cursor becomes a flashing text cursor. If you accidentally select the header, press *F2* to de-select it.

2 If the insertion point is not at the start, press the *Home* key to move it to the start.

3 Type in the new name for the field, followed by a colon – do not put a space before the colon. Do not delete the field name, because Access needs this to know where to get data from.

4 Click on the **Datasheet** or **Run Query** button and the query result with amended field header will be displayed.

In the two previous units you saw how to select the fields you want in the result of a query and how to impose criteria. These can be combined so that the dynaset contains only the records that match the criteria and only the fields specified in the query. To be able to impose a criterion on a field, that field must be in the query grid, which means that it will normally form part of the dynaset.

However, you may not always want to show a field in a dynaset – especially since the selected records may contain the same data in that field. Access lets you choose whether or not a field forms part of the dynaset. By default all fields in the query show in the dynaset as the **Show** checkbox is on; to hide a field, click in this checkbox to remove the tick. The field will then not form part of the dynaset.

Task 2: Renaming and hiding fields in a query

Query 1

This query will list the names and addresses of all the male members who smoke.

1 Create a new query using the *Membership* table.

2 Add the following fields: *Membership No, Title, Lastname, Street, Town, County, Post Code, Smoker, Sex.*

3   In the criteria fields of *Smoker* and *Sex* put **Yes.** Hide these fields.

4   Sort the *Lastname* field in ascending order.

5   Rename **Membership No** as **Member No** and display the dynaset.

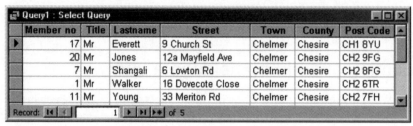

Member no	Title	Lastname	Street	Town	County	Post Code
17	Mr	Everett	9 Church St	Chelmer	Chesire	CH1 8YU
20	Mr	Jones	12a Mayfield Ave	Chelmer	Chesire	CH2 9FG
7	Mr	Shangali	6 Lowton Rd	Chelmer	Chesire	CH2 8FG
1	Mr	Walker	16 Dovecote Close	Chelmer	Chesire	CH2 6TR
11	Mr	Young	33 Meriton Rd	Chelmer	Chesire	CH2 7FH

Record: 1 of 5

6   Save the query as *Addresses of Male Smokers.* Close the query.

Query 2

In this task you create a query which looks at the occupations of the female members of the centre. The result will be selected fields from selected records.

1   Create a new query using the *Membership* table.

2   Add these fields to the query: *Category No, Firstname, Lastname, Occupation, Sex.*

3   In the **Criteria** cell of the *Sex* field type *No.*

4   Clear the checkbox in the **Show** cell of the *Sex* field to hide it.

5   Click at the beginning of the *Category No* header and type *Cat.* (Remember, no space before the colon).

6   Click on the **Datasheet** or **Run Query** button to view the result of the query. The *Category No* field should have the header **Cat** and the *Sex* field should be hidden.

7   Save the query as *Occupations of Female Members.*

Exploring types of query criteria

The queries that we have created so far have only used criteria in one field. Criteria may be applied to all the fields included in a query. Each field may be sorted or hidden. By combining these facilities, more complex queries can be produced.

We have already used some of the operators used in queries. Table 12.1 summarises the mathematical operators.

There are a number of **text** operators, of which the most important is the asterisk. ""*"" can act as a wildcard, standing for any characters. It is used in conjunction with given characters that define part of the text to be selected, for example:

"J*"   text strings beginning with *J*

"*ton"   text strings ending with *ton*

"*k*"   text strings containing the letter *k*

When you use the asterisk in criteria, the keyword **"Like"** is added to the start.

Operator	Meaning
<	less than
>	greater than
<>	not equal to
>=	greater than or equal to
<=	less than or equal to
+	addition
-	subtraction
*	multiplication
/	division

Using logic in queries

You can ask questions in queries which relate to more than one field, for example, to find male smokers (Query 1 in Task 2). The question is 'Is the member male AND does he smoke?' There is a logical AND between the two criteria; both criteria must be true for the record to be retrieved.

A logical AND can be used to set several criteria within one field, for example, members whose date of joining was after 1/1/96 AND before 1/1/97 (Query 2 in Task 3 below). In the **Criteria** cell the word 'and' is used between the two criteria, for example, *>1/1/96 and <1/1/97*. More than two criteria may be specified but remember to put the word AND between them.

The other logical operator that is used in queries is OR. An example of this would be a query which requires as its answer the names and addresses of members who live in Chelmer OR Meriton. There is a row entitled **or:** in the query design grid. The way in which this query is set up is to enter *Chelmer* into the **Criteria** row of the *Town* field and underneath in the **or:** row to enter *Meriton.*

The example below (Query 3 in Task 3) lists the names of the members who are likely to use the fitness suite as their sporting interests are aerobics, fitness training or weight training.

Task 3: Using different types of query criteria

Query 1 – querying text fields

This query picks out people with particular sporting interests.

1   Create a new query using the *Membership* table.

2   Add the following fields: *Membership No, Lastname, Category No, Sporting Interests*.

3   In the **Criteria** field of *Sporting Interests* type **Tennis**. Access will convert this to read **like *Tennis***.

Why are we using **Tennis** instead of just *Tennis*? If you're not sure, run the query and look at the dynaset it generates, then try it with *Tennis*. Without the asterisks,

Access looks for exact matches and will ignore fields which contain other words besides Tennis – and that is no use to us here.

4   Sort the *Lastname* field in **Ascending** order.

5   Rename *Membership No* as **Member No** and *Category No* as **Cat.**

6   Display the dynaset.

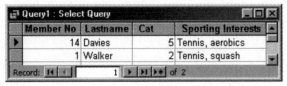

7   Print the dynaset.

8   Save the query giving it the name **Sporting Interest** and close the query.

Query 2 – logic, using AND

This query picks out members who joined in 1996.

1   Create a new query using the *Membership* table.

2   Add the following fields: *Title, Firstname, Lastname, Telephone No, Date of Joining*.

3   In the **Criteria** cell of *Date of joining* type **>=1/1/96 and <1/1/97**. Access will convert this to read >=#01/01/92# And <#01/01/93#.

4   Hide the *Date of joining* field.

5   Sort the *Lastname* field in **Ascending** order.

6   Display the dynaset.

7   Print the dynaset.

8   Save the query giving it the name **When joined** and close the query.

Query 3 – logic using OR

This query picks out members whose sporting interests are aerobics, fitness training or weight training and shows their town so that local interest can be assessed.

1   Create a new query using the *Membership* table.

2   Add the fields: *Membership No, Category No, Lastname, Town, Sporting Interests*.

3   In the **Criteria** cell of *Sporting Interests* type **aerobics**. Access will add the word *Like,* whether you type **aerobics*, '*aerobics*'or "*aerobics*"*.

4   In the **or:** cell of *Sporting Interests* type **fitness training**

5   In the **or:** cell of the row below type **weight training**

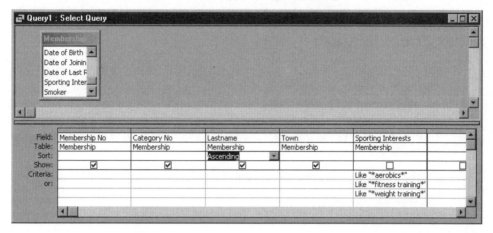

6   Hide the *Sporting Interests* field

7   Sort the *Lastname* field in **Ascending** order

8   Display the dynaset. Notice that when querying text Access is not case sensitive, **aerobics** will find aerobics, AEROBICS or Aerobics.

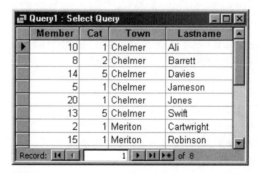

9   Print the dynaset

10   Close the query without saving.

Unit 13

More complex queries

What you will learn in this unit

Queries can perform calculations on the data in the table, as well as just retrieve it. Calculations might count the number of records, add up or take the average of certain fields or create new fields by calculation. New fields can even be created from a calculation using existing fields in the table: for example, if there is a price field which doesn't include sales tax then a *Sales Tax* field can be calculated by multiplying the price by the rate of the tax.

By the end of this unit you will be able to:

❏   edit and rename a query

❏   create new fields by calculation

❏   count and average fields, and group and average fields

❏   use criteria in a summary query.

There is a wide range of different applications where it might be appropriate to perform calculations as part of a query. Here we briefly explain some of the basic concepts and give a few examples. In the following task a new field *Age* is created and the average age of the members calculated.

To create a calculated field, an expression is entered into an empty field cell. The expression takes the form

   Name of calculated field:Expression.

The expression is the formula for creating the value of this field. It can use actual values or values held in other fields. Field names are written enclosed in square brackets, for example:

   Taxable pay:[Gross Pay]-[Free Pay]

   VAT:[Cost]*0.175.

Expressions may be used with date data types and there are several specific date functions available. The two that are used in the task following are:

❏   **Year()** which returns the year of the date/time value enclosed in brackets as an integer number, for example *Year([Date of Joining])* might result in 1996

❏   **Now()** which returns the date and time of the computer's system clock.

Sometimes it is useful to produce some summary statistics as a result of your query, for example the number of fields, the total of values in those fields or the average of the fields. These statistics may be for all the records in the table or just for the ones selected by the query.

Click on the **Totals** button  on the toolbar to show the **Total** row in the query design grid. It appears in between the **Table** and **Sort** rows.

Click in a **Total** cell, then click the down arrow to list the available statistical functions .

The functions of these options are listed below:

Function name	Purpose
Count	will give the number of records
Sum	will give a total of all values in that particular field
Min, **Max**	will give the maximum or minimum value of that particular field
Avg, **StDev**, **Var**	the average, standard deviation, variance of a particular field
Group by	groups records according to this field producing summary statistics for each group
Where	allows criteria to be specified

Editing and renaming a query

Once a query has been saved it can be used again and again. More records may be added to the table; each time a query is used it uses the data currently held in the table. However, as a database develops then the query itself may be changed to accommodate new requirements. If the query is modified you may want to change its name so that its purpose is still clear.

To do this, close the query, select it in the database window and choose **Edit-Rename**. Type the new name and hit *Enter*.

Task 1: Creating a new field by calculation

1 Create a new query using the *Membership* table.

2 Add the fields *Date of Birth* and *Lastname*.

3 Click in the next cell and create a calculated field by typing *Age: Year(Now())-Year([Date of Birth])*

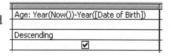

4 Sort the *Age* field in descending order.

5 Display the dynaset and print it.

If you make a mistake in typing in the formula, you will see an error message when you try to run the query – the chances are that you mistyped a field name, as in this example.

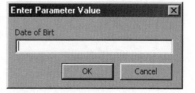

Click **Cancel** and correct the expression.

6 Save the query as *Member ages* and close it.

Task 2: Counting and averaging fields

Continue with the query created in Task 1.

1   Click on the **Totals** button to display the **Total** row.

2   In the **Total** cell for the *Lastname* and *Date of Birth* fields select **Count**.

3   In the total cell for the *Age* field put **Avg**.

Field:	Lastname	Date of Birth	Age: (Year(Now())-Year([Date of Birth]))
Table:	Membership	Membership	
Total:	Count	Count	Avg
Sort:			Descending
Show:	☑	☑	☑
Criteria:			
or:			

4   Run the query.

The result of this query is different from the normal dynaset display. One row is displayed which contains summary information according to the settings in the **Total** row. Return to the design view and click on the **Totals** button to hide the **Total** row; now when you run the query it reverts to the way it was in Task 1.

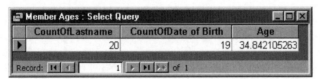

	CountOfLastname	CountOfDate of Birth	Age
▶	20	19	34.842105263

Record: |◀ ◀ | 1 | ▶ ▶| ▶* | of 1

Why is **Count of Lastname** different from **Count of Date of Birth**? Refer back to the section on null values in Unit 6.

If you save the summary form of this query and close it, you'll notice that when you open it again, Access has changed the calculated field to *Age: Avg(Year(Now())-Year([Date of Birth]))* and put **Expression** in the **Total** row.

Task 3: Grouping and averaging fields

Continue with the query in Task 1, by returning to the query design.

1   Add the *Category No* field to the query.

2   In the **Total** cell for the *Category No* field select **Group by** and choose **Ascending** as the sort order for this field.

3   Remove the sort order from *Age* and arrange your query as illustrated below:

Field:	Category No	Lastname	Date of Birth	Age: Avg((Year(Now())-Year([Date of Birth])));
Table:	Membership	Membership	Membership	
Total:	Group By	Count	Count	Expression
Sort:	Ascending			
Show:	☑	☑	☑	☑
Criteria:				
or:				

4   Run the query.

This time a summary row for each category is displayed, showing the total number and average age of members in each membership category.

Member Ages : Select Query			
Category No	CountOfLastname	CountOfDate of Birth	Age
1	7	7	39.142857143
2	5	5	43
3	1	1	17
4	2	2	18.5
5	3	2	39.5
6	2	2	20

Record: |◄| ◄ | 1 | ► | ►| | ►* | of 6

Task 4: Using criteria in a summary query

Continue with the previous query by returning to the query design.

1   In the **Total** cell for the *Category No* field select **Where**.

2   In the **Criteria** row type *1 or 2* (this is equivalent to putting 1 in the **Criteria** row and 2 in the **Or** row).

3   Remove the sort order from the *Category No* field, and hide it.

Field:	Category No	Lastname	Date of Birth	Age: Avg((Year(Now())-Year([Date of Birth])))
Table:	Membership	Membership	Membership	
Total:	Where	Count	Count	Expression
Sort:	▼			
Show:	☐	☑	☑	☑
Criteria:	1 Or 2			
or:				

4   Run the query. The result should be the total number of members in categories 1 and 2 and their average age.

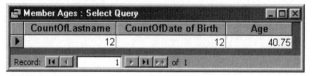

Member Ages : Select Query		
CountOfLastname	CountOfDate of Birth	Age
12	12	40.75

Record: |◄| ◄ | 1 | ► | ►| | ►* | of 1

5   Try this for categories 3 and 4.

6   Save the query and close it.

7   Rename this query as *Average Ages*. To do this, select the *Member Ages* query in the database window, choose **Edit-Rename** and change the name to *Average Ages*.

Task 5: Additional queries

This task takes the form of a series of questions plus the rationale for the questions. All queries are created using the *Membership* table.

1   What is the occupation of members with aerobics as a sporting interest?

If a large majority of members whose sporting interests include aerobics have stated that they are housewives, work from home, or are unemployed or retired, then an aerobics class could be scheduled in the day rather than the evening. Fields appropriate for this query might include *Membership No, Category No, Sex, Title, Lastname* and *Occupation* as well as *Sporting Interests*. Try sorting on *Category No*.

2   What is the home town of male members with sporting interests of weight training?

Should the centre attempt to offer better weight training facilities than the local competition and so attract members from a wide area? The fields that might be appropriate for this query, in addition to *Sporting Interests* and *Sex*, are *Initials*, *Lastname*, *Category No* and *Town*. Sort on the *Town* field.

3   *Which members joined the centre between 1/1/99 and 1/1/00?*

This query can easily be created by adjusting the second query in Task 3, Unit 12. Such queries can be used to assess the success of the centre over time.

4   *Which members are aged between 18 and 25?*

Should the bar consider holding social events targeted at this age group? Are there enough members locally in this age group to make this worthwhile? The fields that might be appropriate for this query are *Name*, *Date of Birth*, all address fields and *Sporting Interests*. Sort the query by *Post Code*.

5   *Which members are over 60, retired and live locally?*

The centre might consider a range of short daytime classes for its less robust members; and since people are less likely to want to travel far for a short class, it will be useful to see how nearby these members live. The fields that might be appropriate for this query, are *Membership No*, *Category No*, *Date of Birth*, *Occupation* and all the address fields. Sort the query by *Date of Birth*.

6   *Which members have sporting interests of keep fit and aerobics?*

The fields that might be appropriate for this query are *Membership No*, *Lastname*, *Category No* and *Sporting Interests*. Sort in **Ascending** order both the *Category No* and *Date of Birth*, with *Category No* having the higher priority.

Designing and using forms

What you will learn in this unit

In this unit you will learn how to create a form for the screen. A form provides a more user-friendly way with which to work with your data. Entering data can be made easier and less prone to error.

 When data is collected manually it is often by means of filling out a form. In a form there are boxes to fill in: name and address, etc, and there may be some that are ticked, like Yes/No boxes. With Access you can create an on-screen form so that data can be entered into a table by filling it in. This should be more user-friendly than filling in the cells in a datasheet, provided that the form has been designed carefully.

By the end of this unit you will be able to:

❏ create a form using the Form Wizard

❏ save a form

❏ use a form

❏ print a form.

 In Units 2 to 9 the tables for the Chelmer Leisure and Recreation Centre were defined. Data was entered into the Membership table, but as yet the other tables are empty. In this and the following two units you will enter the data into these tables. This could be done in the same way as the Membership data, typing directly into the datasheet view of the table, but it will be easier with a form. The fields in a record often do not all fit on the screen at once, and entering data in the datasheet grid can be hard on the eyes if you're doing it in long sessions.

A form can be based upon a table or a dynaset created from a query. A query can use more than one table, so a form created from a query can be used to enter data into several different tables. This will be explored in later sessions. In this session we will concentrate on forms to enter data into one table at a time.

Forms can be used to enter, edit, display and print data contained in your tables. They can also be formatted to a greater extent than a datasheet, and thus present data in an organised and attractive manner.

Standard forms can be created for most applications or jobs: for example, a form for entering a new member's details, as shown in Figure 14.1.

We will use the Access Wizards to create a basic form in this unit, which will then be customised in the next unit. In Unit 16 you will learn how to create a form from scratch. There are two kinds of Wizard for creating forms:

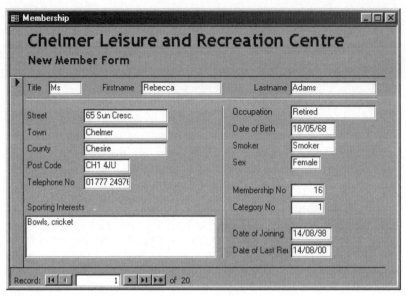

Figure 14.1

❏ AutoForm will create a standard form using all fields in the table that you base the form upon.

❏ Forms Wizard gives you a little more flexibility over the appearance of your form, and which fields are included.

Creating a form with AutoForm

There are three types of form that can be created using AutoForm: columnar, tabular, and datasheet. A columnar form will display from one record at a time, with boxes for the user to fill in which are arranged in one or two columns. The form shown in Figure 14.1 started as a columnar form but has been modified slightly.

Datasheet forms look like a table in Datasheet view, as you might expect. Tabular forms are similarly laid out, but have boxes instead of a datasheet grid. Both display more than one record at once, so if there are a lot of fields an entire record will not fit on the screen; they are most useful for tables with just a few fields, such as the *Membership Category* table.

To create a form using AutoForm:

1 Click on the **Forms** button and then click **New** to show the **New Form** dialog box (Figure 14.2).

2 Click on the down arrow of the **Choose the table or query...** box, and select the table or query for which you wish to create a form.

3 Select one of the AutoForm options.

4 Click on **OK**.

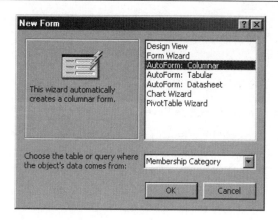

Figure 14.2

Autoforms: a word of warning

For most purposes, the Autoform facility is a useful way of creating forms quickly, but in the current version of Access 2000, there does seem to be a bit of a bug in the way it names forms created with Autoform. For the moment, this is not important, but in later units you will be introduced to macros, small programs which can streamline your database. These macros often need to refer to forms and queries using the object's name, and this can cause problems. This will be explained more thoroughly in Unit 43.

Creating a form using Form Wizard

The Wizard will build the same three types of form as Autoform, plus a further type called a justified form. This displays one record at a time in a row format.

To create a form with Form Wizard, click **New** as above, then select **Form Wizard** and click **OK**. Check that the correct table is listed in the **Table/Queries** box, and if not, select the right one.

The next stage is to choose which fields are to be on the form. The fields that you can have in the form are shown in the **Available Fields** list.

Transfer these to the **Selected Fields** list by selecting each field and clicking ▶. You may set the order in which the fields appear on the form by selecting them in the order you desire.

If you wish to *add all* the fields in the table to the form, click ▶▶.

◀ will remove a highlighted field; ◀◀ will remove all the fields from the form.

When you have added the required fields to the form, click Next >. Choose a **Columnar**, **Tabular**, **Datasheet** or **Justified** form.

You are then asked what kind of style you want for your form and are given a choice. An example of the style is shown to the left of the dialog box. Click on each style in turn to see what it would look like.

Key in an appropriate title for your form into the **Title** box, then click [Finish] to display the form with data in it.

Saving and closing a form

Save a form by choosing **File-Save** or clicking on **Save**.

A form can be closed by **File-Close** or the **Close** button of its window. If the form or the latest changes have not been saved you will be prompted to save. When a form is closed its filename is shown in the Database window in the Forms area.

To open a form from the Database window, click on the **Forms** button, select the name of the form required and click on the **Open** button.

Task 1: Creating a columnar membership form using AutoForm

In this task you will create a single column membership form, which can later be modified to look like the form shown in Figure 14.1. The order in which the fields are selected for the form is important, as will become apparent when the form is used to enter data. To create this form:

1   From the Database window click on the **Forms** button and click **New**.

2   Display the list of tables in the **New Form** dialog box and select *Membership* from the list of tables. Select **AutoForm: Columnar** and click **OK**.

Access creates a form with a title and a list of paired field names and data in a column. The data showing is from the first record in the table – use the **Record** arrows at the bottom of the window to view or edit other records. Notice that there are some differences between this form and the one shown in Figure 14.1. Customising the form will be considered in Unit 15.

3   Choose **File-Save**, and call the form *Membership.*

4   Close the form.

Creating a tabular form

A tabular form is one that displays several records on the screen at once. The field names are column headings and the records are shown in a table, as in Datasheet view. If there are a lot of fields in a record it is unlikely that you will be able to see the complete record on the screen and you may need to scroll to the right. Tabular forms are best suited to tables with only a few fields, like the *Membership Category* table. The advantage is that they display more than one record at a time.

A tabular form may be created either using AutoForm or Form Wizard. The following task deals with creating a tabular form using the Form Wizard.

Task 2: Creating the membership category form

No data has yet been entered into the *Classes* table: this task will create a form which can later be used for this purpose.

1   First close any open forms.

2   In the Database window, click the **Forms** button, and then click **New**.

3   In the **New Form** dialog box select the *Membership Category* table from the drop-down list at the bottom.

4   Select **Form Wizard** and click **OK**.

5   Add all the fields to the form and click on the [Next >] button.

6   Choose a **Tabular** form with a **Standard** style (click [Next >] after each step).

7   Give it the title *Membership Category*.

8   Click on the [Finish] button to display the form. There is no data in this form yet, so there is only one blank record to display. When records have been added, then more than one record is shown in the form, as we shall see later.

9   Close the form.

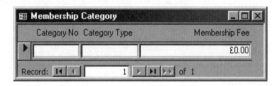

Using a form

To use a form, first display the available ones in the Database window by clicking the **Forms** button. To open a form, select it and click **Open**, or double-click on it.

You can use the form to look at the data in the table (or query) upon which it is based. Whether it is a single column or tabular form use the record movement keys in the status bar or the **Edit-GoTo** options to move around the records in your form.

Using the *Page Up* and *Page Down* keys with a single column form will display the next/previous record, whereas with a tabular form they will either page up or down a screen full of records.

Using the form to enter a new record into the table

Forms should be designed with this purpose in mind, as it is their primary function. Entering data is a labour-intensive task and the design of the form is important because a person entering data may use it for long periods.

To enter a new record using a form:

1   Start a new record use the **New Record** button [▶*] on the status bar. If your form is tabular, click in the first field of the blank record shown at the end of your records.

2   Enter data for the new record by filling in the boxes for each field. When you have completed each field, press *[Enter]* or *[Tab]* to move to the next one.

3   Check boxes are used for **Yes/No** fields. Checked is *Yes*, not checked *No*.

Task 3: Using a form to enter data into a table

In this task we shall enter data into the categories of membership table, using the tabular form.

1   Open the *Membership Category* form.

2   Enter the data as shown below. As you enter each record it is saved to the *Membership Category* table.

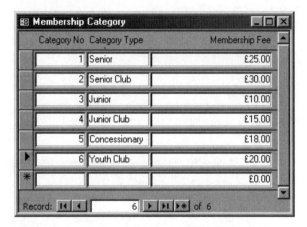

3   Close the form.

4   Now there is data in the form use **Tools-Relationships** to create the link between the *Membership Category* and *Membership* tables (refer back to Unit 8 if you need help). Drag *Category No (Membership Category)* to *Category No* on the *Membership* table. Check the **Enforce Referential Integrity** check box and close the **Relationships** window.

Printing a form

Forms are designed primarily for screen use, i.e. they are intended for data to be entered and they display it on screen. However, Access offers the facility to print from a form in case you need to. Remember to preview a form before printing it.

Previewing

Previewing will display a miniature version of what is to be printed. This allows the layout to be assessed so that adjustments can be made before printing.

To preview a form:

1   Click on the **Print Preview** button in the toolbar, and a miniature version of what is to be printed will be displayed.

2   To zoom in and out, just click on the preview, or use the **Zoom** button. Clicking on the right mouse button will allow you to select the degree of magnification.

3   Choose **File-Page Setup** to make adjustments such as the orientation of the paper

(portrait or landscape), the choice of printer and width of margins. Click **OK** when the required adjustments have been made.

Printing

When you're happy with the layout, you can print from the preview or the form screen.

1   Choose **File-Print**.

2   Select whether all pages of the form will be printed or just selected ones, and specify the number of copies. Click **OK**.

Task 4: Printing the Membership Ccategory form

1   Open the *membership category* form.

2   Click on the **Print Preview** button.

3   Experiment with zooming in and out.

4.   Use **File-Page Setup** and/or **File-Print** to make adjustments to the paper and printer setup before printing. If no adjustments are necessary, then click **Print**.

5.   Close the form.

Unit 15

Customising forms

What you will learn in this unit

Forms are constructed from a collection of individual design elements, which are called controls. If you are familiar with Windows applications you will be familiar with dialog boxes and the controls that they contain. The controls that appear on the forms created so far are:

❏   labels, so that you know what each part of the form is for

❏   text boxes, for entering data.

↔   There are other controls, which will be introduced in Unit 21.

By the end of this unit you will be able to:

❏   display the customising tools (toolbox, palette, properties and field list)

❏   move and size controls

❏   align controls

❏   add text to a form

❏   add the date

❏   add headers and footers to a printed form.

Customising a form

A form may be modified so that it is easier for inexperienced users to enter information into the database. To modify a form you need to display the form in design mode (see the following section). AutoForm or Form Wizard is a good way of quickly creating a form. However, the resulting form is rather standardised in terms of vertical spacing between controls, fonts and colours, so you are likely to wish to make modifications.

Components of a form in Design view

Component	Description
Form header	Typically contains text such as the form's title, but may also hold field headers and graphics.
Detail	Contains the controls (field labels, text boxes and check boxes) that display data from the underlying table.
Form footer	Used like the header, typically holding the date and similar items.

Right margin	The position of the right margin is indicated by a vertical line on the right edge of the form. It can be moved by clicking and dragging.
Bottom margin	A horizontal line that indicates the bottom margin of the form. This also can be positioned by clicking and dragging.
Scroll bars	Vertical and horizontal scroll bars enable movement of the form within its window.

If you have used a Form Wizard to create the form, only the detail band and possibly the header band contain controls. The header band contains information, which will always appear at the top of the form, usually the title. The detail band contains the controls for displaying the data.

Form Design view

So far a form has only been opened in 'form run' or Data view. This is the mode in which forms are usually run where they display and more importantly, accept data. A form can also be shown in Design view, where its layout and appearance can be modified. Data cannot be entered in this view.

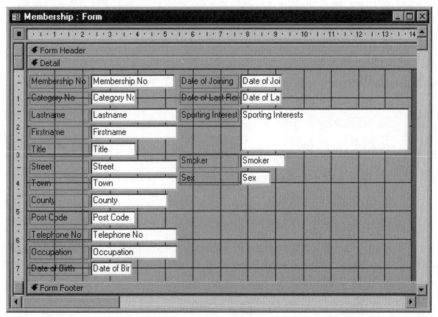

Figure 15.1 Membership form in Design view

Label and text box controls

A field usually has two controls: a label control in which the field name appears and a text box control in which the data will appear when the form is run.

The field names are shown in the controls instead of the data, as in Data view. The labels and controls may be moved, resized or reformatted to produce the desired layout and appearance.

Design aids

Other features of Design view are:

❏ rulers and grid

❏ design aids in the form of other small windows:

    ❖ the Toolbox

    ❖ the Field List

    ❖ the Properties Sheet.

The **Toolbox** offers a selection of tools with which controls and text may be added to the form.

The **Field List** shows a list of fields in the table on which the form was based.

The **Properties Sheet** is a list of properties. The properties will depend upon what part of the form is selected.

You will become familiar with these as you progress through the tasks. To display these windows click on the buttons:

    the Toolbox   the Field List   the Properties Sheet

Or use the menu commands, **View-Toolbox**, **View-Field List** and **View-Proper-ties**.

Colour selection

Colour selection can be made using the drop-down buttons on the Formatting toolbar. These will be considered in Unit 22.

Opening a form in design view

To open a form in Design view, from the Database window:

1   Click on the **Forms** tab.

2   Select the name of the form required and click on the **Design** button.

Once a form is open you may switch between form run (Data) view and Design view by clicking on the button on the toolbar, or by selecting **View-Design-View**, or **View-Form-View**.

    Form View   Design view

Moving and sizing controls

Before you can move or size a control you must select it. A control is selected by clicking anywhere on it. When selected, the control is enclosed by an outlining rectangle with an anchor block at its upper left corner and five smaller blocks. These smaller blocks are sizing handles. On columnar forms, text boxes often have associated labels and when you select one of these they are selected together as a unit.

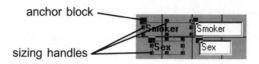

anchor block

sizing handles

Figure 15.2

To...	Do this
Select a text box and its label (if it has one)	Click anywhere on either the label or the text box.
Move a text box and its label (if it has one)	After selecting, move the pointer over the label until it changes shape to a hand. Click and drag the text box to its new position.
Move label or text box separately ing	After selecting, move the pointer over the anchor block at the top left corner of the label or text box. The pointer should change shape to a point-hand. Click and drag to new position.
Adjust the width and height together	Move the pointer over a sizing handle at one of the three other corners (i.e. not the top left). It should change to a diagonal two-headed arrow. Click and drag to size required.
Adjust only the height of the control	Move the pointer over a sizing handle in the middle of the top or bottom of the outline. It should change shape to a vertical two-headed arrow. Click and drag to height required.
Adjust only the width of the control	Move the pointer over a sizing handle in the middle of the left or right-hand side of the outline. It should change shape to a horizontal two-headed arrow. Click and drag to width required.

Selecting and moving a group of controls

You can select and move more than one object at a time. This is useful if you want to keep the relative spacing of a group of objects while you move them to another part of the form.

To select a group of objects, either:

❑ imagine a rectangle that would touch or enclosed the objects; use the pointer and click and drag to draw this rectangle on the form; when you release the mouse button all the objects covered by this rectangle will be selected, or

❑ select one object, hold down the *Shift* key and select the subsequent objects.

To move:

❑ *the whole group*, with pointer as the shape of an open hand, drag

❑ *an individual control in the group*, point to its anchor handle and drag.

To deselect:

❑ *the whole group*, click anywhere outside the selected area

❑ *one object in the group*, hold down the *Shift* key and click on the object.

Using the ruler and the grid

The **View-Ruler** command will select whether or not the ruler is displayed. When a control is being dragged, indicator lines slide along both rulers to aid positioning of controls.

View-Grid will display or hide a grid, which is also an aid to the positioning of controls. The spacing of the grid can be adjusted by adjusting the setting of the **GridX** and **GridY** properties on the form's property sheet. To display the form property sheet use **Edit-Select Form** and click on the **Properties** button.

When **Format-Snap to Grid** is on (indicated by a tick by **Snap to Grid** in the menu), any new controls drawn on the form will have their corners aligned to points on the grid. When **Snap to Grid** is off, the control can be placed anywhere.

Aligning a group of controls

Once you start to move controls around the form they can become untidy as they become misaligned. By selecting a group of controls together they can be aligned. Select labels and text boxes separately for alignment purposes.

To align labels:

1   Select the labels by clicking on each label while holding down the _Shift_ key, or draw a rectangle that encloses part or all of all the labels you wish to select.

2   Choose **Format-Align** and as these are labels select **Right**. The selected group of controls should all align to the right.

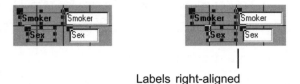

Figure 15.3   Labels right-aligned

To align text box controls:

1   Select the text box controls by clicking on each text box while holding down the _Shift_ key.

2   Choose **Format-Align** and as these are text boxes select **Left**. The selected group of controls should all align to the left.

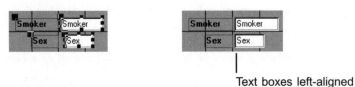

Figure 15.4   Text boxes left-aligned

Changing the form's area

The area of each section of a form – the header, detail and footer – may be altered individually. Also, the position of the right and bottom edge of a form may be adjusted.

To alter the depth of a section of the form:

1 Move the pointer to the bottom edge of the section, where it will change shape.

2 Drag down to increase the depth of the section.

To alter the area of the form drag the right and bottom edges to the required size.

Task 1: Customising the membership form

The aim of this task is to create the form shown in Figure 14.1. We don't give exact instructions as you can experiment with selecting and moving controls. You may find it useful to widen the form so that controls can be moved to temporary positions while you rearrange them, then shrink the form back to the required size when you have finished.

If you wish to keep a group of controls together, select them as a group and then they can be moved as a group. Also try aligning groups of controls to achieve a tidy looking form.

1 Open the *Membership* form in Design view.

2 Select and move the controls as necessary.

3 When you have rearranged the detail section save the form design using **File-Save**.

i If you inadvertently delete a field from the form see the following table for instructions on how to restore it.

Deleting or restoring form fields

To...	Do this
Delete a label and text box	Select the control and press *Delete* or use **Edit-Delete** to delete both label and entry box.
Delete only the label	Click on the control then on the label before deleting.
⚠	*If you delete a field you won't be able to use the form to enter data into it. Use **Edit-Undo** immediately if you accidentally delete one.*
Restore a label and field	Use **View-Field List** to display the list of fields in the table. Click on the field name required and drag into position on the form. If the form is a single column form then both label and field will appear, although the label will require editing. If the form is tabular then just the field will be restored.

Changing the text of a field name label

The text of a field name label may be edited and, if required, additional text can be added to the form.

To...	Do this
Add a label	Click on the **Label** tool in the **Toolbox** (see Figure 21.1), then click on the form in the required position and type the text.
Edit a label	Double-click on the label to display an insertion point in the text. Edit the text as required. Press *Enter* or click on a blank part of the form when finished.

Altering the size and font of controls

To alter the size or font of controls in a form:

1   Select the control(s) to be altered.

2   Open the **Font** list box in the toolbar and select the font required.

3   Open the **Point Size** list box and select the point size required.

4   Click on the **Left**, **Centre** or **Right** alignment button on the toolbar.

⚠   If you increase the size of a font you may need to alter the size of the control and the size of the section.

Task 2: Adding text to the form header

In this task you will add text to the header section of the *Membership* form.

1   Open the *Membership* form in Design view.

2   Widen the form header section.

3   Click on the **Label** tool in the Toolbox window.

4   Click in the space created for the form header and key in the text *Chelmer Leisure and Recreation Centre.*

5   Increase the size of the label and text. You may wish to change the font.

6   Move and size the heading as in Figure 15.5, and add the text *New Member Form.* If you wish you may alter the font or size of this text.

7   Save and close the form.

Task 3: Using the customised form to enter data

To gain a full appreciation of the modifications made to the *Membership* form then it should be used to enter data.

1   Open the form from the Database window by clicking on the **Open** button.

Figure 15.5

2　Move through the records and display a blank form.

3　Compose data for a new member and using the form, enter data into the next record.

4　Close the form.

Reorganising the field order

When data is entered into each field, *Enter* or *Tab* takes you to the next. The order in which the fields are entered is defined by the order in which they were selected in the Wizard. If the layout has been modified, this order may need to be changed.

To change the tab order of the fields:

1　From Design view, choose **View-Tab Order** to display the **Tab Order** dialog box (Figure 15.6). This displays the order of the fields in the **Custom Order** box. In the **Section** box the Detail section is normally selected.

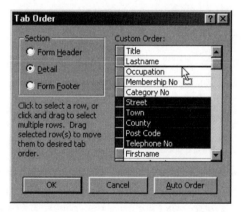

Figure 15.6

2　To alter the order, select the field(s) to be moved and drag to the new position.

3　When the new order has been arranged click on **OK**.

The **Auto Order** button will set the tab order according to the way in which the fields are laid out on the form, working left to right and then top to bottom.

Adding headers and footers

Headers and footers are always displayed on the screen. It is straightforward to add text into these, and simple enough to add calculated text, such as the date.

If a form is to be printed, the header section prints before the first record and the footer prints after the last. Extra sections – *page header* and *page footer* – can be added which will print on each page. You can control whether to display or print these. Calculated text may be added to show the page numbers.

Page breaks may occur in the middle of records, if the record is in single column format. This can be avoided by adjusting the **Keep together** setting of the **Detail** properties from **No** to **Yes** (see Figure 15.7).

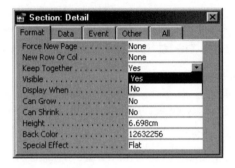

Figure 15.7

To display the Properties sheet check that the **Properties** button is depressed and click on the **Detail** bar.

Task 4: Adding the date

The aim of this task is to put the date in the *Membership Category* form footer.

1 Open the *Membership Category* form in Design view.

2 Choose **Insert-Date and Time**. Select a suitable date format and click on **OK.** The date and time will be inserted into the header.

3 Cut and paste to move the date and time into the footer.

 Note: when moving a control from one section to another, always drag with the open hand pointer ✋*, not the pointing finger* 👆*, as the latter will not do what you expected! Try it to see what happens, then choose **Edit-Undo**.*

4 Switch to run mode by clicking on the **View** button to see the result.

5 Close the form.

Task 5: Adding headers and footers to a printed form

When a form is printed the header is printed at the beginning and the footer is printed at the end of the records. To add a header and footer at the top and bottom of each page of the *Membership* form when printed:

1　Open the *Membership* form in Design view.

2　Choose **View-Page Header/Footer**. Two extra sections appear, **Page Header** and **Page Footer.**

3　Select both title labels in the form header and use **Edit-Copy**.

4　Click on the Page Header bar and use **Edit-Paste.** Position the pasted copy.

5　Click on the Page Footer bar and choose **Insert-Page-Number**. Choose a suitable format and click on **OK.**

6　Click on the Form Header bar. To display the **Properties** sheet, click on the **Properties** button on the toolbar.

7　In the **Section: FormHeader** properties box select the **Format** tab.

8　Click in the **Display When** box to open the list and select **Screen Only**.

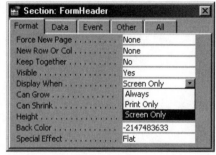

This makes sure that the Form Header section is only displayed when the form is being used on-screen.

If you don't change this setting, the first page of the printed form will have duplicate titles: one from the Form Header and one from the Page Header.

9　Click on the Detail bar and change the **Keep Together** property to **Yes** to prevent page breaks in the middle of records.

10　Preview the form and zoom in and out to see how it looks. Return to Design view and make any adjustments to the layout of the page header and foot.er.

11　Print the form, then save it and close it.

Unit 16

Forms without Wizards

What you will learn in this unit

The previous units have dealt with creating forms using the Form Wizard. This method can be restrictive when creating a custom form, so you may prefer to create a form without the Wizard.

By the end of this unit you will be able to:

❏   open a blank form

❏   choose the type of form

❏   add controls to the form

Creating a blank form

If the columnar or tabular layout is not suitable for the intended form, then it may be easier to start with a blank form and create a custom design from scratch.

When you start with a blank form, then just a blank detail section is displayed, ready for you to add controls in the layout you require.

To create a blank form:

1   Click on the **Forms** button in the database window, click on **New** and choose De-sign view.

2   Select the table upon which the form is to be based and click on **OK**.

3   Display the properties window by choosing **View-Properties** or clicking on the **Properties** button on the toolbar. In the **Form Properties** sheet you should see the Default View property set to Single Form.

Using the ruler and grid

Choose View-Grid to put a matrix of lines on the form, and View-Ruler to display rulers along the top and left edges of the form. These will help with positioning the controls – but neither are visible when the form is run.

Adding header/footer sections

Choose **View-Form Header/Footer** to add the header and footer sections. If you intend to print the form then page header and footer sections may also be added.

Adding a label to the form

A label is the simplest control that you can add to your form. Labels only display the text which you give to them – they are called 'unbound', i.e. they are not related to any data in the underlying table (we will deal with this in more detail in Unit 21). Labels may be added anywhere in the form, e.g. as a title in the header section.

1   Click on the **Label** button in the toolbox. The pointer becomes a label symbol with a cross-hair. Position the pointer in the form where you want the label.

2   Either click to put a small label box on the workspace, which will expand as you add text, or click and drag to draw a larger box. If you drag below the bottom or to the right of the particular section, this part of the form will expand to accommodate the size of label you require.

3   The label is outlined and a flashing insertion point appears inside it, ready for you to enter text. If you don't enter any text and click the mouse button the label will disappear.

4   The size and font may be adjusted by selecting the label and formatting using the appropriate list boxes in the toolbar.

Adding a text box

A text box is the most common type of control found on forms. Text boxes are 'bound' to fields in the underlying table (shown in the Field List window).

To add a text box:

1   Click on the **Field List** button on the toolbar or choose **View-Field List** to display the field list window.

2   Click on the required field in the **Field List** and, holding down the mouse button, drag to the detail workspace. Release the mouse button when the pointer is at the upper left-hand corner of where the text box should go. A label will automatically be placed on the form next to the text box.

3   Reposition and resize the text box and label (if the grid is not showing, choose **View-Grid** to display it). Remember that you need to use the anchor handle if you want to move the label or text box independently of each other.

4   If you need to, change the size and font of text in the control.

5   More than one field can be selected from the field list and placed on the form as a group. To select multiple fields, use the *Shift* or *Ctrl* keys while making the selection.

6   The order in which the fields are selected determines the tab order. If you need to change this, choose **View-Tab Order** and rearrange the order (see the last unit if you need reminding).

Adding a multi-line text box

Multi-line text boxes are usually used to display memo fields. They are larger than the single line boxes. They also have a vertical scroll bar to scroll through text when there is more than can be viewed at one time.

1   From the **Field List** select a field which has the memo data type. Drag the field list pointer to the lower middle part of the detail section and drop.

2   Adjust the size of the text box and position the label.

3   Click on the **Format** tab of the **Text Box Properties** window. The **Scroll Bars** property box will display **Vertical**, which adds a vertical scroll bar to your text box. Note that the scroll bar will only appear when you click in the text box while the form is run, indicating to Access that you are using this control.

4   If you wish to print the form, you will wanbt tomake sure that the whole memo field is printed. In the Properties change both the **Can Grow** and the **Can Shrink** properties to **Yes**. This will not affect the text box while it is being displayed on the screen.

Task 1: Creating a blank form

Although forms have been created either using AutoForm or Form Wizard, this task will explore using a blank form that will duplicate one of the forms already created. You will start with the *Membership* table.

1   Click on the **Forms** button in the database window, click **New** and choose **Design view**. Select the *Membership* table and click on **OK**.

2   Access creates a new blank form, showing the detail section.

3   Add header and footer sections by choosing **View-Form Header/Footer**.

4   Adjust the depth of the detail section by pointing to the top line of the **Form Footer** bar. The pointer should change shape to this double-arrow ╪. Click and drag downward to expand the detail section area.

5   Add all the fields, by clicking and dragging from the field list. Consider the order in which you select and place them. Try selecting and placing a group of fields.

6   Add a title to the form and save the form as *Membership2*.

7   Run the form and use it to add another record to the *Membership* table.

8   Adjust the tab order and layout if necessary, then save the changes.

Forms design: integrative tasks

The following tasks revise some of the topics covered in this and the last two units.

Task 2: Designing and using forms

The *Classes* and *Bookings* tables require forms to be designed.

1 Use AutoForm and Form Wizard to create columnar forms for both these tables, saving them as *Classes* and *Bookings* respectively.

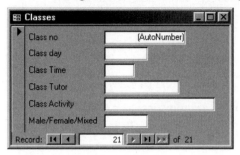

The *Classes* form

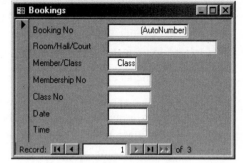

The *Bookings* form

2 Use the forms to enter the data for these tables given in Quick Reference 1.

Note: when entering bookings data, type Yes for a member and No for a class. Remind yourself of the validation rules set in Unit 9 and try testing them while entering the data.

3 Close the forms when the data has been entered.

Task 3: Adding a new table and creating a form

This task recaps on some of the activities met during this and the previous two units. The aim is to create a new table, link it into another table in the Chelmer database and create a form to input data into this table. The table to be created is the *Tutor* table.

The *Tutor* table will contain the fields: *Lastname, Initials, Title, Street, Town, County, Post Code, Telephone No, National Insurance No, Date of Birth* and *Qualifications*.

1 Create this *Tutor* table; make all fields except for *Date of Birth* and *Qualifications* text fields, and choose suitable lengths for each. Use a short date for *Date of Birth* and a memo for *Qualifications*. Set *Lastname* as the primary key. Save the table as *Tutors*. Create a link between this table and the *Classes* table using **View-Relationships**.

2 Use **Relationships-Show Table** to add the Tutor table. Drag the *Lastname* field from the *Tutor* table (the 'one' side of the relationship) to the *Class Tutor* field in the *Classes* table (the 'many' side of the relationship).

3 Consider the pros and cons of checking the **Enforce Referential Integrity** check box. If there is no data in the *Tutor* table you will not be able to enforce referential integrity.

To design a form for this table:

1 Select the **Forms** button in the database window, and click **New**.

2 Select **Design view** for the *Tutor* table. Access creates a new form, showing the Detail section.

3   Check that the **Default View** property in the **Form Properties** box is **Single Form**.

4   Add a header and footer section by choosing **View-Form Header/Footer**.

5   Adjust the depth of the detail section by clicking and dragging the line between the Detail section and the Form Footer.

6   Add all the fields to the form from the **Field List**.

7   Add a title label to the form header and save the form as *Tutors*.

8   Select the text box for qualifications so that its properties sheet is displayed. Set the following properties for this text box: **Scroll bars - Vertical**, **Can Grow - Yes**, **Can Shrink - Yes**.

9   Save the form and run it.

10   Use it to enter the following tutor record: *Evans, P J, Mrs, 25 Lyme Green, Chelmer, Cheshire, CH2 1ED, 01777 560935, XZ 32 99 06B, 17/7/70, Y.M.C.A. Dance to Music, Certificate in Aerobics, First Aid (Red Cross)*.

Report Wizard and AutoReport

What you will learn in this unit

This unit explores the basic design of printed reports that include data from an Access table. It explains how to create a report quickly using Report Wizard. Later units develop some of the themes in this unit more fully.

By the end of this unit you will be able to:

❑ create a report using Report Wizard or AutoReport

❑ save and close a report

❑ use a report to print data from an Access table.

Printing information from a database

Reports are used to print information from a number of records, which can come from a table or a query. Reports may also show summary information relating to the records displayed. Graphs created with Microsoft Graph may also be added.

Reports allow you to select the data to be printed and then to present that data in an acceptable format. Unlike forms, reports are intended to be printed. Forms are normally displayed on screen, though they can be printed if required.

In most applications you will create a number of different standard reports. For example, a mailing list of clients may simply show customer name and address, but a list of outstanding orders to specific clients will also show details of the items customers have ordered, their value and other associated information.

Access has a Report Wizard to help you produce a basic report quickly and easily, and a range of tools for customising or creating a report from scratch. We use the Report Wizard in this unit to introduce the concept of reports and how they work, before you grapple with customising specific features of the report.

Since forms and reports share many design and creation features, you will re-use some of the skills that you acquired earlier in designing a form.

Creating a report using AutoReport

The really easy way to create a report is to allow Access to do all the work for you, by using AutoReport. This does not allow any scope for specifying the contents or style of the report, however; for that we'll use the Report Wizard in the next task.

AutoReports can have a columnar or tabular layout.

Task 1: Creating a tabular report using AutoReport

This task demonstrates how easy it is to create a report using AutoReport.

1   Click on the **Reports** button, then click **New**.

2   In the **New Report** dialog box select **AutoReport: Tabular.**

3   Click on the down arrow button of the **Choose a table or query...** list box, and select the table *Membership Category*.

4   Click **OK**, and the report will be created and displayed on the screen in preview mode.

5   Save the report as *Membership Category* and print it.

Creating a single-column report with Report Wizard

 There are various types of report that can be created with Report Wizard. First we deal with the single-column report, which is used most frequently and is relatively simple to create. A single-column report places all the selected fields in a single column, with their field names to the left.

1   To enter Report wizard from the Database window, either click on **New** in the Database window when you are displaying reports, or click the **New Object** button on the toolbar and select **Report**. A **New Report** dialog box appears (Figure 17.1).

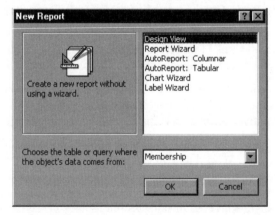

Figure 17.1

2   Select the **Report Wizard** option to create a report using Report Wizard.

3   Click on the down arrow of the **Choose the table or query...** list box, to produce a list of tables and queries and select the table for which you wish to create a report.

4   Click on **OK**.

5   The next stage is to choose which fields are to be in the report. The possible fields are shown in the **Available fields** box (Figure 17.*2)*. These can be transferred to the report by selecting each field in turn and clicking on the ▶ button.

7   If you wish to add all the fields in the table to the report, click on the ▶▶ button.

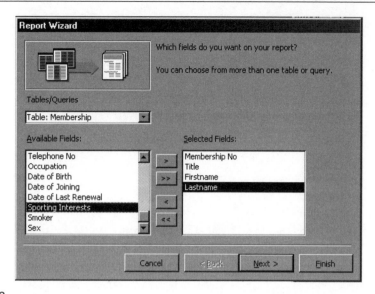

Figure 17.2

8   You may set the order in which the fields appear on the report by selecting them in the order that you desire. The ⟨ button will remove a highlighted field and ⟨⟨ will remove all the fields from the report.

9   Once you have added the required fields to the report continue by clicking on the Next > button.

10   The next dialog box asks you to indicate grouping levels. Leave this for now and ◄► click on the Next > button. We shall return to this in Unit 18.

11   The next step asks you to select the sort order. Select the fields you want the records to be sorted by. If you have only a small set of records, a single sort field will be

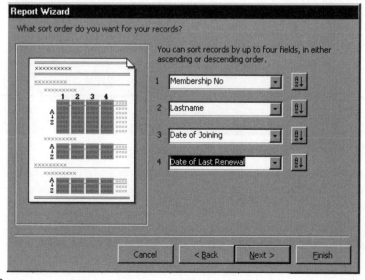

Figure 17.3

adequate. If you want records to appear in the same order as in the table or query, it is not necessary to indicate a sort field. Click the [Next >] button.

12 The next step relates to the report's layout and orientation (portrait or landscape). The choice of layout depends on whether or not grouping is used. For now, choose **Columnar** and **Portrait**. Click on [Next >].

13 You are then asked what kind of style you want for your report. You are given a choice of:

❑ Bold

❑ Casual

❑ Compact

❑ Corporate

❑ Formal

❑ Soft Gray.

14 The style determines the appearance of the field names and field contents in the report. An example of the style is shown on the left of the dialog box. Click on each style in turn to see what it would look like. Click on the [Next >] button.

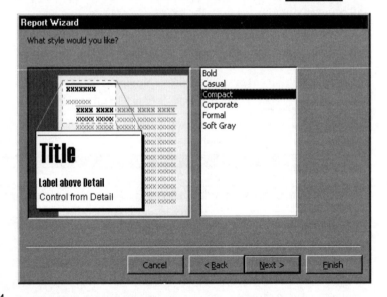

Figure 17.4

15 You are next asked for a title. Report titles are particularly important in flagging the purpose of the report to the reader, so type in something that conveys a clear idea of its contents.

16 Select the **Preview the report** option and click on [Finish]. Note that Access has added a page number and the date at the bottom of every page.

Saving and closing a report

Save a report by choosing **File-Save**. If this is a new report that does not have a name, Access will prompt for a file name with a **File-Save As** dialog box. If you later want to save a report under another name use **File-Save As**, and enter the new name in the dialog box.

Remember that there is a distinction between the name and the title of a report. The title is the text that is displayed at the top of the report when it is printed. The name you give when saving the report is the report's file name, which you need to be able to recognise when you want to open it for use again. These names appear in the Database window when the **Report** button is selected.

Task 2: Creating a vertical (single-column) report using Report Wizard

We wish to create a single-column report, which lists all the members in the database, showing the following fields.

❏ Membership No
❏ Category No
❏ Firstname
❏ Lastname
❏ Occupation
❏ Date of Birth
❏ Sporting Interests.

We want the report to look like the following extract.

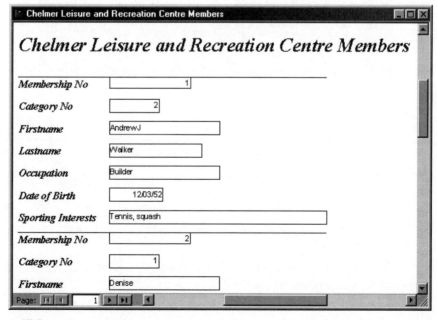

Figure 17.5

1   To enter Report Wizard starting from the Database window, go to **Reports** then
     select **Create report by using wizard**, or click on the **New Object** button on the
     toolbar and select **Report**. At the **New Report** dialog box select the **Report Wiz-
     ard** option.

2   Click on the down arrow button of the **Choose table or query...** list box, to pro-
     duce a list of tables and queries, and select the *Membership* table. Click on **OK.**

3   Select the fields to appear in the report by clicking on the field names above in the
     Available Fields list box, and then clicking on the ▶ button. The selected fields
     should appear in the **Selected Fields** list box. If you include any fields by mistake,
     use ◀ to remove them. Click on Next > .

4   Do not indicate a grouping level; if Access has automatically created one (on *Cat-
     egory No*) then click on ◀ to remove the grouping. Click the Next > button.

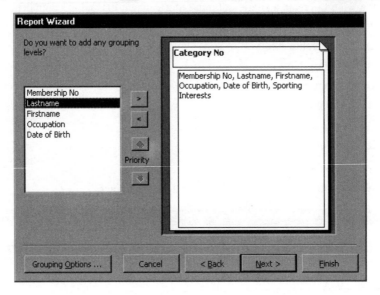

Figure 17.6

6   Choose to sort by *Membership No* by entering it in the first box. Click on Next > .

7   Choose **Columnar** and **Portrait** for the report layout.

8   Choose **Corporate** for the **Style** of the report. Click on Next > .

9   Enter the following report title: ***Chelmer Leisure and Recreation Centre Members***

10   With the option **Preview the report** selected, click on Finish to display the
     report on the screen.

11   Access will save the report with the name *Chelmer Leisure and Recreation Centre
     Members*, the same as the title.

Using a report

To use a report, first display the available report names in the Database window, then double-click on the report name. The Print Preview window will appear showing a preview of how the report will appear when printed. Alternatively, click on the report name and then click on the **Preview** button.

To zoom in and out and to view a complete page on the screen, click on the report.

Printing a report

Before printing any report always view the report in Print Preview.

Previewing

To preview a report:

1   Click the **Preview** button to see a miniature version of what is to be printed.

2   To zoom-in and zoom-out click anywhere on the preview, or use the **Zoom** button. Click on the **Zoom Control** box to select a specific magnification for the preview.

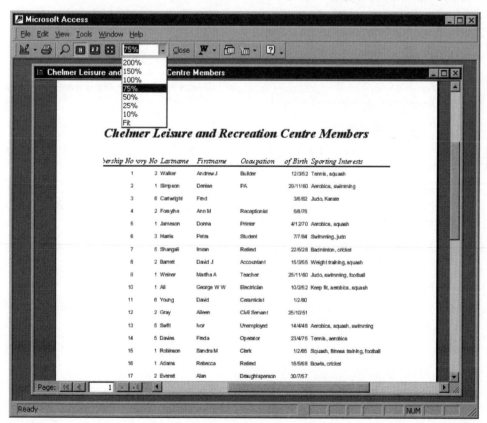

Figure 17.7

3 Choose **File-Page Setup** to make adjustments such as the orientation (portrait or landscape), the choice of printer and the width of the margins.

Some of the options in the **Page Setup** dialog box will be familiar since you will have used them in printing tables and queries, but there are also special options for use when printing report, such as the number of items (records) across the page, item size, and item layout. Click on **OK** when the required adjustments have been made.

Printing

When you're happy with the preview, you can print from either the preview screen or the design screen.

To print from the preview screen:

1 Click on the **Print** button in the Print Preview bar.

To print from the design screen:

1 Choose **File-Print.**

2 Select whether all or certain pages of the report will be printed and the number of copies. Click on **OK**.

Task 3: Using and printing a report

To use the report *Chelmer Leisure and Recreation Centre Members*, first select it from the file names displayed in the Database window, by double-clicking on the report name. The Print Preview window will appear showing a preview of how the report will appear when printed.

To print the report:

1 Choose **File-Page Setup**. Experiment with the Setup options. Close the **Page Setup** dialog box between each trial in order to view the new layout in **Print Preview.**

❏ Set two columns to the page by selecting the **Columns** tab and entering *2* in the **Number of Columns** box. You may need to adjust the **Width** in the **Column Size** section to less than half your page width.

❏ With two columns, explore the effect of **Down, then Across** and **Across, then Down** in the **Column Layout** section.

❏ Increase the column **Height.**

2 When you are happy with the layout, print it, by selecting the **Print** button.

Grouped reports

What you will learn in this unit

This unit explores creating reports where records are arranged in groups according to the value of fields in a table or query.

By the end of this unit you will be able to:

❑ create a report with grouped records.

 Note: You may choose to omit this unit for the moment and return to it later when you are ready to design this kind of report.

Understanding grouped reports

 A grouped report places its fields in a row and groups the records according to the values in one or more selected fields. This approach can also be used simply to create a report in a table form with fields shown in columns, if you do not specify groups. The advantage of this type of report is that it displays more records to the page. However, it is not ideal for records with several long fields, which therefore cannot be accommodated next to each other on the page in parallel columns.

Records can be grouped by several different fields, although we shall use only one field for grouping in this case.

Apart from the need to define how records will be displayed in groups, the process of creating a grouped report is similar to that for a single-column report. The process is basically:

1 Select the fields to appear in the report.

2 Select how the records in the table or query will be grouped for the report. Groups are divisions that include all records that have a value for a specific field, e.g. all members in category 1.

3 Select the order in which you want the groups created (if using more than one).

4 Select how the records are to be sorted for the report.

5 Select a layout.

6 Select a style.

7 Add the report's title.

8 Use Print Preview to display the report on screen.

9 Save the report.

10 Print the report and close it.

Task 1: Creating a grouped report using Report Wizard

We wish to create a grouped report that lists all the members for which there are records in the database, showing the following fields:

❏ Category No

❏ Lastname

❏ Firstname

❏ Telephone No.

The records are to be grouped according to *Category No*, i.e. all those with a given *Category No* are shown together. We wish to create a report, which looks like this.

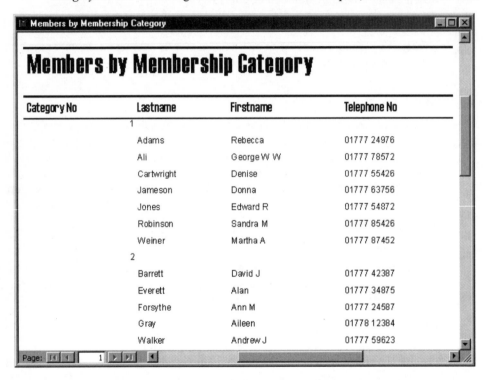

Figure 18.1

1   At the Database window, go to **Reports** then select **Create report by using wizard** or click on the **New Object** button on the toolbar and select **Report**. At the **New Report** dialog box select the **Report Wizard** option.

2   From the **Choose the table or query...** drop-down list box select the *Membership* table. Click on **OK**.

3   Select the fields to appear in the report by clicking on their names in the **Available Fields** list, then clicking on the ⟩ button. The selected fields should appear in the **Selected Fields** list. If any fields are included by mistake, click on them in the **Selected Fields** list and click ⟨ to remove them. Click on Next > .

4   You may find that Access has automatically grouped the records by *Category No*. If not, select *Category No* in the list of fields then click on ▶ to display it in the heading box in the preview. Click on Next >.

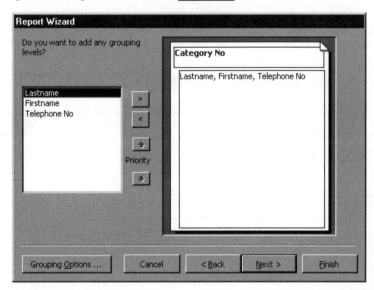

Figure 18.2

5   Sort records within groups alphabetically by the *Lastname* field. Click on Next >.

6   Select **Stepped** and **Portrait** for the layout of the report. Click on Next >.

7   Select **Compact** for the style of the report. Click on Next >.

8   Enter the report title: ***Members by Membership Category***.

9   Choose **Preview the report** and click on Finish. As the wizard has created the report it is saved with the name of its title i.e. *Members by Membership Category*.

10 To print the report directly, click on the **Print** button.

11 To change print options display the **Print** dialog box using **File-Print** and make the choices you require before clicking on **OK**.

Task 2: Creating a grouped report using more than one group

In this task you will create a grouped report which lists all the members for which there are records in the database, showing the following fields:

❑   Category No

❑   Lastname

❑   Firstname

❑   Town

❑   Telephone No.

The records are to be grouped according to *Category No* and *Town*, so that, all records with a given *Category No* are grouped together and within this grouping all records with a given *Town* will be grouped together.

We wish to create a report, which looks like the one shown below.

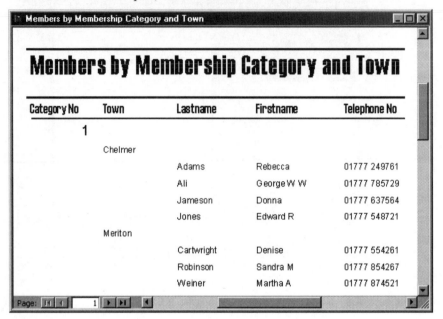

Figure 18.3

1   Follow the first four steps as for the previous task. If Access has not automatically grouped the records by *Category No*, click on *Category No* in the list of fields and then click on ☐ > ☐ to display it in the heading box in the preview.

2   To add *Town* to the grouping select it and click on ☐ > ☐. Click on ☐ Next > ☐.

3   Sort records within groups alphabetically by the *Lastname* field. Click on ☐ Next > ☐.

4   Select **Stepped** and **Portrait** for the layout of the report. Click on ☐ Next > ☐.

5   Select **Compact** for the style of the report. Click on ☐ Next > ☐.

6   Enter the following report title: ***Members by Membership Category and Town***.

7   Choose **Preview the report** and click on ☐ Finish ☐. The report will be saved with the name of its title i.e. *Members by Membership Category and Town*.

8   To print the report directly, click on the **Print** button.

9   To change print options display the **Print** dialog box using **File-Print** and make the choices you require before clicking on **OK**.

Task 3: Selecting the order of grouping

1   Create a report that is the same as the one in Task 2, with the records grouped according to *Category No* and *Town*. This time show all records with a given *Town* grouped together and within this grouping show all records with a given *Category No* grouped together.

2   Create this report as in Task 2, and when you have added *Town* as a grouping, click on the **Priority** up arrow to change the priority of grouping.

3   Continue as before but title this report ***Members by Town and Membership Category.*** Note the difference between this report and the previous one.

Unit 19

Mailing label reports

What you will learn in this unit

Mailing label reports allow the creation of mailing labels, from, say, a table of names and addresses. A mailing label report fits its fields into a rectangle designed to print labels. Unlike other Report Wizard reports, this type does not show field names. It does, however, make it easy to add text such as commas and spaces.

By the end of this unit you will be able to:

❏   create a mailing label report

❏   use a query as the basis for a Report Wizard report

❏   perform a mail merge to create an accompanying letter.

Creating a mailing label report

The procedure for creating a mailing label report is similar to that for creating any other type of report, except that you use a special Label Wizard.

To create a mailing label report:

1   With **Report** displayed in the Database window, select **New**.

2   Click on the **Label Wizard** option and select a table or query to provide the data for the labels report. Click on **OK** to start the Label Wizard (Figure 19.1).

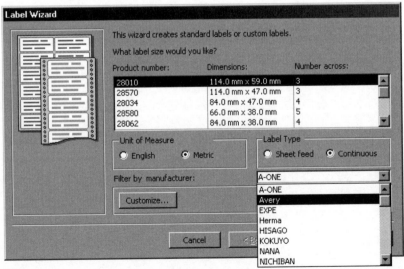

Figure 19.1

3. Select the size of labels from the list. Label sizes are listed according to their manufacturer's product number. Select the brand name of your labels from the drop-down **Filter by manufacturer** list, then choose the particular product from the list above.

 Note: if you do not know the brand and product number for a label size, look at the Dimensions and Number Across columns to find the size that matches your labels.

4. Change the **Unit of Measure** to **English** to see label sizes in inches. If you cannot see your label type listed, you may need to switch the **Label Type** from **Sheet Feed** to **Continuous**. Click on Next > .

5 Select the **Font name**, **Font size**, **Font weight** and **Text color**. You may also check **Italic** and/or **Underline** (Figure 19.2). Click on Next > .

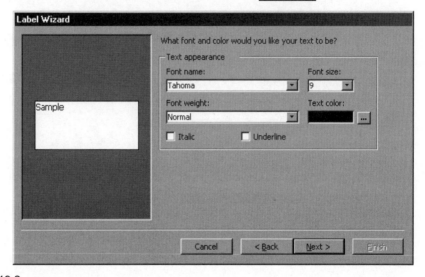

Figure 19.2

6 Select fields as with other report types, so that they appear on the prototype label but remembering that more than one field can be added to a line.

7 Add text, fields and punctuation to a line, e.g. click on *Title*, then type in a space and click *Lastname* and type in a comma. Advance to a new line by pressing *Enter* (see Figure 19.3). When you have created the label, click on Next > .

8 Select how the records are to be sorted, i.e. the order in which mailing labels are to be printed (Figure 19.4). Click on Next > .

9 Either accept the suggested name or type in a different name for the report. With **See the mailing labels as they will look printed** selected click on **Finish** to display the labels on screen.

10 Save the report.

11 Print and close the report.

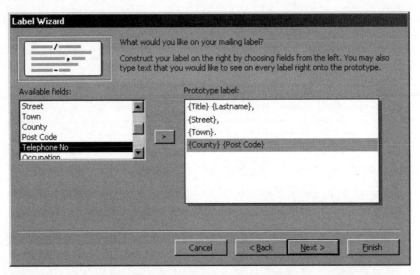

Figure 19.3

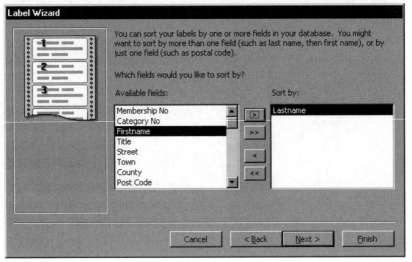

Figure 19.4

Task 1: Creating a mailing label report wizard report based on a query

We wish to create a mailing label report, which lists all members who have joined since 1/1/99. An extract from such a report is shown below. First we need to define and execute a query to select the appropriate records, and then we need to define the mailing label report that is to be used to display this set of records.

Mr Gray	Miss Robinson
4 The Parade	16 Lowton Lane
Chelmer	Branford
CHESHIRE, CHI 7ER	STAFFS, STI 0 2D Z

Query design and execution were introduced earlier, and you may wish to review this topic at this point.

To define the query:

1   Starting from the Database window, click on the **Queries** button, and click on the **New** button to create a new query.

2   Select **Design view** and click on **OK**.

3   The **Show Table** dialog box appears. Select the table *Membership* and click on the **Add** button, then click on the **Close** button.

4   Include all fields in the query by double-clicking on the title bar of the **Field List** box of the table in the upper section of the window. Click anywhere in the selected area and drag to the field row to transfer all the fields to the lower section.

5   In the *Date of Joining* criteria cell enter the query criteria *>=1/1/99*. To view the result of this query click on the **Run** button on the toolbar.

6   Save the query by choosing **File-Save**.

7   At the **Save As** dialog box, enter the **Query Name** *Members since 99*.

8   Close the query.

To design a report to display the records retrieved by the query:

1   Click on the **Reports** tab in the Database window and click on **New**.

2   Select the **Label Wizard** option to create a report using Label Wizard.

3   From the **Choose a table or query...** drop-down list select the query *Members since 99*. Click on **OK.**

4   Select the size of the labels. You may need to experiment with different label sizes. If you do not have labels to print from right now, try metric, sheet feed, Avery number L7160 just to see the result on screen. Click on [Next >].

5   Leave the font as default and click on [Next >].

6   Select the fields to be included. These are, in the order that follows.
   - Title
   - Lastname
   - Street
   - Town
   - County
   - Post Code

7   Add the field *Title* followed by a space and then the field *Lastname* to the first line. Press the *Enter* key to move onto the next line.

8   Add *Street* to the next line and press *Enter*.

9   Add the remainder of the fields, each on a separate line, except for *County* and *Post Code*, which should be on the same line separated by a space. Click on [Next >].

10   Choose to order the records in alphabetical order according to *Lastname*.

11 Accept the title *Labels Members since 99.* The report is automatically saved.

12 With **See the labels...** selected, click on [Finish] to display the report on the screen.

13 To print the report directly select the **Print** button.

14 To display the Print dialog box use **File-Print**.

Mail merging

When a circular is to be sent out, creating mailing labels takes the tedium out of addressing the envelopes. The process can be further automated by using Access in conjunction with Word to perform a mail merge. In Word a standard letter can be produced and Access can provide the data (usually names and addresses) to be merged with the standard letter.

Task 2: Mail merging

For this task you will need both Access and Word. A standard letter will be sent to all the fitness instructors informing them of the times of opening over the Easter holiday. If you have not already done so you will need to add some records to the *Tutors* table. The names of fitness instructors are in the *Classes* table, and you can invent their addresses and qualifications. Add at least four records to the table.

1 With the **Tables** buttonselected, highlight the *Tutor* table in the database window.

2 Open the **Office Links** drop-down list (on the toolbar) and select **Merge It with MS Word**.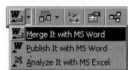

3 Choose the option to create a new document and click **OK**. This causes Word to be loaded in mail merge mode.

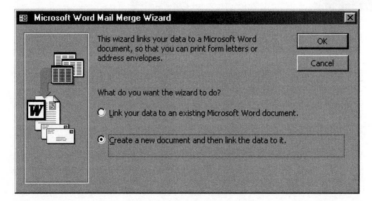

 Note: This will not work unless there is data in at least one tutor record.

4 Next create a standard letter as shown in Figure 19.5. The parts of the letter that are replaceable fields are shown enclosed in <<double chevrons>>. To insert a replaceable field click on the **Insert Merge Field** button on the mail merge toolbar and select the required field from the drop down list.

Chelmer Leisure and Recreation Centre
Park View Road, Chelmer
Cheshire CE9 115

Tel: 01777 563444
Fax: 01777 560112

19 March, 2001
<<Street>>
<<Town>>
<<County>>
<<Post Code>>

Dear <<Title>> <<Lastname>>

Please note the following times when the Centre will be open during the Easter break.

Good Friday   9:00am to 5:00pm
Easter Saturday 9:00am to 1:00pm
Easter Sunday   Closed
Easter Monday   9:00am to 5pm
Tuesday   Normal hours

If you wish to reschedule any classes please let me know as soon as possible.

Yours sincerely

G V Richards
Manager

Figure 19.5

5   It is best to check the merge for errors first; do this by clicking on the **View Merged Data** button ⧉. Check the merged data and save the document.

6   To complete the task, design a mailing label report for envelopes to accompany the letters produced.

Unit 20

Customising a report

What you will learn in this unit

This unit explores some of the basic tools for designing customised reports instead of using the standard reports that can be created using Report Wizards.

By the end of this unit you will be able to:

❏ appreciate the component parts of a report

❏ create a blank report as a basis for later design work

❏ move and size controls

❏ change the report's area

❏ delete, add and restore fields to a report

❏ change the text of a field name

❏ add headers and footers.

Understanding customised reports

Although Report Wizard produces a useful basic report, eventually you may wish to create your own from scratch, so that you can exercise greater control over the design. If you examine the Report Wizard reports that you have created recently you will note that they have these limitations: the title length is restricted; the spacing is fixed; horizontal spacing that makes it difficult to distinguish between records; and the fixed format gives the same standard appearance time and time again.

This unit explores some of the simple tools for customising a report. These may be applied either to a report created initially with Report Wizards, or to create your own report. Before attempting to create or modify a report it is useful to identify the components of a report. These are listed and described below. If you examine the reports that you have just created using Report Wizards, you should recognise that they have these components. If you display an existing report in Design view, by clicking on the **Design** button with the report selected in the Database window, the report will be displayed with these areas clearly marked.

Components of a report

Component	Description
Report header	Contains any headings or other introductory text that might appear at the beginning of the report.

Page header	Contains headings that will appear at the top of each page, such as a running title and page numbers.
Detail	Shows data from the records in the database. Sets up the format for records in general which is then used for every record included in the report.
Page footer	Appears at the bottom of each page.
Report footer	Contains information at the end of the report, such as a final summary or a statement such as 'This is the end of the report'.
Group header	Marks the beginning of a group; usually contains the group name.
Group footer	Marks the end of a group and often contains sections that summarise the records that are part of a group.

 Working with report design allows you to adjust the content, size and position of everything that appears on the report. As with forms, each item of a report is called a *control*. Controls include a field's data, text, picture and calculations. Many of the features relating to forms that you experimented with earlier also apply to reports.

Modifying an existing report

To customise an existing report it must be selected in Design view.

1 Select the report in the Database window and then click on the **Design** button

Or

2 Right-click on the report name and choose **Design** from the shortcut menu.

Creating a new blank report

To create a new report, without the aid of Report Wizard:

1 Open the **Reports** tab in the Database window and click on **New**.

Or

Choose **View-Database Objects-Reports** and then click on the **New** button in the Database window.

Or

Click on the down arrow of the **New Object** button and select **Report**.

3 Select the **Design view** option to create a report without using Report Wizard.

4 Click on the down arrow of the **Choose the table or query...** box to open the list of tables and queries and select the one for which you wish to create a report.

5 Click on **OK**.

Design aids

When you create a new blank report the Toolbox window will be displayed. This is useful for adding controls to the report. There are a number of such windows, which you will encounter as you advance in report design. These are listed below.

Window	Description
Properties sheet	To change different features of the report's contents
Field list	To add controls bound to fields
Toolbox	Contains the design tools (can be dragged to left of screen where it locks as a toolbar)

All of these windows can be moved or closed in the same way as any other window. They can also be opened and closed from the **View** menu.

Tools for aligning controls

There are also some useful features to help you create a neatly arranged report:

❑ The **Ruler** measures the distance from the top and left corner of the report. It can be removed or replaced by choosing **View-Ruler**.

❑ The **Grid** shows guidelines in design view, and can be turned on or off by choosing **View-Grid**. Note that Access automatically aligns moved or sized controls with the grid. To disable this feature, choose **Format-Snap to Grid**.

❑ The **Align** option. Use **Format-Align** to position controls relative to each other. Select two or more controls together, choose **Format-Align** and then the appropriate alignment, e.g. **Left**.

Task 1: Examining the components of a report

1   Examine one of the reports that you have created with Report Wizards.

2   In the Database window, click the **Reports** tab, then the **Design** button.

Note that Report Wizards create reports with default settings in many areas.

3   Examine the report that you have displayed. Click the Properties Sheet button, then click on each control in turn. What are the default settings for the following?

❑ Report Header

❑ Page Header

❑ Detail

❑ Page Footer

❑ Group Header

❑ Group Footer

❑ Report Footer

Task 2: Creating a blank report

Create a blank report for the *Classes* table, showing all of the fields in the table.

1   Click on the **Reports** tab in the Database window, and then the **New** button. Select the *Classes* table from the **Choose the table or query...** drop-down list.

2   Select the **Design view** option. Click on **OK.**

3   Consider the layout and decide where to put title, field labels and the fields them-
    selves.

4   Add all the fields to the report from the field list. Display the field list; double-click
    on the field list title bar to highlight all the fields.

5   Click and drag the highlighted fields onto the **Detail** section of the report. Controls
    for all the fields should appear.

6   Save as *Classes* and close.

Moving and sizing controls

To move a control, select it and drag it to where you want it, just as you did with
form controls in Unit 15.

Task 3: Moving and sizing controls on an existing Report Wizards report

We wish to improve on the design of the report **Chelmer Leisure and Recreation
Centre Members,** so that the final report looks like this.

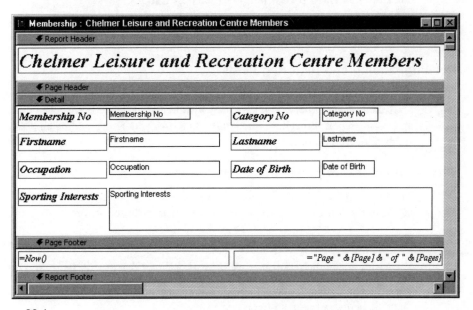

Figure 20.1

1   First open the existing report. Select the report *Chelmer Leisure and Recreation
    Centre Members* in the Database window and then select the **Design** button.

2   Move the controls on the report until it resembles the design screen shown above.
    Several controls can be moved as a block if you use the *Shift* key to select more
    than one at a time.

If the toolbox is in the way, remove it by using **View-Toolbox**.

Note: there should be gridlines showing to help you line controls up neatly – if not, choose **Grid** from the View menu.

3   View the new report on screen using **Print Preview**.

4   Save the report as *Members2* using **File-Save As**.

Customising a report

Changing the report's area

The areas in each section of a report – the header, detail and footer, may be altered individually. It is also possible to adjust the position of the right and bottom edge of a form.

To alter the depth of a section of the form:

1   Move the pointer to the bottom edge of the section, where it will change shape. Drag the pointer to a new location.

2   To alter the area of the report, drag the right and bottom edges to the size required.

3.   Click on the **Print Preview** button to see how it looks.

 Note: if you make the report too wide for the page, a message will warn you when you try to preview the report.

Deleting, adding and restoring fields

When you create a report from scratch it is necessary to add appropriate fields from a selected table or query. You may also wish to add or delete fields when changing an existing report. Procedures are similar to those for deleting, adding and restoring fields to or from a form.

Changing the text of a field name label

The text of a field name label may be edited and if required additional text can be added to the form. Again, procedures are similar to those for forms.

Task 4: Creating a customised report

We wish to open the report that we created earlier, *Classes*, add fields and modify field labels, in order to create a report like the one shown in Figure 20.2.

1   Open the *Classes* report in Design view.

2   Click on the fields and their labels and move them into a more satisfactory position.

 Note: If you inadvertently delete a field, display the **Field List** window and drag the field onto the report.

4   Edit the field label *Class No* so that it reads **Number**. Select the field label control, click where the text editing is required and modify its name. Modify other labels as necessary in the same way.

Chelmer Leisure and Recreation Centre: Sports, Fitness and Exercise Classes

Classes

Number:		1	Class Tutor:	Evans
Class Day	Monday		Class Activity:	Ladies' Aerobics
Class Time		10:00	Male/Female/Mixed:	Female
Number:		2	Class Tutor:	Franks
Class Day	Monday		Class Activity:	Weight Training
Class Time		11:00	Male/Female/Mixed:	Male

Figure 20.2

5   Press *Enter* or click on another part of the report to complete changes. If you want to begin a new line inside a text box (as with the report title, for instance), press *Shift* + *Enter*)

6.   Try tidying up the form using **Format-Align-Left** to align a group of controls (use the *Shift* key to select them as a group first).

7.   **Print preview** the report and go back to Design view to make any changes.

8.   Save *Classes* and close it.

You have now created a report showing all of the basic information, and it looks better than it did before. However, there is still plenty of room for improvement.

A few ideas are explored later in this unit, and we'll look at further possibilities over the next few units.

Reformatting a report

Altering the size and font of controls

To alter the size or font of text on a report:

1   Select the controls to be altered.

2   Click on the **Font** list box in the toolbar and select the font required.

3   Click on the **Font Size** list box and select the point size required.

i   *Note: If you increase the size of a font you may need to alter the size of the control and the size of the section.*

Adding headers and footers

Report headers and footers (sections which appear at the very beginning and end of a report) and page headers and footers (sections repeated on every page in a long report) can be easily added to a report.

1. Choose **Page Header/Footer** from the **View** menu.

2. Click on the **Label** tool **Aa** in the Toolbox.

3. Place the pointer in the appropriate header or footer box and drag it to make a box large enough to accommodate the text.

4. Type *Chelmer Leisure and Recreation Centre: Sports, Fitness and Exercise Classes* into the new box.

5. Repeat these steps to insert text in the report footer, page header and page footer areas.

i   *Note: On long tabular reports, field labels should be put in the page header so that all information is seen in context.*

Task 5: Reformatting a report

This task reformats the report created in the last task using some of the additional features that have been introduced above.

1   Open the report called *Classes* in Design view.

2   Select the controls in the **Report Header**, open the **Font Size** list box and increase the point size. Click on the **Bold** button to make the text bold and on the **Centre** button to centre the text within the control. If necessary, click on the corner of the box and stretch it to fit all of the text in.

3   Move the field labels into the page header band by first selecting them as a group then dragging them.

4   Rearrange the labels in the page header to make column headings. Select these as a group and format them, making them bold, italic and slightly larger.

5   Adjust the depth of the page header so that it just accommodates the labels, by dragging the bottom of the page header.

6   In the Detail area, rearrange the controls to align with the labels in the page header. If necessary expand the boxes to accommodate the longest field value. For example make sure that the control box for **Activity** accommodates "Badminton".

7   In turn, select the text boxes for *Class No* and *Time* and right justify them using the **Align** button.

8   Select the **Male/Female/Mixed** control box and delete it by pressing the *Delete* key.

9   Select and format the report footer in italics.

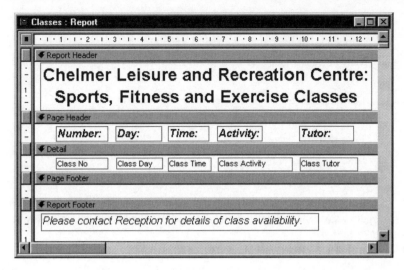

Figure 20.3

i *Note: you will probably find that you switch between print preview and design view several times as you make changes and check the effect of the changes.*

10   Print preview, save as **Classes2**, close and print as required.

Chelmer Leisure and Recreation Centre: Sports, Fitness and Exercise Classes

Number:	Day:	Time:	Activity:	Tutor:
1	Monday	10:00	Ladies' Aerobics	Evans
2	Monday	11:00	Weight Training	Franks
3	Monday	15:00	Body Conditioning	Latham
4	Monday	19:00	Step Aerobics	Wheildon
5	Tuesday	10:00	Men's Multi-gym	Jackson
6	Tuesday	14:00	Ladies' Multi-gym	Evans
7	Tuesday	19:00	Family Multi-gym	Jackson

Figure 20.4

Integrative tasks

Use the following tasks to practise the report creation skills you have gained from this and the last three units.

Task 6: Creating a single-column report using Report Wizard

Produce a report, based on the *Membership* table, which lists these details for all members who are smokers.

- ❏ Membership No
- ❏ Category No
- ❏ Title
- ❏ Firstname
- ❏ Lastname
- ❏ Occupation
- ❏ Date of Birth
- ❏ Sex.

1 First define a query, which selects the records for the members who are smokers.

2 Save this query and use it in the design of a report using Report Wizards. Don't forget to save the report, as *Smokers*, and preview it on screen before printing.

Task 7: Creating a groups/totals report using Report Wizard

You wish to create a report that lists all the classes offered by the centre, based on the *Classes* table. The report is to be organised in groups according to *Class Activity*. All fields in the *Classes* table are to be included.

1 Produce a second groups/totals report, based on the *Classes* table, which details all the information in the *Classes* table.

2 Sort the report in classes order.

3 Save this report as *Classes List*.

Task 8: Creating a customised report

Instead of using Report Wizard to create the report in Task 6, attempt to create the same report independently of the Report Wizards tool, i.e. as a customised report.

Types of form controls

What you will learn in this unit

This unit describes the additional features that you can add to forms and reports.

By the end of this unit you will be able to:

❏   identify the tools in the Toolbox

❏   understand the function of the different types of control

So far you have met forms and reports created by AutoForm, AutoReport and the Wizards, which tend to use limited controls, and created a simple report from scratch.

In this unit we will introduce more sophisticated controls that you can use in both forms and reports to add to the professionalism of your work.

Types of form controls

You have already met labels and text box controls, but if you are familiar with Windows applications you will have seen other types of control on dialog boxes. These include list boxes, check boxes and option buttons.

There are three categories of control:

❏   *Bound controls.* A bound control is associated with a field in the table or query that was used to create the report or form, and displays or alters the data in that field. Text boxes are the most common type of bound control.

❏   *Unbound controls.* An unbound control is independent of the data in the table or query field. Labels used as titles are examples of unbound controls.

❏   *Calculated controls.* A calculated control is an expression, which usually performs a calculation on data in the report or form.

The Toolbox

The Access Toolbox allows you to add control objects to forms and reports. The Toolbox only appears when you are in design mode. If it is not visible in design view then use **View-Toolbox** to make it visible. The Toolbox is composed of a set of buttons, each of which gives access to a different tool. The icon on the button indicates the function of the tool, as outlined in Figure 21.1. Click on a button to access a particular tool, then click in the report template to place the control where you want it.

Figure 21.1

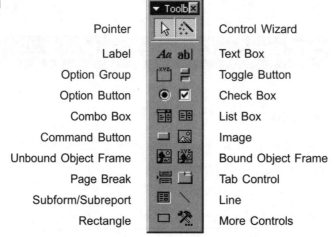

Pointer		Control Wizard
Label		Text Box
Option Group		Toggle Button
Option Button		Check Box
Combo Box		List Box
Command Button		Image
Unbound Object Frame		Bound Object Frame
Page Break		Tab Control
Subform/Subreport		Line
Rectangle		More Controls

Pointer

This is the default tool when the Toolbox is displayed. Click on it to deselect a previously selected tool and return the mouse pointer to its normal function.

Label

Click and drag to draw a box on the form, into which text can be inserted.

Option Group

Creates a frame of adjustable size into which several controls can be placed. Only one of the controls within the frame can be selected. Usually the controls are of the same kind, e.g. option buttons or check boxes. When a control within an option group is selected all others in the group are deselected.

Option Button

Creates an on-off button (sometimes also known as a 'radio button' – a white circle which has a black dot in it to indicate 'on'). Option buttons are most commonly used within option groups to select between values in a set.

Combo Box

Creates a box which is a combination of a text box and a drop-down list box (see below). This gives the choice of either selecting from a list or keying in an entry.

Command Button

Creates a button to which you can assign a macro which will execute when the button is clicked (see Unit 39).

Unbound Object Frame

Adds an OLE object, something created in another application which supports OLE, such as an Excel spreadsheet. (See Unit 31, *Pictures in Forms and Reports*.)

Page Break

When printing the report, the printer will start a new page where the page break is on the form or the report.

Subform/ Subreport

↔ Adds a subform or subreport to a main form or report. Don't use this unless the subform or subreport already exists - see Unit 33 for more details.

Rectangle

Creates a decorative rectangle that can be sized and moved. Select width, colour and fill from the properties and palette.

Control Wizards

Certain controls, such as list boxes for example, have wizards to help you set them up. When the Control Wizards button is depressed, these will start up when you insert the control. If you do not want to use the wizards, turn this option off.

Text box

Creates a frame in which text is displayed or edited.

Toggle Button

Creates a grey on-off button which switches between raised and depressed when clicked.

Check Box

Creates a check box that toggles on and off. Multiple check boxes can be used in groups, but should not be placed within an option group, otherwise only one check box can be selected.

List Box

Creates a drop-down list box from which an item or value can be selected.

Image

Creates a frame for displaying a static picture on a form or report. Useful for a company logo or just to improve the look of your report.

Bound Object Frame

Where the data table contains OLE objects, for example, digitised photographs in a personnel table, this tool is used to create an object control in a similar way to the text box control.

Tab Control

Creates an area of the form which allows you to place several 'pages' on top of each other, with tabs along the top to switch between them. (Choose **Options** from the **Tools** menu on any Microsoft application to see an example of a dialog box which uses tabs.)

Line

Creates a straight line that can be sized and relocated. The colour and width of the line can be changed using the properties and palette.

More Controls

Displays a list of advanced dynamic controls.

Unit 22

Adding controls to forms

What you will learn in this unit

Data entry can be made more efficient by using the kind of features encountered in dialog boxes – list boxes, option buttons, option groups, etc. The person entering the data simply selects an option from a list of rooms in a leisure centre for example, rather than having to key in the entry each time. This has the advantages of reducing errors and maintaining consistency.

Calculated controls may be added to either forms or reports. They display information calculated from existing data. As an example in this session you will find out which members have not renewed their membership, based on their last date of renewal.

By the end of this unit you will be able to create:

❑   a list box

❑   a calculated text box

❑   an option group

❑   a combo box

❑   a check box.

Adding controls to forms

Use the Toolbox to add controls to forms (if the Toolbox isn't visible in Form Design view choose **View-Toolbox** to display it). A brief summary of the tools' functions was given in the previous unit, so this will be a practical one, consisting entirely of tasks. By completing these tasks you will learn the techniques you need to design your own form.

Task 1: Adding a list box

List boxes are useful for picking values from a static list of options. You may define a list or use a table as a source of the list. The following example adds a list box to the *Bookings* form. The list box will be defined for the *Room/Hall/Court* field and will use a static list of rooms at the centre. At Chelmer Leisure and Recreation Centre there are six bookable rooms: the Fitness Suite, Sports Hall 1 and 2, and three courts.

To add a list box to the *Bookings* form:

1   Open the form in Design view.

2   Select and delete the *Room/Hall/Court* text box.

3   Open the **Field List** window and choose *Room/Hall/Court*.

4   Check that the **Control Wizard** button in the Toolbox is depressed and click on the **List Box** tool.

5   Go back to the Field List and click and drag *Room/Hall/Court* to the right position. Dragging is important as it links the control with the field.

6   Rearrange the other controls on the form so that there is room to have a list box deep enough to show all six rooms (if the list box is made smaller it will be shown with a vertical scroll bar). You may prefer to try a slightly different layout, as illustrated later in this task.

7   The List Box Wizard dialog box opens. Select the option **I will type in the values that I want** and click on <u>N</u>ext > .

8   Enter *1* into the **Number of columns** box. Click in the first cell (under Col1) and type *Fitness Suite*. Use the *Tab* or down arrow keys to go to the next cell.

9   Complete the column with *Sports Hall 1*, *Sports Hall 2*, *Court 1*, *Court 2*, and *Court 3* in the next five rows. Click on <u>N</u>ext > .

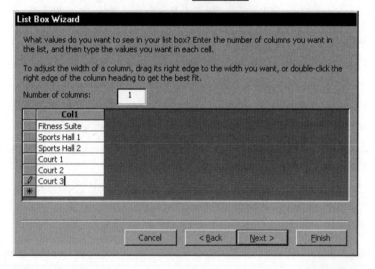

10 Choose the option **Store that value in this field** and click on <u>N</u>ext > .

This will record the choice in the *Room/Hall/Court* field in the database; the other option is to temporarily store the information for use later in the form – perhaps on a 'booking fee' field for calculating the cost of several bookings.

11 Accept the label for the list box, which should be ***Room/Hall/Court*** and click on <u>F</u>inish .

12 Click on the **View** button on the toolbar to display the form. If adjustments to the position of controls are needed then return to Design view to make them.

The form should now look something like this:

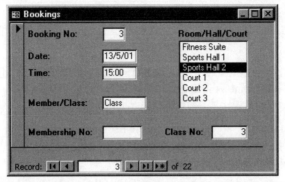

13   Save the form as **Bookings2.** Try testing the form to enter a booking.

Note: you may find it helpful to amend the Tab order for easier data entry.

Task 2: Adding a combo box

The combo box is very similar to the list box: it presents a list of options, but also allows the user to enter alternative text if none of the options are appropriate.

In this task you will add a combo box for the choice of county to the *Membership* form. Three counties will be listed, but any other can be typed into the text box if necessary.

1   Open the *Membership* form in Design view.

2   Select and delete the *County* text box.

3   Check that both the **Field List** window and the **Toolbox** are displayed. Check that the **Control Wizard** button in the Toolbox is depressed.

4   Click on the **Combo Box** tool in the Toolbox, then click and drag the *County* field from the field list onto the form.

5   Using the Wizard in the same way as for a List Box, choose to type in the values and set the number of columns to one.

6   Enter the list of counties, **Cheshire**, **Staffs**, and **Derbyshire**.

7   Choose to store the data in the *County* field, and edit the label if required.

8   Click on [Finish].

9   Preview the form. The *County* text box should now have a **List Box** button, which when clicked will display the list of counties. Note that when entering a new record, Cheshire is still the default county.

10   Experiment with entering data. If adjustments are needed, return to Design view, then save when you're happy with it.

Task 3: Adding option groups

Option buttons are commonly employed to select one from a set of mutually exclusive choices. In this example we'll add a group of option buttons for the membership categories. Open the *Membership* form in Design view. If necessary, adjust the area of the form to allow room for the option group at the bottom or side.

To create an option group:

1 Check that the **Control Wizard** button in Toolbox is depressed. Click on the **Option Group** frame tool in the Toolbox.

2 Choose *Category No* from the Field List and drag to a suitable position on the form.

3 Enter the label names as shown here and click on   Next >   .

4 Select **No, I don't want a default** and click on   Next >   .

5 In this case the default values are correct, so click on   Next >   .

6 Choose **Store the value in this field: Category No** and click on   Next >   .

7 Choose the **Option** buttons type of control with an **Etched** style and click on   Next >   .

8 Give the option group the title *Category No* and click on   Finish   .

9 To test the form click on the **View** button. Experiment by entering a new member's record.

10 Save the form as *Membership*.

Since we did not delete the old *Category No* text box control, this will also be visible, and you'll see that it confirms the entry made in the option group. Data could be entered into this field using either of the controls, though in a finished version, you'll probably only want one to avoid confusion!

Task 4: Check box controls for logical fields

In this task the *Smoker* control in the *Membership* form will be changed to a check box control.

1 Display both the **Toolbox** and the **Field List**.

2 Delete the *Smoker* field.

3 Select the **Check box** in the **Toolbox**. Click on the *Smoker* field in the Field List and drag onto the form.

4 Save the form.

Task 5: Creating a calculated text box

In this task the calculated control that is to be created is one which flags members whose renewal is due. This control will be added to the *Membership* form created in Task 1 in Unit 14.

When people join Chelmer Leisure and Recreation Centre they pay for one year's membership from that date. They renew their membership annually. To calculate whether the member's subscription is overdue then the renewal date is compared with today's date. If the renewal date is more than one year before today's date then the fee is overdue.

To create a realistic result, you'll need to amend or add records to the *Membership* table so that some members' renewal fees show as overdue. Open the *Membership* table and change the *Date of Last Renewal* entry for three or four members so that it is more than one year ago from today's date.

To add the calculated text box:

1 Open the *Membership* form in Design view.

2 Click on the **Text box** tool in the Toolbox.

3 Click on a suitable place on the form for the text box and its label.

4 Edit the label to read ***Subscription***.

5 Click in the text box and key in the expression

=iif(DateAdd("d",365,[Date of last renewal])<Date(), "Overdue", "Up to date")

If you have trouble seeing the expression on-screen, you can display it in a zoom box: open the **Properties** sheet and select **Control source**, then press *Shift* + *F2* to open the zoom box for easier editing.

Don't worry for now about how we created this expression – if you wish to create your own expressions, look in the Access Help system for lists of the available functions. But for the curious:

The expression is an in-line IF... THEN... ELSE statement (**iif** = **i**nline **if**). ***DateAdd("d",365,[Date of last renewal])*** adds ***365 d***ays to the ***Date of last renewal*** field. This is compared to today's date. IF the result is less than today's (***<Date()***) THEN the text displayed in this field is "***Overdue***" ELSE it is "***Up to date***".

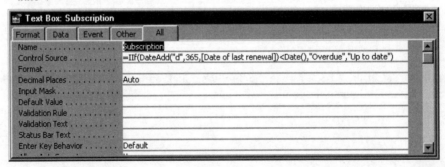

i   *Note: if you miss out a bracket, when you press <u>Enter</u> Access will display an information box. Click on **OK** and you will be returned to the control so that you can edit the expression.*

6   Open the **Properties sheet** for this control and click on the **All** tab. Change the Name to *Subscription*.

7.   Run the form to test it, and save when you're happy with it.

If you have errors, return to the Design view and check that you have keyed in the expression correctly. For example, if you have misspelt the control name, then the message **#Name?** appears in the control. Check all control names carefully and correct them.

i   *Note: if you rename a control in an underlying table then this kind of error may result. Names in expressions using that control will need to be updated accordingly.*

Formatting displayed values

↔   Font and size formatting and alignment have already been discussed in Units 14 and 15. Formatting can be applied in the same way to the controls introduced in this session: select a control and use the usual buttons on the formatting toolbar.

Unit 23

Using filters to select records

What you will learn in this unit

A filter acts on a table, form or query and picks out only those records which match the criteria you specify. In this respect they are similar to queries, but filters are a little more rough-and-ready – unlike a query, you cannot determine which fields are displayed; the entire record is shown. On the other hand, a simple filter can be applied to a table, form or query with just two clicks of the mouse without leaving preview mode.

It is often useful to be able to pick out records in this way: Chelmer Leisure Centre might use it to get a quick overview of how many people it had in a particular membership category, for instance. Perhaps a class tutor is going on holiday for a week and is to be replaced by a new instructor; filter on the tutor's name and see instantly which classes need to be dealt with.

By then end of this unit you will be able to:

❏ use a filter to select records using one field as a criterion

❏ use a filter to select records using more than one field as criteria

There are two kinds of filters you can apply: **Filter by Selection** is a simple filter which filters on one field only. More complex filters can be created using the **Filter by Form** option to select several fields as criteria.

Filter by Selection

Click on any field which holds the information you want to match, and click the **Filter by Selection** button. This will select records that match the chosen value.

Task 1: Selecting with a filter

In this task you will filter the Membership form to display only those records where the Town field is Meriton.

1   Open the Membership form in form view.

2   Move through the records until you one with Meriton in the Town field.

3   Click in this field and click on the **Filter by Selection** button ![button]. Only the records with Meriton in the Town field will be displayed. To sort the records displayed via the filter use the sorting buttons on the toolbar as shown in Unit 6.

4   Click on the **Remove Filter** button ![button] to display all the records again. Click it again to reapply the filter.

5   Close the form. Choose **Yes** when asked if you want to save changes.

6   Open the form again, and click on the **Apply Filter** button – the filter you set up a moment ago is reapplied.

Filter by Form

A filter created by this method will select records that match the value of more than one field. Filters can be designed narrowly, where a record must match several criteria; or widely, where a record can match any of several alternatives to qualify.

For instance, you might set up a narrow filter to find all senior members from Meriton who smoke; or a wide filter to find all members from Meriton OR Chelmer.

To filter by this method:

1   Open a table, form or query and click the **Filter by Form** button 📇 in the toolbar. This displays a filter form – the one illustrated here is for the *Membership* table.

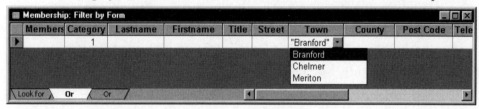

2   Click in a field to open a drop down list that displays all the different values used for that field in the underlying data. Select the value you want to look for.

3   You may specify 'AND' criteria by setting values in more than one field, e.g. where the Town is Meriton *AND* Category No is 1.

4   You may specify 'OR' criteria using the **Or** tab. This will display another sheet of the form filter, where more criteria can be applied in the same way. You can set up as many alternatives as you like; just click on a new **Or** tab to display another form filter sheet.

i   *Note: the rules of 'AND' and 'OR' logic apply to sheets of the form filter in the same way as rows in the query QBE grid.*

5   To deselect a criterion, click on it and press *Delete* then *Enter*.

6   Click on the Apply Filter button on the toolbar; the filter form disappears and is replaced by the underlying datasheet, duly filtered.

7   To remove the filter and display all records again, click on the Remove Filter button.

Task 2: Selecting with a filter form

In this task you will apply a filter with three criteria to the *Membership* form.

1   Open the *Membership* form and click on the **Filter by Form** button to display the Filter Form window.

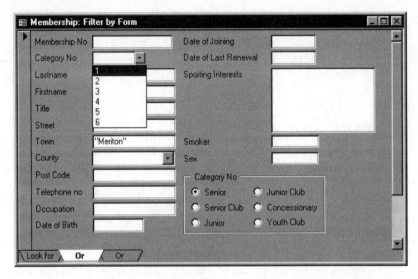

i Note: When filtering a form, Access uses your form design for the filter form, so it looks different to the Membership table filter form illustrated in Figure 23.1 above.

2   In the *Category No* field select **1**, and in the *Town* field select **Branford**.

3   Click on the **Or** tab and select **Category No 1** and **Meriton**.

Note: if you do not repeat the Category No *filter on this 'OR' sheet, the filter will return all senior members from Branford, and ANY member from Meriton.*

4   Click on the **Apply Filter** button to see the selected records displayed in the *Membership* form.

Editing a filter

Filters do not exist independently of the table, form or query to which they were applied, so you can't save several filters for a table and switch between them. When you apply a filter to a table and then save the table, the filter criteria are saved with it, ready to use again next time. To apply a different filter, the old one has to be edited, replacing the old criteria with the new.

Task 3: Editing a filter

This follows on from Task 2.

1   Click on the **Filter by Form** button to re-display the form filter.

2   Remove the *Town* criteria by deleting them. Set criteria in the *Category No* field to filter out categories **3** or **4**.

3   Click on the **Apply Filter** button to see the records.

4   Experiment with different filter forms, using criteria for different fields.

5   Remove the filter and close the form.

Using controls in reports

What you will learn in this unit

Sorting and grouping enhance the presentation of data in reports – if you're printing a list of members, for instance, it makes sense to group them by membership category, so that all Senior members are together, then all Senior Club members, and so on. The control for the field that is being used for grouping can usefully be put in the group header to identify the group within the report.

Calculated controls can be added to group footers to produce subtotals or averages for the group. Records can then be sorted within groups, e.g. members may be listed alphabetically by last name within their category grouping.

By the end of this unit, you will be able to:

❏ save a formas a report

❏ change the way a report is grouped

❏ add calculated controls to grouped reports.

Saving a form as a report

If you have a nicely laid-out form, you can change this to a report for printing instead of having to design the report all over again.

Task 1: Saving a form as a report

In this task you will save the *Bookings* form as a report.

1. Click on the **Forms** button in the Database window, then right-click on the form *Bookings*.

2. Choose **Save As...** from the shortcut menu. Give the report a name – select **Report** from the **Save as** menu and click **OK**.

3. Click on the **Reports** button in the Database window. Preview the new report; you will see that it has the same formatting and settings as it had when it was a form.

Editing the grouping of a report

The easiest way to group a report is to set up a grouping by a particular field when constructing the report using the Report Wizard. However, once you've made the report, you can still add or change groupings directly in design view, as well as add group headers and footers.

Task 2: Changing the grouping of a report

In this task, you will group the *Bookings* form according to the room they are held in, and add a heading to each group.

1   Open the *Bookings* report in Design view.

2   Click the **Sorting and Grouping** button on the toolbar.

3   Choose *Room/Hall/Court* from the **Field/Expression** drop-down menu.

4   Change the **Group Header** option to *Yes*. An extra section will appear on the report now, to hold group header information.

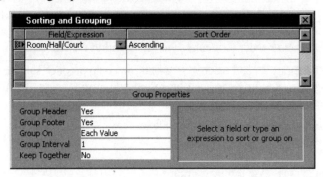

Figure 24.1

5   Open the **Field List** and drag the *Room/Hall/Court* field into the group header.

6   Format the control and preview the report. Make any design changes necessary, and when you're happy with it, print and save.

i   *Hint: to distinguish the group heading from the other controls, you might want to use a larger font size, or change the text box style (see Unit 27 for more on this).*

Calculated controls

Calculated controls are useful in reports. For example, if a report has been produced from a table that contains data about stock in the form of quantity sold and price, then the total sales revenue can be calculated by multiplying the quantity sold by the price.

Task 3: Adding a calculated control to the *Members2* report

A calculated control was used in the *Membership* form to find out whether a member's subscription was overdue. In this task this control will be copied and pasted into the *Members2* report that you added in Unit 20.

1   Open the *Membership* form in Design view. Select the calculated control and copy it, using **Edit-Copy**. Close the form.

2   Open the report *Members2* in design view.

3   Click on the Detail bar and use **Edit-Paste** to paste in the control. Move it to a suitable place and, if necessary, rearrange the other controls.

4   Save the report, preview and print it. The new control should print either "Up to date" or "Overdue" as illustrated in Figure 24.2.

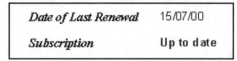

Date of Last Renewal	15/07/00
Subscription	Up to date

Figure 24.2

Controls in grouped reports

Calculated controls can be added to give summaries of the data in a group - sub-totals or average sales in a particular category, for instance.

Task 4: Adding calculated controls to a grouped report

1   Open the *Members2* report in Design view.

2   Click on the **Sorting and Grouping** button and set the options as illustrated in Figure 24.3. This report sorts the members into alphabetical order within the category number groups.

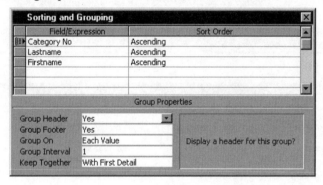

Figure 24.3

3   For *Category No* set the **Group Header** and **Group Footer** to *Yes*, and set **Keep Together** to *With first detail*, which will prevent a page break between the group heading and the next record.

4   Move the *Category No* control from the detail section to the group header.

5   In the Category No Footer add a text box control and key into it the expression

   =Count ([Membership No])

This will display the total number of members in each category.

6   Add the label *Number of Members.*

The report should now look like the one in Figure 24.4.

7   Preview the report, save and print it. It should look something like this extract, which shows the end of the Category 1 group and the beginning of Category 2.

i   *Note: you may have to view more than one page in order to see the calculated control in the group footer in action!.*

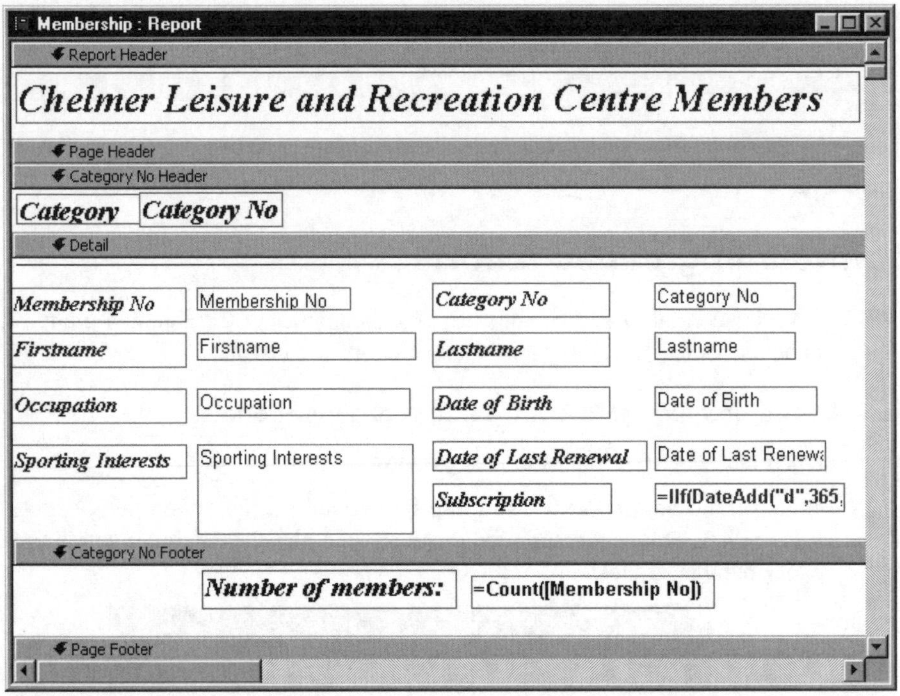

Figure 24.4

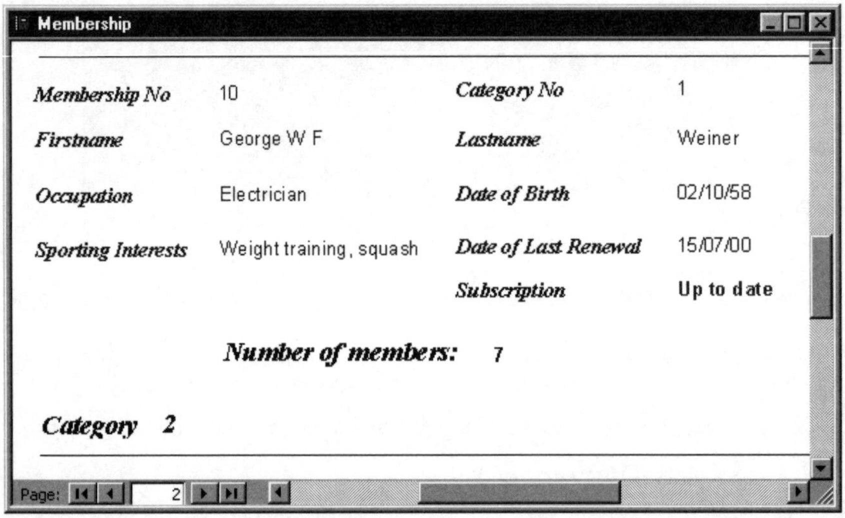

Figure 24.5 A sample of the finished report

Task 4: Groups within groups in a report

This task follows on from the previous task. The aim is create a report that groups
by town within each category group. Open the report in Design view and display
the **Sorting and Grouping** dialog box.

1   In the fourth row add the field *Town*. Access applies the grouping and sorting rules in the order they appear in this window. We want this grouping to take priority over the sorting by name, so we must move the *Town* row up: click on the row to select it, then click again and drag it to below the first row.

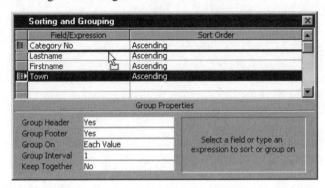

Figure 24.6

2   Select *Yes* for **Group Footer** and **Group Footer**.

3   In Design view, move the *Town* control from the Detail section into the Town Header.

4   Copy the calculated control for number of members from the Category No Footer and paste the copy into the **Town Footer**. Amend the labels for both these controls so that you know which is which.

i   *Note: to make things even more clear, you could add an extra **Town** control field in between the label and the calculated control, as shown below:*

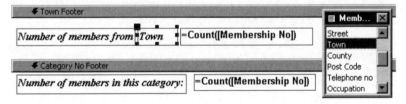

Figure 24.7

5   Preview the report, save and print it.

6   Experiment with different sorting and groupings.

Controls design: integrative tasks

The following tasks revise some of the topics covered in this and the previous two units.

Task 5: Adding a combo box to the classes form

In this task you will add a combo box for the choice of tutor to the **Classes** form. Six tutors will be listed but the text box will accept an alternative – perhaps a guest instructor – which may be keyed in.

1   Open the *Classes* form in Design view.

2   Select and delete the *Class Tutor* text box.

3   Check that both the **Field List** and the **Toolbox** are displayed, and that the **Control Wizard** button is depressed in the Toolbox.

4   Click on the **Combo Box** tool in the Toolbox. Click and drag the *Class Tutor* field from the field list to a suitable position on the form.

5   Using the Wizard, opt to type in the values and set the number of columns to one.

6   Enter the list of tutors:

Adams	Evans	Franks
Jackson	Latham	Wheildon

7   Choose the **Store that value in this field** option and edit the label if required.

8   Click on **Finish** and preview the form. The *Class Tutor* text box should have a list box button, which will display the list of tutors' last names when clicked.

9   Experiment with entering data. If adjustments are needed return to design view; save the form when you're happy with it.

Task 6: Getting combo box values from another table

This kind of static list is all very well for a limited number of tutors and a single report, but what if you have dozens of tutors coming and going and several reports? It would be better to link the combo box to a table holding details of the tutors; then all you have to do is keep the tutors table updated, and the controls on the report will gather the right information by themselves.

1   First complete some more tutor details in the *Tutor* table.

2   When you drag the *Class Tutor* field to the *Classes* form, and the Wizard starts up, choose **I want the combo box to look up the values in a table or query** instead of opting to type the values in yourself.

3   Select the *Tutor* table and select *Lastname* from the **Available Fields** list.

4   Adjust the width of the column and continue with the wizard as usual.

Task 6: Adding a calculated control to a report

Use the *Classes3* report created in Unit 20 and group it by *Class Tutor*.

1   Move the *Class Tutor* control to the Class Tutor Header.

2   Add a calculated control in the Class Tutor that will count the number of classes. *Hint: count the **Class No** field.*

3   Within the *Class Tutor* grouping, group classes by activity and count the number of classes of each activity held by each tutor.

4   Save and close the report.

Adding lines and rectangles

What you will learn in this unit

This unit is the first of a series that deal with techniques to change the appearance of the information on a report or form, and to make their presentation more exciting. Access offers a wide range of tools for formatting forms and reports and supports the imaginative creation of interesting designs. Forms and reports created using Wizards use some of these features to a limited extent, but by the time you have completed these units you should be able to improve on Wizard designs.

By the end of this unit you will be able to:

❏ add lines and boxes to forms and reports.

Understanding design

Although the tools we explore in these units allow you to be very adventurous with your designs, remember that in good design, less is often more. Be sparing in your use of coloured boxes and lines, and don't go wild with fifty different fonts! A few tips to bear in mind are listed below, but before you start, ask yourself a couple of questions:

❏ Are you designing a form or a report? Forms will be used on-screen, whereas reports are likely to be printed out on paper to be read once or occasionally referred to. This has implications for layout, font sizes and colours.

❏ Who will be reading/using it? Data entry personnel may have to use your forms for long periods at a time, so be functional, use toned-down colours with clear but not harsh contrast between text and backgrounds. Reports for presentations on the other hand need to be eye-catching, with plenty of space around the important bits, and may carry the organisation's colours and branding.

Design tips

❏ Keep forms simple and easy to read. Don't use unnecessary text and graphics, and try to ensure that the whole form fits onto a normal screen comfortably to avoid scrolling where possible.

❏ Use colour sparingly – if there are logically distinct sections of a form, it may be helpful to mark them off, but don't let colour become a distraction.

❏ Think of how the form will be used and place controls in sensible places – for instance, if a user is entering membership data from a paper form filled in by a new member, make sure that the fields on the form appear in the same order so that you can work through it easily.

❏ Maintain a consistent appearance for related forms. This looks more professional and makes it easier for a user to get used to a series of forms.

❏ Design reports with your printer in mind. Is it colour or black and white? Do large pictures slow it down unacceptably? Can it handle fine detail or subtle colour graduations?

❏ What is the purpose of the report? Focus on the particular piece of information which is important. If you have a lot of information on one report, but different bits are relevant to different people, split it into smaller reports targeted to specific audiences.

Adding lines and rectangles to forms and reports

Lines and rectangles can be added to emphasise portions of the form or report or to separate one part from another. Here you'll learn how to add plain lines and rectangles – colours and special effects are dealt with in Unit 27.

To add a line:

1 Select the **Line** tool in the **Toolbox**.

2 Point to where you want the line to start.

3 Click and drag the pointer to where the line should end, and release the mouse button.

To add a rectangle:

1 Select the **Rectangle** tool in the **Toolbox**.

2 Point to where you want one corner of the rectangle to be.

3 Drag the pointer to where the opposite corner should be, and release the mouse button.

To delete a line or rectangle, just select it and press *Delete*. To move or resize one, select it and click and drag on the edges as you would for any other control.

Changing layer order

When you add lines and rectangles to a form or report, imagine that they are drawn on a transparent sheet (called a 'layer') which is placed over the top of any features already on the screen. You'll see if you try overlapping a line or rectangle with a control that the control is partially obscured by it. Rectangles have a transparent fill by default, but when you add coloured fills to rectangles in Unit 27, you'll find that controls underneath it seem to disappear altogether!

To remedy this, you'll need to change the order of the layers so that the controls sit on top of the rectangle or line, not underneath it.

1 To move a control back beneath other controls, select it and choose **Send to Back** from the **Format** menu.

2   To move a control from behind other controls and put it on top, choose **Bring to Front** from the **Format** menu.

i   *Note: if you are having difficulty selecting a control which is "stuck" behind another one, select a nearby control and use the <u>Tab</u> key to hop from one control to the next until you have the hidden one selected.*

Task 1: Adding lines and rectangles

Open the **Classes** form. Experiment with adding lines and rectangles to the form until it looks similar to the form shown below.

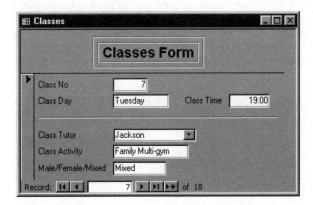

Figure 25.1

1   Move and size the controls so that they are in the positions shown above.

2   Edit the text of the labels appropriately.

3   Place two rectangles around the text in the form header.

4   Insert a line underneath the controls for Day and Time.

5   Save the form as *Classes3*.

Unit 26

Style enhancements

What you will learn in this unit

Style enhancements include alignment, colour, 3-D effects, fonts and borders. These properties are listed in the bottom half of the property sheet window and may also be set using buttons on the toolbar. When a control is selected that can or does use any of these style enhancements, the toolbar buttons shown below become active.

By the end of this unit you will be able to:

❑ use different alignments

❑ use different fonts

❑ set dimensions

❑ set colours

❑ set borders.

Setting alignment and fonts

This activity uses the toolbar to set font style, size and text alignment. Select a control, then click on an appropriate icon on the toolbar to apply the style.

Button	*Action*
Font	
Arial	sets the font style of characters
8	sets the font size of the characters
B	sets characters in bold type
I	sets characters in italics
U	underlines characters
Alignment	
	left aligns text
	centres text
	right aligns text

These buttons work in much the same way as Microsoft Word, so if you are familiar with that program, you'll be at home here. The main difference is that to apply a style, you have to select the *control*, not the *text* on the control – you'll find that when you have the text itself selected for editing, the style buttons are inactive. The other difference is in the way alignment works: alignment refers to the text's position inside the control box, *not* the control box's position on the screen.

For those of you not familiar with formatting text in MS Word, a 'font' is a style of lettering; this style can be further modified by changing the font size (measured in 'points'), or applying bold (heavy print), italics (slanting letters) or underline (you work it out!). Experiment with different fonts, sizes and styles until you have a good feel for how they work – but remember not to go font- and style-crazy when producing a final design. You should also bear in mind that not all printers and not all computers will necessarily have the same fonts available as you, so for professional purposes, stick to common ones such as Arial, Comic Sans, Courier New, the Lucida family of fonts, Times New Roman and Verdana. If in doubt, have a look on a couple of other computers and see which fonts are common to all.

When printing reports, try to use True Type fonts only – these are designed so that they print out exactly as they appear on he screen. True Type fonts have a symbol like this next to them in the **Font Name** menu: ⊤.

The alignment buttons determine where the text sits inside the control box:

❏ left align means that the text starts at the left-hand edge of the control box

❏ right align means that it ends flush with the right-hand edge

❏ centre align places it right in the middle.

 These alignment buttons should not be confused with the **Align-Left/Right/Top/Bottom** options available when you right-click on a group of selected controls – those set the position of the controls on the page relative to each other, whereas these buttons affect the text inside the control boxes.

Task 1: Setting alignment and fonts on forms

Open the *Classes3* form. Set the alignment and fonts as shown in Figure 21.1.

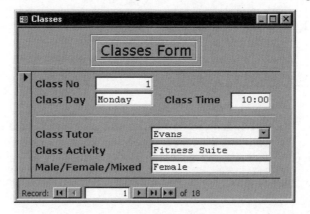

Figure 26.1

1   Change the font of *Class No*, *Class Day* and *Class Time* to Verdana, make them Bold, and set the field controls to Courier New.

2   Increase the font size of all of them to 10 point. You may need to increase the size of the controls to accommodate the text of the labels and the data in the larger size.

3   Set the title *Classes Form* in 14 point Verdana, Underlined.

4   Click on each control in turn and check its alignment. Left align controls for all fields except *Class No* and *Class Time* which should be right aligned.

Note: You can copy the formatting from one control to another using the **Format Painter** – select the control with the style you like, click the **Format Painter** button, and then click on another control to apply the same formatting to it.

Task 2: Borders, lines, alignment and fonts on reports

The last two tasks have involved forms. In this task you are required to apply borders, lines, alignment and fonts to a report.

Design a new report *Classes4* based on the *Classes* table. Format the report so that it looks like this.

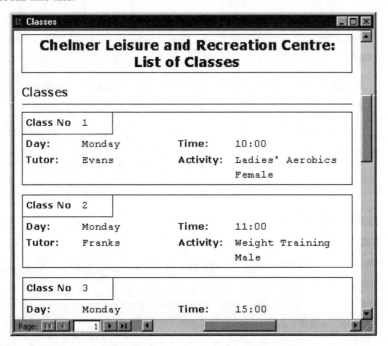

Figure 26.2

1   In the **Report Header** insert a label control and type in the title text shown above. Move the control to the centre, and centre align the text. Format the text to an appropriate font size and embolden it. Add a rectangle around the text.

2   In the **Page Header** section type in *Classes*. Format this text and place a line underneath it.

3   In the **Detail** section, add the controls and labels using the **Field List**. Click on the field list window title bar to select all fields, and then drag one of the fields to where you want the fields to start. Arrange the controls to roughly the layout shown above.

4   Edit the field names and format them as shown in the illustration.

5   Resize controls to fit the text in if necessary, and fine-tune their placement.

6   To align a group of controls select the group, right-click and choose **Align-Left/ Right/Top/Bottom**. Most of these controls are left and bottom aligned relative to each other.

7   Check the alignment of text within the controls. Ensure that all controls are left aligned.

8   Add a rectangle around the *Class No* controls. Add another rectangle to enclose all text in the Detail band.

9   At the top of the Page Footer band insert a line.

10   Preview the report, making sure that you have made your controls large enough to display their information (check the *Class Activity* in particular, because some of the entries, e.g. 'Body Conditioning', are quite long).

11   Make any necessary adjustments, preview again, and save the report as *Classes4*.

Unit 27

Special effects, colours and borders

What you will learn in this unit

You can make a control look three-dimensional, add colour or change border widths to make reports and forms look more interesting. Remember the design tips given in Unit 21 when adding colours and special effects to controls on printed reports – especially since most reports are likely to be printed in black and white.

By the end of this unit you will be able to:

❏ set colours

❏ set borders

❏ set 3-D effects.

Using the Formatting (Form/Report Design) toolbar

Special effects, colours and borders can be set using the Formatting (Form/Report Design) toolbar:

From left to right, these tools give you control over **Fill/Back**(ground) **Color**, **Font/Fore**(ground) **Color**, **Line/Border Color**, **Line/Border Width** and **Special Effects** (3D).

You can also set these properties through the Property Sheet. Double-click on the control or area to be changed and set the properties on the **Format** tab. Generally, it's easier to use the Formatting toolbar so we shall restrict ourselves to that here.

Back, fore and border colours

A control can have separate colours for background, foreground and border. To set a colour:

1   Select the control.

2   Click on the down arrow of the **Fill/Back Color** button to drop down the colour selection box, and choose a colour.

3   If the **Transparent** button in the colour selection box is clicked, the selected control is made transparent so that it shows whatever controls are behind it. This is usually what you want, and controls have a transparent background by default.

4   Repeat for **Font/Fore Color** and **Line/Border Color**.

5   Experiment with different colours until you have chosen a colour combination that is legible and draws attention to the right parts of the screen – test it on a black and white printer if necessary, as you may be surprised how little contrast there is between two apparently distinct colours when they're converted to greyscale!

Note: If you fill a rectangle with a back colour, it will obscure any controls underneath it, and you will need to use **Format-Send to Back** to make them visible again ↔ (see Unit 25).

Border widths

All controls have adjustable borders. Some, such as label controls have no border set as a default. Other controls, such as option groups, list boxes and combo boxes, have a thin black border as a default.

To select a border width, click on the drop-down arrow of the **Border Width** button on the toolbar. Choose a suitable border width from the options are shown (the numbers give the line thickness in points).

Special effects

There are six special effects to choose from: Flat, Raised, Sunken, Etched, Shadowed, and Chiselled. These options are displayed by clicking on the drop-down arrow of the **Special Effects** button on the toolbar. Rather than try to explain these in words, we recommend that you try each one in turn to see how it looks.

Using special effects with colours and borders

When you select any 3-D effect (i.e. not Flat), the 3-D effect is given the same colours as buttons on the toolbar and command buttons to achieve the effect. The 3-D effect colours are set by the Windows Control Panel, and you can only change the fore and back colours here. If you choose Shadowed, the back colour is the shadow colour.

If you change the border width on a 3-D control, it will revert to Flat; click the Special Effects to reapply the effect and remove the border.

Task 1: Setting dimensions and borders

Open the *Classes3* form and experiment with setting colours, borders and 3-D effects. For example, try:

1   Setting all the field labels as Raised.

2   Setting the Form Header as Sunken.

3   Increasing the width of the line in the Detail section.

4   Apply some colours to different parts of the screen to add interest.

Unit 28

Control default properties

What you will learn in this unit

In earlier units we have set the properties of controls after adding them to the form. It is also possible to set default properties for controls, which then apply to all controls of that type when you add them to that form or report. If you want to use a set of default control properties for multiple forms or reports, you can create templates that store default settings, and use these templates whenever you create forms and reports. Templates will be explored in the next unit.

By the end of this unit you will be able to:

❑ examine the default properties of a control

❑ set default properties of a control.

 Note: once you set a default property for a tool, it will always apply in that form or report from now on. If something goes wrong and you can't work out how to set it right, you may have to scrap the report and start again! To avoid this, make a note of any settings before you change them, so you can easily change them back if necessary.

Setting property defaults

Setting property defaults for a tool is similar to setting an individual control's properties, only you use the Properties Sheet for the tool itself.

1 Click the **Properties Sheet** button on the Toolbar.

2 Click on a tool in the Toolbox.

3 The Property Sheet window now shows the default properties of that tool which you can edit.

Note that the window's title bar says **Default** and then the name of the tool you have selected.

To change the properties in the property sheet window:

4 Click on a property and either a drop-down arrow or a 'More' button (...) appears. Click on this to show the available options.

5 Choose the default settings you want and repeat for other properties.

6 From now on, any control of that type that you add to the form or report uses these new settings.

Default text box

Click on the **Properties Sheet** button on the toolbar, then select the **Text Box** from the Toolbox. You will see that there are a lot of properties you can set, some of which will be familiar, others not so familiar. In particular there are five properties which only appear when setting defaults:

Property	Description
Auto Label	Adds labels automatically with new controls.
Add Colon	Adds colons to the end of labels.
Label X and Label Y	Sets the relative distance of the label from the upper left-hand corner of the selected control.
Label Align	Sets the position of the text on the label.

Task 1: Changing the default properties of a control

Before you modify any of the default properties of the control in this task, you will make a note of every setting on the properties sheet, and at the end of the task you'll restore the original defaults. This is to ensure that when you come to other tasks later in this book, things still work the way they're supposed to!

1   Open any form or report, and make sure the **Properties Sheet** is showing.

2   Click on the **Label** button in the Toolbox. Make a written note of all the default properties for this tool.

3   Try changing some of the properties, then add a new label control to see how it is affected.

4   Open the default Properties Sheet again and copy the original settings back in from your notes.

5   Now do the same for a **Rectangle** control, remembering to note down the original settings before you change anything. Test your settings with a new rectangle.

6   Restore the original settings and close the form.

Unit 29

Report and form templates

What you will learn in this unit

When a form or report is created without using a Wizard, Access uses a template to define its default characteristics. You can design your own templates for producing reports or forms which maintain a house style, or simply to save time formatting them the way you want them. Even if you only want to format two or three reports to a similar design, it may be worth creating a template to avoid duplicating effort.

By the end of this unit you will be able to:

❏   create a report template

❏   create a form template

Understanding templates

A template determines the default settings for form, report, section and control properties, section sizes and whether the form or report includes headers and footers.

To create a template from an existing form or report:

1   Create a blank form or report with default settings for the controls.

2   Display the form or report header and footer and page header and footer, if you want these to be included in the template.

3   Set section sizes to determine their default size.

4   Save this form or report.

5   To use it as a template, choose **Tools-Options** and click on the **Forms/Reports** tab.

6   Type in the name of the form or report in the **Form Template** or **Report Template** box. Click on **OK**.

The next time you create a new blank report or form, the selected template will be used as a basis.

Note: The default for both form and report templates is Normal.

Task 1: Creating and using a report template

In this task we use a report that you have previously created to define the properties of a template. The most obvious properties that will be set are the section sizes (e.g. the size of the Page Header) and whether or not headers and footers are included. Other section and control properties can also be set.

1   Choose **Options** from the **Tools** menu and click on the **Forms/Reports** tab.

2   In the **Report Template** box at the bottom of the dialog box, enter the name of the report *Classes4*.

3   Click on **OK**; from now on, this will be used as the default report template.

4   Now click on the **Reports** tab in the Database window.

5   Create a new blank report using Design view instead of the Wizard.

6   You should see that this report has the same headers, footers and section sizes as the *Classes4* template.

Task 2: Creating and using a form template

In this task we will create a blank form and define the properties of the form to be stored in the template. We'll also change the default properties of the Label tool.

1   In the Database window, click on the **Forms** tab, then double-click on **Create form in Design view**.

2   Right-click and choose Page Header/Footer, to include these in the template. Adjust their size if you want to.

3   Set the default properties for the Label tool to Times New Roman, size 14, bold and shadowed (see previous unit if you can't remember how to do this).

4   Save this form as *Chelmer* and close it.

5   To use the form as a template, choose **Tools-Options** and click on the **Forms/Reports** tab.

6   In the **Form Template** box at the bottom of the dialog box, type the name of the form: *Chelmer*.

7   Click on **OK**; this will now be used as the template for new forms.

8   Create a blank new form using design view instead of the Wizard.

i   *Note that the form has the same headers and footers and section sizes as the template. If you add a label control you will see that it has the same properties as set in the template.*

Task 3: Returning form and report templates to Normal

When you no longer want to use these designs for new forms or reports, reset the templates to *Normal*.

1   Choose **Tools-Options** and click on the **Forms/Reports** tab.

2   In the **Form Template** text box, enter *Normal*. Repeat for the **Report Template**.

3   Click on **OK**.

Unit 30

Report and form charts

What you will learn in this unit

Analysis of the data in a database can often be more quickly and clearly using a chart. For example, it might be useful to examine the membership of the Leisure Centre by Membership Category or to look at the distribution of bookings as a visual chart, instead of going through text records and counting them.

Charts can be created by using Microsoft Graph, which is a component of both Access and Word. Here we introduce a few tasks that make use of Graph in order to demonstrate how it can be used to insert charts into a report or form. These tasks first take you step-by-step through the creation of a simple chart, and then demonstrate how that chart can be inserted in a Report or form. Charts can be based on tables or queries.

i *Note: there are many more features to MS Graph than we have time to cover in this book. Press [F1] to use the Access Help system, or consult* Word 2000 Basic Skills.

By the end of this unit you will be able to:

❑ add a chart to a report or form

❑ edit a chart

❑ understand the links between the database and the chart

❑ use the clipboard to copy or move charts

❑ add a chart to a report that is based upon a query

Understanding charts

Charts are most appropriate in reports where some summary data can be displayed visually. As such they will often be included in the report's footer, at the end of the detailed information.

Charts can also be added to forms. They may be used to chart items within individual records, in which case they can be included in the Detail section. We'll start by creating a form and inserting a chart giving a visual indication of various stock levels in Chelmer Leisure Centre's fitness shop. To complete the tasks, you need to create a new table called *Stock Levels* and enter into it the data in Quick Reference 1.

Later we'll experiment with some simple charts that use queries to show counts of specific field values, for example to show how many bookings each room, hall or court has. We also experiment with moving charts between forms using the clipboard.

Adding a chart to a form

Charts can be used on forms to display data on screen at a glance. The simplest use is where the data comes from the tables, and the data from each record is shown on a separate chart for each record. This is the type of chart that we shall explore here.

To use a chart in a form to display data from a table:

1 Display or create a form in design view.

2 Open the Detail section by clicking on it.

3 Choose **Insert-Chart**. Click and drag a chart box on the Detail section.

4 When you release the mouse button, Access will start a wizard to help you define your chart.

5 Go through the dialog boxes making appropriate selections for fields to chart and labels for the chart, and insert a chart title.

6 To complete the chart, click **Finish**.

7 Access inserts a control in the Detail section which holds the chart.

8 Save and close the form. The chart is saved as part of the form.

Task 1: Adding a chart to a form

In this task we wish to add a chart to a form for a new table, called *Stock Levels*.

1 First you will need to create the *Stock Levels* table. Give it the following fields:

Field Name	Data Type
Item Code	Autonumber Primary Key
Item	Text
Stock	Integer
Re-order Level	Integer

2 Enter the data from Quick Reference 1 into the table, using the Datasheet view.

3 Create a form with the **Form Wizard**, using the *Stock Levels* table.

4 Click on the Detail section and choose **Insert-Chart**. Click on the Detail section and drag to the required size.

5 When the **Chart Wizard** opens, select a data source for your chart – in this case, the *Stock Levels* table. Click [Next >].

6 Select *Stock* and *Re-order Level* as the fields that contain the data you want for the chart. Click [Next >].

7 Select a chart type. Choose a 3D column chart and click [Next >].

8 You will probably find that Access has added **SumOfStock** to the Data section of the preview chart (top left). In this case however, you just want to display the value

in the *Stock* field, so there's no need to Sum it. Double-click on the **SumOfStock** button and select *None* as the **Summarize** option. Click **OK**. The button should now just read *Stock*.

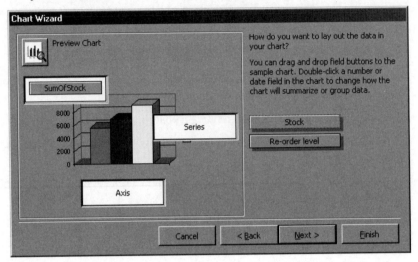

Figure 30.1

9   Drag the *Re-order Level* button to underneath the *Stock* button. Do the same as above to remove the **Sum** function from it. Click Next > .

10   The next dialog box shows the link between chart and document as **Item Code**. This link will mean that the chart display will change from record to record, as we want. Click on Next > .

11   Give your chart the title *Stock Levels*. Choose the option **No, don't display a legend**. To complete the chart, click Finish .

     Access now inserts a control for the chart in the Detail section. To see the chart on the form click on the View button.

12   You may need to adjust the size of the chart control in design view, and the chart may need editing; this is discussed in the following section. For now, just save the form as *Stock Levels* and close the form. The chart is saved as part of the form.

Editing a chart

Charts can be edited in order to change the data that it is based on, or the way it is displayed. For example, a chart of membership fees could show £ symbols on the y axis figures. Graph is a useful chart creation tool which has a range of options for creating and designing effective charts. In the following task, we demonstrate how to use Graph to make a few simple alterations to a chart.

To edit a chart:

1   In Design view, double click on the chart.

2 Access starts **Graph** and displays the chart in the Graph application window.

3 Change overall chart properties using **Chart-Chart Options**.

4 Select specific components of the chart using the **Chart Objects** menu on the toolbar.

5 Make any changes that you require.

6 Click outside the chart area to return to the form in Design view.

7 Save and close the form or report. The chart is saved as part of the form or report

Task 2: Editing a chart

This task edits the form that you created in Task 1. You will experiment with some basic editing techniques to appreciate the principles of editing charts. Before you start, run the form and look through the charts for different stock items. What might you want to change?

1 Open the *Stock Levels* form in Design view and double-click on the chart control to start Graph.

2 Close the sample data spreadsheet by clicking on the **Close** button at the top right.

i *Note: the sample chart data shown in Design view is just for preview purposes – the correct data will be displayed when you run the form.*

3 Choose a different type of chart by clicking on the down arrow of the **Chart Type** button and selecting a **Column Chart**.

4 Add or remove the gridlines by using **Chart-Chart Options** and choosing the **Gridlines** tab.

5 Use the **Chart Objects** menu on the toolbar to select the **Value Axis** (the *y* axis), then click the **Properties** button next to it. Click on the **Scale** tab and uncheck the **Automatic** checkbox for the **Minimum** option. This ensures that all the charts start at 0. Click **OK**.

6 Open the **Value Axis Properties** dialog box again and experiment with the **Font**, **Number**, and **Alignment** options to see what effect they have.

7 Insert an axis label for the *y* axis by choosing **Chart-Chart Options**, clicking on the **Titles** tab and adding the text **Units** in the **Value (Y) Axis** field. Click **OK**.

8 Select the **Value Axis Title** from the **Chart Objects** menu and open its properties dialog box. Choose a different font and make the text bold and italic. Click **OK**.

9 Click on the main title to select it and press **Delete** to remove it.

10 Select the **Plot area** and open its properties dialog box. Set the **Border** option to **None**, then click on the **Fill Effects** button. Experiment with gradients and patterns, then click **OK** to see the result (the example below uses a horizontal gradient, one colour, maximum lightness).

11 Click outside the chart to return to the form's Design view.

12 If necessary, adjust the size of the chart control by dragging its border. You may then need to return to Graph and alter the size of the Chart in a similar way.

13   Save the form and run it to see how it looks.

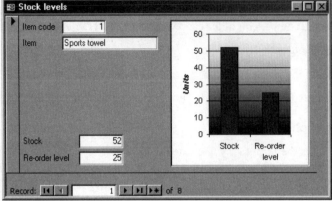

Figure 30.2 The form after editing

Demonstrating that charts are linked to the database

The charts that you create in Access and that use data in the database are updated when you update the data. So, for example, the charts that we have just created should be automatically updated if we change the values in the **Stock Levels** table.

Task 3: Testing links between the database and associated charts

In this task we wish to demonstrate how the chart changes to display updated data in the *Stock Levels* table.

1   Open the *Stock Levels* form in Data view.

2   Change the value in the *Stock* field of the first record to *30*.

3   Use the **Record Navigation** buttons to move on to the next record.

4   Now go back to the record you just changed. The new data should be reflected in the chart.

Using the clipboard to copy or move charts

Since you can spend some time formatting a chart, it is useful to be able to copy and paste it into other forms or reports, having created it once. The Clipboard can be used to move charts in the same way as other controls.

Task 4: Using the clipboard to copy a chart

1   Open the *Stock Levels* form in Design view and click the chart control to select it.

2   Choose **Edit-Copy** to copy the chart to the clipboard.

3   Close the form.

4   Create a new report based on the *Stock Levels* table using the **Report Wizard**. Include all fields.

5   Sort by *Item Code* and save the report.

6   Open the new report in Design view. Click on the Detail section and choose **Edit-Paste** to insert the chart from the clipboard.

7   Move the chart to a suitable position and preview the report.

8   Save the report as ***Stock Levels***.

Adding a summary chart to a report

The tasks above show how to add charts which reflect data from one particular record at a time. A useful chart for Chelmer to have in a report might be the number of bookings in each room, hall and court, or the number of members in each category. The **Chart Wizard** gives you the option to do this too.

Suppose we wish to display the number of bookings for each room, hall or court. We need to display the values in the *Room/Hall/Court* field against the number of bookings for each of these. When the Chart Wizard creates this chart, it in effect creates a query which groups by *Category* and counts the number of *Booking No* records in each group, and then base the chart on that query.

1   Use the **Report Wizard** to create a report based on the *Bookings* table. Use all fields.

2   Save the report as ***Bookings*** and open it in Design view.

3   Choose **Insert-Chart**. Drag a chart control in the report footer.

4   Access takes you through the creation of a chart using the **Chart Wizard**.

5   Choose **Tables** and then *Bookings* as the data source for your chart. Add the *Booking No* and *Room/Hall/Court* fields to be displayed on the chart.

6   Choose a **Column Chart** type. In the **Chart Preview** dialog box, make sure that the *Room/Hall/Court* button is on the *x* axis of the chart, and *Booking No* is on the is on the *y* axis. The *Booking No* field should automatically change to ***CountOfBooking No*** – which is what we want in this case. Click ▐ Next > ▐.

7   In the **Linking Fields** dialog box choose **<No Field>** for both fields. This stops the chart from being linked to a particular record and allows it to draw from the data in the whole table.

8   Give your chart the title ***Bookings by Hall***.

9   To complete the chart, click ▐ Finish ▐.

10. To view the chart on the report, click **View** and go to the end of the last page of the report.

11   Return to Design view to make any changes necessary, then save and close the report.

i *Note: If the control is too small to display a chart effectively, you cannot size the chart in Report Design View directly. First you need to re-size the chart control in Design View, then double-click on the chart to resize it in Graph.*

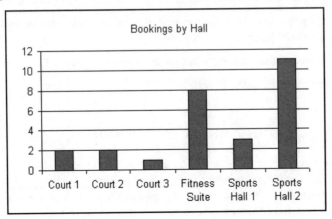

Figure 30.3 The summary chart on the *Bookings* report

Adding a chart to a report using a query

Another interesting chart that we might add to a stock levels report is one which summarises items which are in short stock. To do this we will create a query which selects all items where the stock level is less than the re-order level.

Task 5: Adding a chart to a report using a query

First we need to create a query to use as the basis for the chart.

1 Create a new query using the **Stock Levels** table.

2 Add the **Item**, **Stock** and **Re-order** fields.

3 Sort the query by the **Item** field.

4 In the **Criteria** cell for the **Stock** field type *<[Re-order Level]*.

Field:	Item	Stock	Re-order level
Table:	Stock levels	Stock levels	Stock levels
Sort:	Ascending		
Show:	☑	☑	☑
Criteria:		<[Re-order level]	
or:			

5 Display the dynaset and check that the query counts the items which are in need of re-stocking as you would expect it to.

	Item	Stock	Re-order level
▶	Ankle support	3	5
	T-shirt (medium)	17	20
✱		0	0

6 Save the query as ***Short Stock***.

To use this query to create a chart:

1   Create a report using the **Reports Wizard** based on the *Stock Levels* table. Include all fields.

2   Make 5 to 8cm (2 to 3 inches) of space in the report footer. Choose **Insert-Chart**.

3   In the grey area below the report footer section, draw a control that is about 5 cm (2 inches) deep and 15 cm (6 inches) wide.

4   Choose to take the chart data from the *Short Stock* query that you have just created.

5   Go through the **Charts Wizard** making appropriate selections for fields to chart and label for the chart, and inserting a chart title.

5   To complete the chart, click [Finish].

6   Access now inserts a control in the report footer for the chart and resizes the footer to make room for the new control.

7   View the chart and return to **Design** view to edit it as necessary.

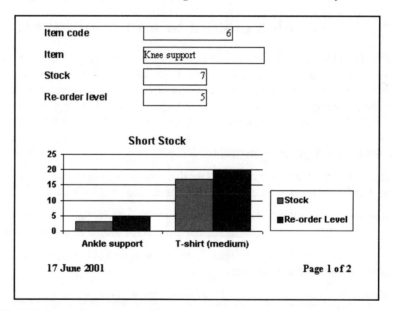

Figure 30.4 Report with summary chart

Unit 31

Pictures in forms and reports

What you will learn in this unit

We have just experimented with adding charts to forms and reports. You can also insert other objects, including pictures, worksheets from Excel, or any object from an application that supports what is known as 'object linking and embedding' (OLE).

By the end of this unit you will be able to:

❑ add pictures and objects to forms

❑ add pictures and objects to reports

Adding a decorative picture to a form or report

Picture can be created using any image editing application, including Paint, or even Word. You might also use a digital camera or scanner to import a photo or graphic. Select the picture in whichever application it was created or imported in, and copy it using **Edit-Copy**. Then return to your form or report in Design view, click on the section header where the picture is to go, and paste it in with **Edit-Paste**.

Task 1: Adding a logo to a form

If you wish to create your own logo for this task you can; alternatively you can scan in the one below, or create a simple text-based logo with Word.

1   If you are using Word, select **Insert-Picture-WordArt**. Select a style, click **OK**, enter your text and click **OK** again. Now select the picture and choose **Edit-Copy**.

2   If you are using another application, create or open your image in that program. Select it and choose **Edit-Copy**.

3   Return to Access and open the *Membership* form in Design view.

4   Click on the form header section.

5   Choose **Edit-Paste**, size the header section and position the logo.

6   Run the form to see how it looks. Return to Design view and make any changes necessary.

7   Save and close the form.

Storing and retrieving pictures from the database

You might want to have pictures of members or products stored in the database, and display them on forms and reports. To do this, we will create an extra field in the *Membership* table using the data type **OLE Object**, then we can add that field to a form or report.

Integrative tasks

Task 2: Using pictures from the database

If you do not have a scanned photo or other image to use for this task, just use a WordArt image for now, so you can learn the process.

1   Open the *Membership* table in Design view.

2   Add a field called *Picture* and set the data type to OLE Object, then save the table.

3   Switch to your image application, select the image and copy it using **Edit-Copy**.

4   Go back to Access and switch to Datasheet view of the *Membership* table.

5   Click in the *Picture* field and choose **Edit-Paste**. Access will add a note to the field explaining what is in it: "Picture" or "Adobe Photoshop Image" for example.

6   Save and close the *Membership* table and open the *Membership* form in Design view.

7   Show the Field List (click on the **Field List** button if it is not already showing).

8   Click and drag the *Picture* field onto the form. Position it and rearrange the other controls if necessary.

9   Run the form to see how it looks, and make changes if required. Close the form.

Task 2: Creating a chart for the Members by Membership Category report

The *Members by Membership Category* report was created in Report Wizards as a Groups/Totals report. It shows members grouped in categories. It might be interesting to create a simple chart which counts and displays the number of members in each category. (It would be even better if the category labels were shown as *Category Type* instead of *Category No*, but this would involve the use of a query which used multiple tables, and these are not introduced until later units.)

To create this chart:

1   First create an appropriate query to count members by *Category No*. You will have created such a query earlier but probably did not save it.

2   Revisit Unit 13 to discover how to create a query which shows *Category No* and
↔   *CountofLastname*, then save it as *Categories*.

3   Open the *Members by Membership Category* report.

4   Go through the steps necessary to create a chart in the report footer, choosing the *Categories* query as the data source.

    5.   Edit the chart as appropriate and save the report.

Task 3: Adding a logo to reports

In order to start to create some kind of house style to our reports, we would like to add the Chelmer Leisure logo to some of the reports generated from the *Membership* table. The easiest way to do this is to copy and paste the logo that we created in Task 1 onto the clipboard, and then paste it into the report header.

1   Open the *Membership* form in Design view.

2   Click on the Chelmer Leisure logo to select it. Choose **Edit-Copy**.

3   Close the form.

4   Open the *Chelmer Leisure and Recreation Centre Members* report. Click on the report header, and choose **Edit-Paste**. The logo should appear in the report header.

5   Repeat this operation for the other reports you have created.

Using multiple tables in a query

What you will learn in this unit

This unit introduces queries that use more than one table. Tables that are linked by their relationships can act as if they are one large table for the purpose of a query.

By the end of this unit you will be able to:

❏   add and delete tables from a query

❏   create queries using multiple tables

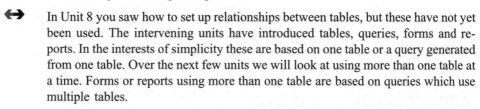 In Unit 8 you saw how to set up relationships between tables, but these have not yet been used. The intervening units have introduced tables, queries, forms and reports. In the interests of simplicity these are based on one table or a query generated from one table. Over the next few units we will look at using more than one table at a time. Forms or reports using more than one table are based on queries which use multiple tables.

Through constructing queries using more than one table you should appreciate how versatile a relational database is. By keeping data in a series of linked but separate tables the need to duplicate data is reduced and it is simpler to update it (refer to Unit 8 to remind you of this).

Multiple tables in a query

When you use more than one table in a query there should be links between the tables chosen. If tables are added to a query and there is no relationship defined between them then Access will try to link them, which can be a time-consuming and unproductive process. Try to establish relationships between tables first if you want to run a query using more than one table.

This is a good opportunity to review the relationships between the tables in the Chelmer Leisure and Recreation Centre database.

❏   The *Membership* table is linked to the *Bookings* table through *Membership No*.

❏   The *Membership Category* table is linked to the *Membership* table through the *Category No*.

❏   The *Bookings* table is linked to the *Classes* table through *Class No*. The *Tutor* table is linked to the *Classes* table through *Lastname*.

Joins between tables

Before you can use joins (relationships) between tables, you must know the contents of their fields and which fields are related by common values. Assigning identical names to fields in different tables that contain related data is a common practice. This has generally been adhered to in the *Chelmer Leisure and Recreation Centre* database, as the summary shows. The exception is *Class Tutor* (*Classes* table) and *Lastname* (*Tutor* table), which could be remedied by using *Tutor Name* as a field in both tables.

Joins are indicated in Access query designs by lines between field names of different tables, as illustrated in Task 1.

Access allows different types of joins between tables, but only the most common type will be considered here. This type is called an 'equivalent' or 'inner-join' and has already been created when the relationships were defined. Inner-joins display all the records in one table that have corresponding records in another table. This correspondence is determined by identical values in the fields that join the tables. In the case of the Chelmer database all joins are one-to-many relationships based

 on a unique primary key field in one table and a field in the other table (see Unit 8).

Adding tables to a query

When creating a query this is simply a matter of selecting more than one table from the **Show Table** dialog box. Tables are shown in the query window with lines between them indicating the relationships. Choose **Query-Show Table** to display the **Show Table** dialog box if it is not showing.

Knowing what is in your tables will help when you need to add tables to a query so that you add tables containing the right data – and you will know when you need additional tables to create links between existing tables. Each of the following tasks starts by considering what data we need and where to find it.

Deleting tables from a query

Just click on the title bar of the particular table and press the *Delete* key to remove it from the query. Check first that the table was not providing an indirect link between two tables, and remove references to it from the query if necessary.

Task 1: Adding tables to the query window

In this task you will add all the tables in the Chelmer database to a query.

1   Click on the **Queries** button in the Database window and click **New**. Select Design view and click **OK**.

2   From the **Show Table** dialog box add all the tables. These are *Membership, Membership Category, Bookings, Classes* and *Tutors*.

3 By rearranging the tables, your query window will appear as illustrated below. If there are no lines indicating the relationships or some are missing, abandon the query and check the relationships using **Tools-Relationships** (refer to Unit 8).

4 A link may be displayed between *Lastname* in the *Membership* table and *Lastname* in the *Tutors* table, because Access is guessing that you want this relationship, based on the fact that the field names are the same. However, the relationship is actually false, so remove the link by clicking on it and pressing *Delete*.

5 Delete the *Tutors* and the *Membership Category* tables. Consider why you should not delete the *Bookings* table.

6 Close the query without saving it.

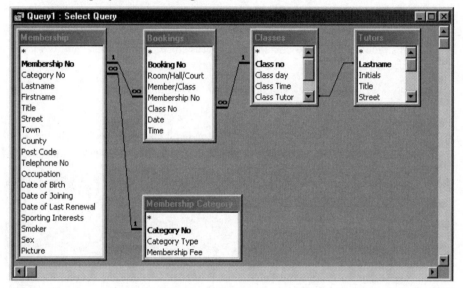

Figure 32.1

Using multiple tables

In this section a series of tasks ask questions of the database, and queries containing multiple tables are devised in order to answer them.

Task 2: Membership fees

How much membership fee money has been collected in the last six months?

First decide which tables are needed. The data needed is the members who renewed their membership in the last six months, their membership category and the fee. This data can be found in the *Membership* table and the *Membership Category* table. Is there a link between these two tables? Yes, between *Category No* (primary key *Classes* table) and *Category No* (*Membership* table), so only these two tables will be required.

Before continuing you should review the dates of renewal in the *Membership* table and, if necessary, update them so that this query will produce some tangible results.

To create the query:

1   Click on the **Queries** button in the Database window and click **New**. Select **Design View** and click **OK**.

2   From the **Show Table** dialog box select the *Membership* and *Membership Category* tables. These two should be shown in the query window with a link between them.

3   Add the fields *Membership No* and *Membership Fee* to the query.

4   Create a calculated field which works out the time between the date of last renewal and today's date. In the next field cell enter this expression:

   Rejoin: DateDiff("d",[Date of last renewal],Date())

5   Run this query to see the result.

6   Return to the query design. Add the criteria ***<183*** (i.e. less than six months - 183 days: you may need to check your records to see if this query will work) to find those with renewal dates less than six months old.

7   Run this query to check and then return to Design view.

8   Click on the **Totals** button to show the **Total** row.

9   In the **Rejoin** field select ***Where*** in the total cell and hide the field. In the *Membership No* field select ***Count*** and in the *Membership Fee* field, ***Sum***. (Figure 32.2)

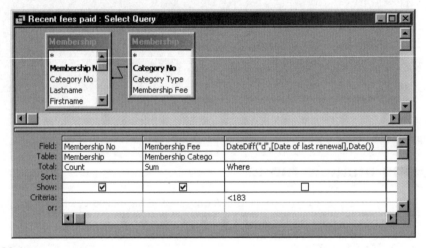

Figure 32.1

10   Run the query. The result should be the number of members who rejoined in the last six months and the total of fees paid.

11   Save the query as ***Recent fees paid***.

To create the report:

1   Click on the **Reports** button in the database window and click **New**.

2   In the **New Report** dialog box select the query *Recent fees paid* and use **AutoReport: Tabular** to design a report.

3   Switch to Design view and edit the labels so your report is similar to the one in Figure 32.3. Save the report as **Recent fees paid**.

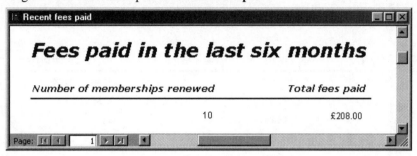

Figure 32.1

Task 3: Class activities in the fitness suite

What class activities are being held in the fitness suite?

The tables that are needed to answer this question are the **Bookings** table and the **Classes** table. There is a direct link between these tables through **Class No**.

To create the query:

1   Click on the **Queries** button in the database window and click **New**. Select **Design View** and click **OK**.

2   From the **Show Table** dialog box select the *Classes* and *Bookings* tables. These two tables should be shown in the query window with a link between them.

3   Add the fields *Member/Class*, *Room/Hall/Court*, *Class Day*, *Date*, *Class Time* and *Class Activity* to the query.

4   In the *Member/Class* column set the criterion to *No* to select only classes, and hide this field.

5   In *Room/Hall/Court* put *"Fitness Suite"* in the criteria row and hide this field.

6   Run the query and save it as *Activities in Fitness Suite*.

To create the report:

1   Click on the **Reports** button in the database window and click **New**.

2   In the **New Report** dialog box select the query *Activities in Fitness Suite* and use the **Report Wizard** to design a tabular report.

3   Edit your design to create a report similar to the one illustrated in Figure 32.4. Save this report as *Activities in Fitness Suite*.

Task 4: Class attendance

Which members are attending which classes?

Our database is unable to answer this question yet because the data needed has not been recorded. The database must be modified so that this data can be added. What

173

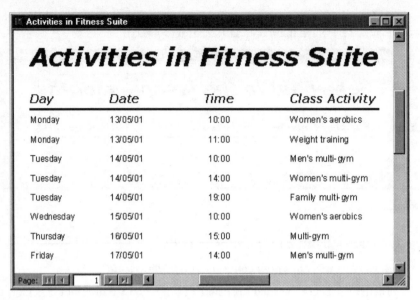

Figure 32.4

would be the best way to go about this? One method could be to introduce an extra field Class to the Membership table. However, this leads to problems if the member attends more than one class or a class is cancelled. A better alternative is to create another table that keeps lists of members in classes. This table would be linked to both the *Membership* and *Classes* tables. *Class List* would be a suitable name.

To create the Class List table:

1   Click on the **Tables** button in the database window and click **New**. Select **Design View** and click **OK**.

2   Create a table with two fields, *Class No* and *Membership No*. Make both numeric, of type long integer. This is so that they are of a type which will correspond to the counter types used by the fields *Membership No* (*Membership* table) and *Class No* (*Classes* table) to which they will be related.

3   Each record is unique, even though the membership numbers and class numbers themselves are not unique (i.e. one member might be in more than one class, and presumably each class will have more than one member in it – but each member will be in each class list only once). Therefore the primary key must be both fields. To set both as the primary key select both before clicking on the **Primary Key** button in the toolbar.

4   Save the table as *Class List* and close it.

5   Define two relationships as described below. In both of these relationships referential integrity is enforced. This will prevent a class or a membership number being entered which does not exist in the *Classes* or *Membership* table

6   Click on the **Relationships** button and then click on the **Show Table** button. Add the *Class List* table.

7   Drag *Class No* from the *Classes* table to *Class No* in the *Class List* table. Check the **Enforce Referential Integrity** check box.

8   Now do the same for *Membership No* with the *Membership* table.

9   Save the layout and close the relationships window.

 Before a form can be created, we need a query which links the member's name to the class activity. A form can be created from this query which lists the members in each class (this will later become a sub-form in a main/sub form in Unit 33).

10 Click on the **Queries** button in the database window and click **New**. Select **Design View** and click **OK**.

11 From the **Add Table** dialog box select the *Class List* and *Membership* tables. These two tables should be shown in the query window with a link between them.

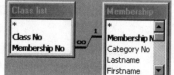

12 Add the following fields to the query: **Class No**, **Membership No**, **Firstname** and **Lastname**. Save the query as **Class Member List**. Close the query.

13 Click on the **Forms** button in the database window and click **New**. In the **New Form** dialog box select the **Class Member List** query just created and use the **Form Wizard** to create a tabular form.

 *Be careful with form names if you use **AutoForm** to create this form instead of the Wizard. If you do not use the default name assigned by Autoform, you may find that the macro you will write in Unit 43 does not work properly! See Unit 43 for more.*

14 Display this form in design view, hold the <u>*Shift*</u> key and click on the *Class No*, *Firstname* and *Lastname* controls. Now click on the **Properties** button to display the property sheet for these three controls. Set the **Enabled** property to **No** and the **Locked** property to **Yes**. This prevents a user from accessing or changing the data in the field. You will see why we do this in the next unit.

Figure 32.5

15 Add a title to the form as illustrated and save it as *Class Member List*.

16 Try entering data into the table using the form.

Unit 33

Main/subforms and main/subreports

What you will learn in this unit

Subforms and subreports are another way to use the links between tables. Information from one form or report can be inserted as a subsection into another main form or report, so that each main record has an extra subset of data displayed with it.

An example would be keeping academic information about students. A student may study several modules and for each one a performance record is kept. The details about the student (Student No, Title, Surname, Forenames, Date Enrolled, Tutor) could be kept in a *Student* table. The module results for all students could be kept in a *Results* table, with the fields Student No, Module No, Coursework Grade, Exam Grade, Overall Grade, Date Completed, etc. The tables *Student* and *Results* would be linked through the *Student No* field.

One form can then be based on the *Student* table and another based on the *Results* table, and the two combined into one known as a 'main/subform'. This form would display the student details as heading information, with a subsection for entering results data for that student. Similarly, a *Student* report would be the main part of the main/subreport and a *Results* report would be the 'sub' part.

By the end of this unit, you will be able to:

❏   create and use main/subforms

❏   create and use main/subreports

Creating and using main/subform forms

What is a subform? A main form is usually created from one of the primary tables in a database and a subform is a table that is related to it. This is best described by means of an example. Consider a wholesaler's database where there is a table of customer names, addresses, etc, and a table of purchase transactions made by customers. A form showing the customer's details plus a list of transactions made by that customer can be created using a main/subform.

The *Customer* table will be the main part of the form, and that particular customer's transactions will be the subform. This type of form is useful for all areas of transaction processing, such as sales made by salespeople, or bookings made by members of our leisure centre.

A main/subform is created by inserting one form into another as follows.

1   Create the main form and the subform separately. Ideally these should be linked through an existing relationship. The main form should be created in single column format and the subform in tabular format.

2 Open the main form in Design view.

3 Switch back to the Database window (shortcut key _F11_) and if necessary move it so that you can clearly see the main form window beneath it.

4 Click and drag the subform onto the main form.

Task 1: Creating and using a main/subform

This task creates a main/subform for the _Class List_ table. This form shows the class details and lists members enrolled in the class in a subform. It can be used to book members into a particular class. Open the _Classes_ form and use **File-Save As** to save the form as _Class Lists_, so that you have a copy to work from. Display this form in Design view and set the locked property for all the controls to **Yes**. This is the reason for making a copy of the form – the original _Classes_ form can be used to enter classes data but this new one cannot.

 If you run this form you'll see that the form window is captioned **Classes** _though you've changed the filename to_ **Class Lists**_. To amend this, open the_ **Properties sheet**_, and click on the dark grey area beneath the form footer to see the properties for the form. Change the text in the_ **Caption** _field to give your new form a new title._

1 Choose **Window-Tile Vertically** to display the _Class Lists_ form window (in Design view) and Database window side by side.

2 Click on _Class Member List_ (the sub-form created in Task 4 in Unit 32) and drag to the _Class Lists_ form.

3 A sub-form box appears on the form. Reposition and resize as necessary.

4 Run the form. It should look something like the one illustrated in Figure 33.1.

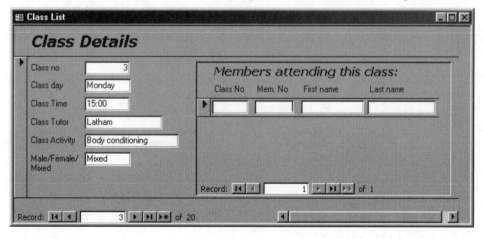

Figure 33.1

5 Save the form and try using it to enter data. A class list can be quickly built up by entering just the membership numbers of those members who are attending the class. Notice that the correct class number is automatically entered for each record you add. In practice, you would set the Visible property to No for this field on the

subform because you already have it on the main form, but it is useful for now to see how it ties the two forms together.

6   So that a report can be generated later, enter data for three class lists as follows.

Class No	Membership No
1	2
1	5
1	16
4	4
4	6
5	7
5	10
5	1

Creating and using main/subreport reports

Like forms, reports can include subreports. An example of such a report is one in which a customer's details are shown in the main report and purchases made by that customer in the subreport. To insert a subreport into a main report:

1   Create the main report and the subreport separately as reports. Ideally these should be linked through an existing relationship.

2   Open the main report in Design view. Use **Sorting and Grouping** if you want to group by customer or by company, perhaps, and add a group footer.

3   Display the database window and click and drag the subreport to the required section in the main report.

Task 2: Adding a subreport to a report

↔   For this task check that you have the *Classes2* report created in Task 5 of Unit 20. Open it and save a copy of it as *Class List2*.

In this task you will create a report of classes and the members enrolled in each one. This is done by adding a *Class Member List* subreport to the *Class List2* main report.

↔
1   Save the *Class Member List* form as a report (see Unit 24) with the same name.

2   Open this new report in Design view.

3   Reorder the fields so that *Class No* is last in the row. Set the **Visible** property for this field to **No** so that it does not print. Remove the label for *Class No*.

4   Edit the header to read ***List of Members***. The report design should be similar to the one shown in Figure 33.2.

5   Use the palette to alter the colour of fill and borders. Preview the report to check your settings.

6   Save the report and close it.

7   Open the *Class Lists2* report in Design view.

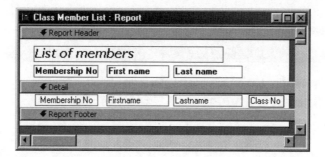

Figure 33.2

8   Click on the **Sorting and Grouping** button and select **Class No Ascending** in the dialog box. Set the group header and footer to **Yes**.

9   If necessary, widen the group footer section to make room for the subreport.

10   Display the Database window and click and drag the *Class Member List* report into the group footer section. You may need to re-arrange your windows so that you can adjust the position of the subreport.

11   In the subForm/subReport properties window note that the link between the two reports is **Class No**.

12   Set the **Can Shrink** and the **Can Grow** properties of the **Class No Footer** section to **Yes**. (Click on the section header to select the section.)

13   Delete the *Class Member List* label and adjust the size of the control as illustrated overleaf. Preview the report.

14   The report would look better if the field labels were in the *Class No* header. Cut and paste the headings from the page header to the *Class No* header (Figure 33.3).

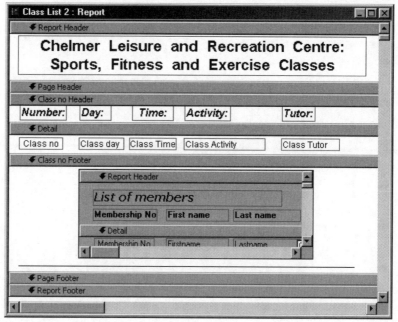

Figure 33.3

179

15 Preview, make final adjustments so that it looks similar to the following extract, then save and print the report.

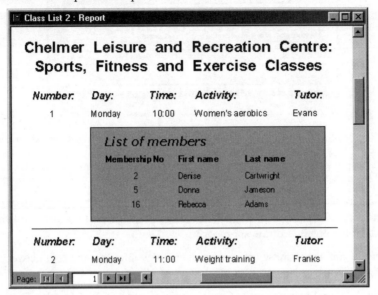

Figure 33.4

Action queries

What you will learn in this unit

Usually queries are passive in nature, i.e. they do not change any of the data, they just retrieve and display it. However, special queries known as action queries can be designed to change the data. An example could be a bank amending its customer credit limits. The bank wishes to amend the credit limit of customers whose present limit is £200 or less and who have been with the bank for six months or more. First, a query which selects the appropriate customer records would be constructed. By converting this search query to an action query the values in the *Credit Limit* field, for each selected record, would be updated with the new credit limit.

By the end of this unit you will be able to:

❏ design action queries to modify data

Designing action queries to modify data

There are four types of action query: update queries, delete queries, append queries and make table queries.

An action query changes the data in your table or copies data from one table to another. Unlike the select queries we have already seen, an action query doesn't show the records it has retrieved for modification.

If you wish to see the result of the change made by an action query then will you need either to convert your action query to a select query or open the relevant table to view changes. The following activities explore the various action queries.

Make table and delete query

These two action queries will be used together to deal with members who have not renewed their membership for more than a year. This operation would be carried out periodically, say annually or every six months, to keep only current members in the *Membership* table.

Members who have not renewed their membership could simply be discarded or their information could be kept in a separate file for a further period as historical information. Chelmer Leisure Centre follows the latter course and makes a table of old members before deleting them from the current membership table.

 A make table query does just what it says and creates one table from another or others. Data is selected by means of a query to create the new table. A delete query deletes a group of records from one or more tables. The query you design will select the records that are to be deleted. When you run the query, Access retrieves the records you asked for and deletes them from the table.

In this activity we will create a table in which to store old member details before deleting all the members whose last renewal date was in 1999 or before. So that some records meet these criteria open the Membership table and add a couple of records where the *Date of Last Renewal* is before the end of 1999. To prevent any problems with referential integrity in later tasks in this book, alter the renewal date of the existing records so that they are all after 1/1/2000.

Task 1: Archiving and removing out-of-date members

1   Start a new query using Design view. Add the *Membership* table to the query.

2   Add all the fields from the table to the query by double-clicking on the table's title bar and dragging the contents to the Query Design grid.

3   In the *Date of Last Renewal* column, enter *<1/1/99* into the criteria cell.

4   At this point you should run the query to check which records are selected.

i   It is always a good idea to check that your query will select the correct records before it changes or deletes anything. You can do this by running your query as a select query before making it an action query.

5   Assuming the correct records are selected, choose **Query-Make Table Query**, or click on the **Query Type** button and select **Make Table Query**. Name the table *Archive 99*.

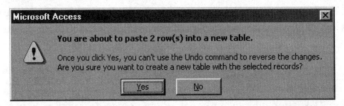

This table will go into the current database so leave the default setting. Click **OK**.

6   Click on the **Run** button. A message box confirms the number of rows (records) that are being added to the new table. Click **Yes** to create the new table.

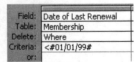

7   Change the query to a Delete query: use **Query-Delete Query**, or click the **Query Type** button and select **Delete Query**. Check that the criterion in the *Date of Last Renewal* field is as shown here.

8   Click on the **Run** button. A message box confirms the number of records that will be deleted. Click Yes. There is no need to save this query as it has performed its function.

9   View the *Membership* and *Archive 99* tables to see the effect of the make table and delete actions.

Update query

An update query updates data in your tables. You choose the records and fields you want to change. When you run the query, Access retrieves the records you asked for (the dynaset) and makes the changes you specified. An example would be increasing the credit limit of all customers who have limits of less than, say, £2000.

Task 2: Update query

An example of an update query that Chelmer Leisure and Recreation Centre might use is when a member of staff changes. The update query can change the name of the *Class Tutor* in the *Classes* table.

1   Start a new query using Design view. Add the *Classes* table to it.

2   Create a query with three fields. *Class No*, *Class Tutor* and *Class Activity*. In the criteria cell for *Class Tutor* put **Franks**.

3   Run the query as a select query to check that it selects the right records.

4   Choose **Query-Update Query**, or click on the **Query Type** button and select **Update Query**. An **Update To:** row appears in the query design grid.

5   In the **Update To:** cell of the *Class Tutor* column type **Knight**.

6   Run the query. A message will appear telling you how many rows will be updated and giving you the opportunity to cancel. Click **Yes** to continue.

7   Save the query as **Update tutor** and close it.

8   Create a select query using the new tutor's name as a criterion. Satisfy yourself that the action query has worked.

9   Delete the action query: in the database window click on the **Queries** button, highlight the update query and delete it by pressing *Delete*.

Integrative tasks

The following tasks reinforce concepts introduced in this and the preceding units.

Task 3: Tutors' names and qualifications

What are the names and qualifications of the tutors taking class on 13/5/2001?

The tables needed are *Bookings* and *Tutors*. There is no direct link between them so the *Classes* table must be included in the query. Before creating this query, review the data in the *Tutors* table and create records for the tutors employed by the centre.

To create the query:

1   Click on the **Queries** in the database window and click **New**. Choose **Design View**.

2   From the **Show Table** dialog box select the *Bookings*, *Classes* and *Tutors* tables. These three tables should be shown in the query window with links between them.

3   Add the *Date*, *Lastname* and *Qualifications* fields.

4   In the *Date* column set the criterion to ***13/5/01*** and hide this field. Run the query and save it.

5   Create a report based on this query.

Task 4: Counting the number of non-smokers in aerobics classes

How many members that attend women's aerobics classes are non-smokers?

The tables needed are *Membership*, *Class Lists* and *Classes*.

To create the query:

1   Click on the **Queries** in the database window and click **New**. Choose **Design View**.

2   In the **Show Table** dialog box select the *Membership*, *Class List* and *Classes* tables. These three tables should be shown in the query window with links between them.

3   Add the *Lastname*, *Smoker* and *Class Activity* fields.

4   In the *Smoker* column, set the criterion to **No** and hide this field.

5   In the *Class Activity* column, set the criterion to ***Women's Aerobics*** and hide the field.

6   Click on the **Totals** button, select **Count** for the *Lastname* field (only **CountofLastname** will show).

7   Run the query to discover the answer to the question.

8   Change the *Smoker* criterion to find the number of smokers in the same class.

Task 5: Attendance profile

What is the attendance profile of classes on Wednesdays?

The *Classes* and *Class List* tables are required for this query. Before constructing it you'll need to use the *Class Lists* form to enter some sample data into Wednesday's classes. Add at least 20 members to various classes being held on Wednesday. A report containing a chart is a good method of presenting the answer to the query.

1   Create a query as illustrated below.

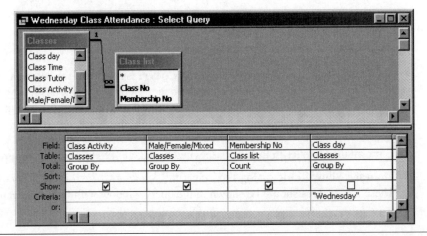

2   Click on the **Totals** button to display the **Total:** row. Hide the *Class Day* field.

3   Save the query as ***Wednesday Class Attendance***.

4   Create a columnar report based on this query using the Report Wizard and sort on *Class Activity*.

5   Display the report in Design view. In the report footer create a chart using **Insert-Chart**. Base the chart on the *Wednesday Class Attendance* query. Select all three fields for the chart.

6   Accept the options offered by the Wizard but choose no link between the chart and report. You will want to display the legend to distinguish between male/female/mixed classes. Click **Finish**.

7   The chart can only be seen properly in Report view; in Design view the default chart is shown. Some editing of the default chart in terms of size and scale can be achieved to produce a result similar to that shown below. Switch between Design view and Report view to adjust and preview the chart until you're happy with the result.

8   Save the report as ***Wednesday Class Attendance***, and preview before printing.

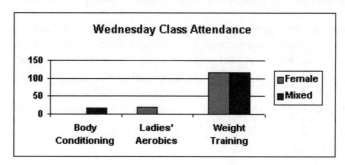

Unit 35

Importing data

What you will learn in this unit

These next few units explore various issues associated with importing and exporting data. You should select and attempt those activities for which you have the appropriate software and data.

By the end of this unit you will be able to:

❑ understand the distinction between importing data and linking data

❑ import data from databases created in earlier versions of Access

Understanding importing, exporting and linking files

Importing and exporting data is relatively straightforward with Access, especially between other standard packages and other Office applications. Its developers have recognised that users may well have significant databases established in earlier versions or in other database packages and need to transfer data from these environments into Access. Equally, users need to be able to integrate data in database, spreadsheet and word processing programs into appropriate documents.

Access offers two different approaches to making use of existing data compiled with other database software.

❑ Linked data behaves as if it is part of the Access database although it is not. The data can be edited in both Access and the other application and can be viewed as an Access table, although no Access table is actually created.

Linking is useful when you wish to maintain the data in its original file format, while creating Access forms and reports.

❑ Imported data has been converted from its original format into an Access table. A copy of the data is placed in a table in an Access database, and the original data is left unchanged when this copy is edited in Access.

Other database objects such as tables, forms or reports can be imported from another Access database. When importing, all or a subset of these objects can be chosen. In this way a database created in an earlier version of Access can be imported to Access 2000. If importing an Access 97 (or earlier) database, create a new database using Access 2000 first.

If you want to add data from an application to an existing Access table, you can append the data, as long as its format matches that of the existing table entries, i.e. it has the same fields with similar definitions.

Either link or import; do not do both, because this will create more than one copy of the data. With more than one copy of the data it is difficult to be sure which is the most recent, and to maintain file integrity.

Exporting data puts Access data into a format that other applications can use and creates a separate file containing the data.

Importing data into an Access table

To import the data in a file into a table in the current Access database:

1   Display the Database window.

2   Choose **File-Get External Data-Import**. or click on the **New Object** button and choose **Table**, then select **Import Table** from the list.

3   Choose the format of the data to be imported from the **Files of type** list box in the **Import** dialog box.

4   Browse to the folder and file you want to import, and click the **Import** button.

5   When Access has imported the file you have selected, it displays a message to say that it has successfully imported the file. If Access needs some guidance on formatting the file as an Access table you will be prompted by a series of wizards.

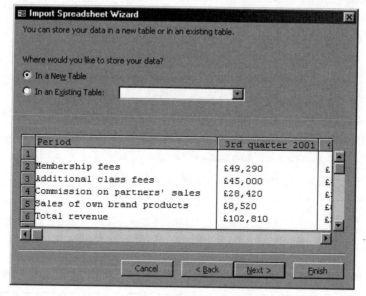

The next unit deals with importing Excel spreadsheets (as illustrated above) in more detail.

6   If the database window is displaying the database's tables, the newly imported table will appear in the list of tables.

Importing Access database objects

You can import tables, queries, forms, and reports from another Access database whether or not the database was created in a previous version of Access.

To import Access database objects:

1   Display the database window and choose **File-Get External Data-Import**.

2   Choose **Microsoft Access** from the **Files of type** list box in the **Import** dialog box.

3   Browse to the folder and file you want to import and click the **Import** button.

4   The **Import Objects** dialog box is displayed. Click the tab of the type of object you wish to import. Select one or more of the objects listed and click **OK**.

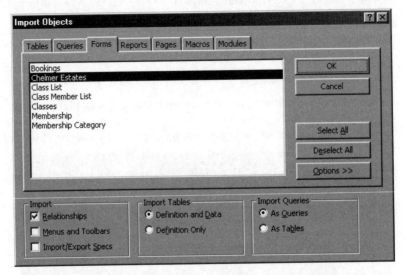

5   The Options button provides choices such as importing a table structure without the data or importing queries as tables.

6   When imported, the objects will be listed in the appropriate part of the database window.

Linking a table

To link data stored in another file as a table in the current database:

1   Display the database window and choose **File-Get External Data-Link Tables**, or click the **New Object** button, choose **Table** and select **Link Table** from the list.

2   Choose the format of the data that you want to import from the **Files of Type** list box in the **Import** dialog box.

3   Browse to the folder and file that you want to link, and click the **Link** button. If you are using certain kinds of older files, such as a dBase index file, there may be a further dialog box to give Access the information it needs to import it successfully.

4   Click **OK** and **Close**.

Linked tables are used in the same way as any other Access table. The link icon (an arrow) is displayed in the database window, showing that this table is a linked table, not one actually in the current database. The table can be used with queries, forms and reports just like any other table – though you will not be able to modify it as normal in Design view.

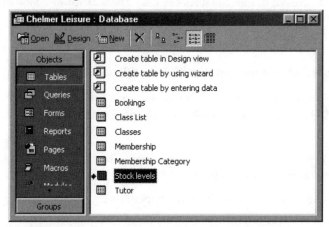

To delete a linked table, if you no longer require the link:

1   Select the icon for the linked table that is to be detached.

2   Choose **Edit-Delete** then click **Yes** to confirm.

This deletes the link but the table remains intact, and could be re-linked at a later stage.

Differences between linking and importing

To import or link? That is the question... If you intend to use your data only in the current Access database you should import it, as Access works faster with its own tables. If the data is likely to be linked into more than one database, you should link so that it is stored and edited in one place only – otherwise you have duplicate sets of data and it will be problematic to keep them all current and consistent.

Imported and linked tables differ in the following respects.

❏   **Deleting a table.** When you delete an imported table, the table and its contents are deleted. When you delete a linked table, only the link between the current database and the database that contains the table is deleted. The data itself is still available in the original database and any other databases that use the table as a linked table.

❏ **Adding data.** Imported data can be added to an existing table or placed in a new table. Linked tables are separate from existing tables in the database.

❏ **Speed.** Linked tables are not as fast as tables stored in Access files because the data from the linked table must be constantly read from the original file. The process can however be speeded up by appropriate use of queries and indexes.

❏ **Table design.** Linked tables can only be modified to a limited extent in table design. Features such as field names, data type, the order of fields, adding new fields or deleting fields can not be performed on linked tables.

Task 1: Importing, exporting and linking files

This task asks you to review some of the basic concepts associated with importing, exporting and linking files. Answer the following questions.

1 What are the advantages of importing a file compared with linking it?

2 How can you tell when viewing filenames with the database window, which files are imported and which files are linked?

3 Why should you not both link and import a file?

4 What does exporting do?

Importing text/spreadsheets

What you will learn in this unit

It is possible to import spreadsheet data and text files into Access, in the following spreadsheet and text formats:

❑ Excel (versions 3.0, 4.0, 5.0, 7(95) and 97)

❑ Lotus 1 -2-3

❑ Delimited text (where text is separated into groups by commas, tabs or other characters)

❑ Fixed width text (where values are arranged so that each field has a certain width)

❑ HTML files

By the end of this unit you will be able to:

❑ import spreadsheet data into an Access database

❑ import delimited text files into Access

Importing spreadsheet data

There are a number of options for in importing spreadsheet data and text files, because you need to define how the table should be created from the imported data. If you have several worksheets in a spreadsheet, or several distinct sections on one worksheet, you will have to import each one as a separate table.

Importing spreadsheet data is easiest if the data is in an appropriate format, so it may be worth spending a few minutes tidying up a spreadsheet before trying to import it. The spreadsheet data must have the same type of data in each field and the same fields in every row. In addition, it is preferable if column headings of an appropriate type are inserted in the first row of the spreadsheet so that these can be used as field names. Access will look at the first row of data and assign a data type for each field on the basis of this first row. For example, if the first value for a field is a date, then Access assigns date/time data type to that field and assumes that all values for that field will be dates.

To import spreadsheet data into Access:

1 Display the database window and choose **File-Get External Data-Import**.

2 Select the appropriate format for the data that you want to import (e.g. Excel) and browse to the folder that contains the file to be imported.

3   Select the spreadsheet name and click **Import**. The **Import Spreadsheet Wizard** will start (Figure 36.1).

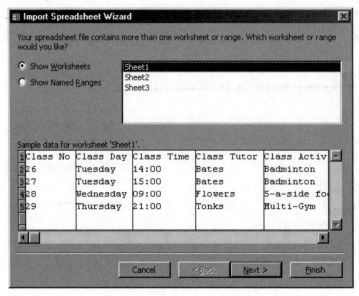

Figure 36.1

4   At the first stage, select the sheet or data range. Select the appropriate part of your spreadsheet (previewed in the sample area), and click [Next >].

5   Tick the **First Row Contains Column Headings** check box if the spreadsheet range has labels in the first row that you want to use as field names. Click [Next >].

6   The next stage asks you whether to import the data into a new table or add it to an existing one. If you want to add it to a table, choose one from the drop-down list.

7   If you are adding the data to an existing table, click [Finish] now. If the data is going into a new table, work through the next steps, which set properties for the imported fields, a primary key and a name for the table. Click [Finish].

8   When Access has imported the table, click **OK**. If you have imported data into a new table then it should be displayed in the list of tables in the database window.

Task 1: Importing spreadsheet data

 Note: To complete this task you need access to Excel or other compatible spreadsheet.

1   Create a spreadsheet in Excel into which you can enter data that matches the *Classes* table. Save this file as *Classes2*. Enter the field names in the first row, then enter some records for specific classes, one record per row, as illustrated in Figure 36.2.

2   Open Access and display the Database window.

3   Choose **File-Get External Data-Import**.

4   In the **Files of type** list box choose the format for the data that you want to import (e.g. Excel) and browse to the folder that contains the file to be imported.

	A	B	C	D	E	F
1	Class No	Class Day	Class Time	Class Tutor	Class Activity	Male/Female/Mixed
2	26	Tuesday	14:00	Bates	Badminton	Mixed
3	27	Tuesday	15:00	Bates	Badminton	Mixed
4	28	Wednesday	09:00	Flowers	5-a-side football	Male
5	29	Thursday	21:00	Tonks	Multi-Gym	Female

Figure 36.2

5   Select the spreadsheet name and click **Import**. Access displays the **Import Spreadsheet Wizard** dialog box.

6   Tick the **First Row Contains Column Headings** check box and click [Next >].
    Choose the option to import the data into a new table and click [Next >].

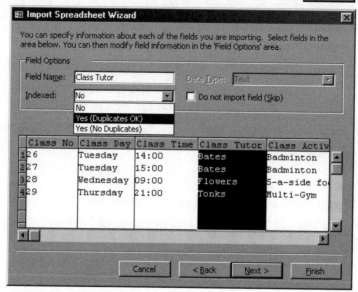

Figure 36.3

7   The next dialog box allows you to specify information about each of the fields that you are importing. By clicking on each field in turn you can set: field name, indexed (or not) and whether the field is to be imported. Use the default settings (i.e. don't make any changes), and click [Next >].

8   Select **Choose my own primary key** (Access will create one for you if necessary, but we want to use the class number in this case). Choose *Class No* and click [Next >]. Enter the table's name, e.g. *Classes2*, and click [Finish].

9   When Access has finished importing the table it will display a confirmation alert. Click **OK** to complete the process. The new table should be displayed in the list of tables in the Database window.

10 Repeat this task, but import the data into the *Classes* table instead of a new one.

i   *Note: If you choose to allow Access to analyse your table it will, when you ask, run the Table Analyzer Wizard, and inform you of the faults in your table design. Try this if you are interested. What is wrong with the design of this table?*

Importing delimited or fixed width text files

A *delimited text file* is one in which fields are separated by a special character, such as a comma or a tab. In a *fixed width file*, fields are aligned in columns with spaces between each field.

Data in a text file intended for importing into a table must be in a suitable format, with the same type of data in each field and the same fields in every row. Again the first row may be used as field names, and Access uses the first row of data as a basis for assigning data types.

i   *Only delimited and fixed width text files saved as .txt files can be imported. So, for example, if you create a file in Word, you must save it as a .txt file (using Text only or Text only with line breaks) and not a .doc file if you wish to import it into Access.*

To import a text file:

1   Open the database window and choose **File-Get External Data-Import**.

2   Choose the appropriate format for the data you want to import (e.g. Text files) and browse to the folder that contains the file to be imported.

3   Select the text file and click **Import**. The **Text Import Wizard** will start.

For delimited text files:

4   Choose **Delimited** as the format and click `Next >`.

5   Specify the text delimiter that has been used, (Tab, Comma, etc).

6   Click on the **First Row Contains Field Names** box if appropriate. Click `Next >`.
For fixed-width text files:

4   Choose **Fixed-width** as the format and click `Next >`.

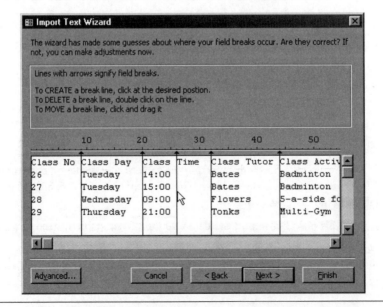

5   Based on the layout of the text file, Access will guess how to divide the file into columns and display a sample with column markers. These are usually good guesses, but you may need to tidy them up a bit, as in the screenshot. The column markers can be moved, deleted or new ones added according to the instructions on-screen.

6   When you have the column markers in the right places, click [Next >].

7   Specify whether you would like to store your data in an existing or new table.

8   Specify the following information about each of the fields you are importing: field name, data type, whether it should be indexed, and whether the field should be included. Click [Next >].

9   Choose the Primary Key and click [Next >].

10   Name the file and click [Finish]. (Access creates a new table with the same name as the original text file, unless you chose to append data to an existing file.) Click **Close**.

Task 2: Importing a delimited text file

i   *Note: To complete this task you need access to a word processing package, such as Word.*

Create a delimited text file into which you can enter data that matches the *Classes* table. If you are working with Word 2000 you may choose to do this by creating a table, but you will need to convert the table to text before saving as a .txt file. Text delimited by commas or tabs may be saved directly as a .txt file. Save this file as *Classes3* and close it.

Enter the field names in the first row, and then enter some records for specific classes, one record per row, as required, as shown below.

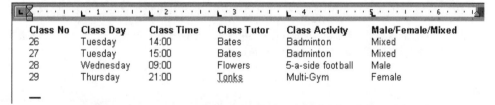

Class No	Class Day	Class Time	Class Tutor	Class Activity	Male/Female/Mixed
26	Tuesday	14:00	Bates	Badminton	Mixed
27	Tuesday	15:00	Bates	Badminton	Mixed
28	Wednesday	09:00	Flowers	5-a-side football	Male
29	Thursday	21:00	Tonks	Multi-Gym	Female

1   Open Access and open the database window.

2   Choose **File-Get External Data-Import**.

3   In the **Files of type** list box choose the appropriate format for the data that you want to import (e.g. Text files) and browse to the folder that contains the file to be imported.

4   Select the text file and click **Import**. The **Text Import Wizard** will start. The delimiter in the following illustration is a tab, represented in the dialog box by a square character.

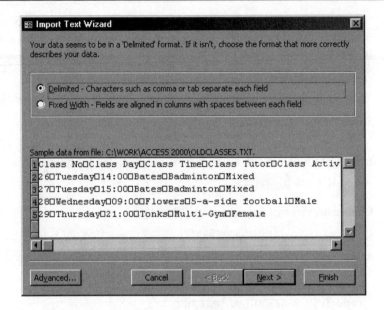

5   Choose **Delimited** as the format. Click [Next >].

6   Specify the text delimiter that has been used, e.g. Comma or Tab.

7   Tick the **First Row Contains Field Names** check box. Click [Next >].

8   You may choose to import your data into a new table or an existing one. Choose the new table option (if you want to import the data to an existing table then specify the table using the drop down list). Click [Next >].

9   Accept the data types for the fields and click [Next >].

10 Set *Class No* as the primary key and name the new table *Classes3*. Click [Finish].

11 View this table in Datasheet view, and then in Design view. Change the data and data type of *Class Time* to a time format.

Notes

We have just explored a further way of creating text and entering it in a database. Normally, it is more satisfactory to enter data directly into a database, but on occasions you may want to add data from an existing word processed file without having to re-enter it by hand, or you may just want to make use of Access' querying tools to extract data from a text file quickly.

Exporting and publishing data

What you will learn in this unit

Data can be exported from Access tables to text files, spreadsheets and to any of the database formats from which you can import data. Data can also be exported to a Word mail merge data file, which can then be used to create form letters, mailing labels and other merged documents. Data may be exported to other database applications so that it can be merged with other data in other files.

If you want to make data available to others via the Internet, Access provides a Wizard to enable you to do this.

By the end of this unit you will be able to:

❑ export a table to a spreadsheet

❑ export a table to a word processor

❑ export a table to another database

❑ use the Publish to Web Wizard

Understanding exporting

 Access allows table and field names that are up to 64 characters and can include spaces. Some older database packages and other applications work with shorter maximum table and field names, and may not allow spaces in names. When you export a table with table or field names that are not acceptable to an application, Access truncates the names to an acceptable length. It is therefore important to check that you will still have a set of unique field and table names afterwards.

To export data in a table to a file in a format that other applications can use:

1 Display the database window, click on the button for the object type you wish to export and highlight the name of the object, e.g. the *Membership* table.

2 Choose **File-Export**.

3 In the **Export To** dialog box, browse to the folder you want to save the file in.

4 Select the type of file to be created from the **Save as type** list box and give this version of the table an appropriate filename. Click **Save**.

Task 1: Exporting a table to a spreadsheet

i *Note: To complete this task you require a spreadsheet package such as Excel.*

Export the table that was imported in Unit 36, *Classes2*.

1   Switch to the database containing the table *Classes2* and highlight it.

2   Choose **File-Export**. In the **Export To** dialog box, choose the folder where you want to save the file.

3   Select the type of spreadsheet file to be created from the **Save as type** list box, e.g. **Microsoft Excel 97-2000**, and name this table *Classes4*. Click **Save**.

Exporting a table to a text file

There are times when you will want to select a set of records from a table and export them to a word processor for further formatting or for integration into a text based document.

To export an Access table to a text file:

1   Open the database containing the table that you wish to export and select the table.

2   Choose **File-Export**. In the **Export To** dialog box, choose the folder where you want to save the file.

3   Select **Text Files** from the **Save as type** list, and give the file a name. Click **Save**.

4   The **Export Text Wizard** will allow you to select the format of the text, i.e. delimited with a particular delimiter character, or in a fixed width format.

Task 2: Exporting a table to a text file

Suppose Chelmer Leisure and Recreation Centre has invested in some new equipment and wants to create a brochure advertising classes using the gym. This leaflet will be essentially a word processed document containing text about the activities and the Centre. However, embedded in the document will be a list of Body Conditioning and Multi-gym classes. In order to extract this information from our Access Classes table, and insert the data into the leaflet, we need first to select the appropriate records by the use of a query, convert the result of the query to a table, and then export the data in the table to a word processor file.

To execute the query:

1   Click on the **Queries** button in the Database window and create a new query using Design view.

2   In the **Show Table** dialog box, choose *Classes*. Click on **Add** then **Close**.

3   Add the appropriate fields to the query.

4   Use criteria to select the required records.

5   Run the query to display the dynaset. Save and close the query, choosing an appropriate name.

To export the data to a word processor file:

1   Select the newly created query in the Database window.

2   Choose **File-Export** and browse to the folder in which you wish to save the file.

3   Select **Text files** from the **Save as type** list box and choose an appropriate filename. Click on **Save**.

4   Work through the stages in the **Export Text Wizard** to select a delimited format with a tab delimiter. You can use Word to convert this to a word processed table.

Exporting Access data to another Access database

Exporting and importing from and to Access databases are two sides of the same process.

❏   You import when the current database is the one where you need a copy of the table or other object.

❏   You export when you are in the database that contains the object or data you want copied to another database.

To export a query or report, follow the steps for exporting a table but click on the appropriate button in the Database window.

After exporting, the object is in both databases but there is no link between the two copies of the object, so if the object is updated in one database it will not be updated in another.

Publishing a database on the World Wide Web

Some or all of the data in a database may be information that could be made available to customers or clients over the internet. Access provides a Wizard which allows you to create a Data Access web page, which users can use to view, edit or add data to a table or query via a web browser.

Many organisations use 'intranets' which are local 'Webs' that operate in the same way as the WWW, except that published pages are only accessible to internal users. This is a useful way to make certain company data available to employees.

To publish Access tables or queries:

1 Click the down arrow on the **New Object** button on the toolbar, and choose **Page**.

2 Choose a table or query from the drop-down list. You then have a choice of **Page Wizard** or **Autopage: Columnar**. The Autopage option will generate a page with all fields selected. The Wizard gives you a bit more control over what appears on the page and how. Select **Page Wizard** and click **OK**.

3 Select the fields to be displayed and click Next >.

4 Select **Sorting and Grouping** options as if you were creating a report.

5 Give the page a name and click Finish.

6 Access now displays the Data Access page in Design view. Click on the title section and enter a title for the page.

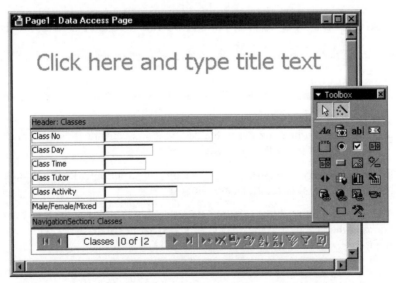

7 You can now format the page in much the same way as for a report. Click on the **View** button on the toolbar to switch to preview mode and then click the Design button to return to Design view and make changes.

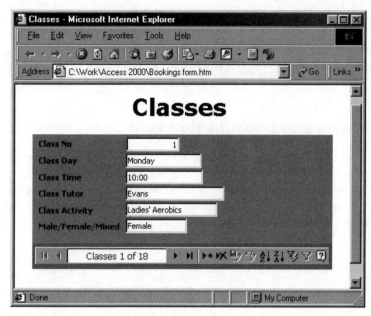

8   When you are happy with the page, choose **File-Save**. Give the file a name and click Save.

Task 3: Using the Web Wizard

This is a simple task that introduces the basics of publishing in HTML format.

1   Follow the steps described above. Select the *Classes* table, add all fields and sort by *Class No*.

2   Save the file as *Classes via web*.

3   Open the file in a web browser and experiment with the navigation controls to view and edit data.

4   Return to Access and look at the *Classes* table – you will see that the data amended via the browser has been saved in the database.

5   If you wish, experiment with creating other pages.

Unit 38

Using the Clipboard to transfer data

What you will learn in this unit

As well as the methods of data transfer already discussed - importing, linking and exporting - information can be also transferred between applications using the clipboard. Transferring data using the Clipboard is very straightforward, provided the data is in an acceptable format. It is especially easy if you are working with Excel and Word alongside Access.

The clipboard can be used for:

❏ moving Access data into an Excel (or other) spreadsheet

❏ moving Access data into a Word document in the form of a table

❏ moving Access data into other text applications as tab-delimited text files

❏ moving Access objects from one database to another

By the end of this unit you will be able to:

❏ use the Clipboard to transfer data

The Clipboard is temporary storage space where Windows can store information from any applications designed to use it. The basic procedure is to:

1 Select the data to be moved.

2 Select **Edit-Copy** or **Edit-Cut** depending upon whether you want to keep the data in its original location or not.

3 Switch to the application into which you wish to import data.

4 Select **Edit-Paste**.

Task 1: Using the Clipboard to move Access data into a Word document

Chelmer Leisure and Recreation Centre may want to send out a leaflet targeted at those members who are children, i.e. members of the Junior or Junior Club categories. First we need to create a query to select appropriate records, then we can select the records on-screen and copy and paste them into a word processed document.

To create a query:

1 Click on the **Queries** button in the database window, click **New** and choose **Design view**.

2 In the **Show Table** dialog box, choose *Membership*.

3 Add the following fields to the query: *Category No, Firstname, Lastname, Date of Birth, Date of Joining, Sporting Interests, Sex*.

4   Use a criterion in the *Category No* field to select categories 3 OR 4. Run the query to display the dynaset.

5   To select the whole dynaset, choose **Edit-Select all Records**. If you just wanted to select certain records, click and drag on the row selectors to the left of the records you want.

6   Copy the selection to the Clipboard using **Edit-Copy**, switch to the word processor and paste in the table with **Edit-Paste**.

7   Close the query without saving.

How would you amend the query to produce a leaflet targeted at the male adult members?

Task 2: Using the Clipboard to move data into an Excel spreadsheet

Access can calculate averages and other basic statistical functions, but Excel is capable of more advanced analysis, such as forecasting using a linear regression technique.

This task investigates how *Bookings* table data can be pasted into an Excel spreadsheet to perform additional analysis.

1   Create a query based on the *Bookings* table.

2   Add the fields *Booking No* and *Date*.

3   Click on the **Totals** button to create totals.

4   Select **Count** for *Booking No* and **Group By** for *Date*. Run the query.

5   Use **Edit-Select All Records** and copy them.

6   Switch to Excel and paste the data in.

Unit 39

Creating and editing macros

What you will learn in this unit

This unit introduces macros. A macro is basically a list of instructions, rather like a short program. When using Access there may be occasions when the same series of actions is performed again and again. To save time these may be recorded as a macro so that one command, to run the macro, can replace a whole set of commands.

By performing a series of actions, macros can automate your database application. Macros in Access are powerful and can be used without having to understand any complicated programming languages. Creating macros, however, does require a clear understanding of your database application so that you can plan exactly what you want each macro to do. Over the next four units, you will be introduced to some basic macros, after which you may feel confident enough to investigate more advanced macro functions on our own.

By the end of this unit you will be able to:

❏   create and edit simple macros

The Macro window

Macros are designed in a macro window, just as queries are designed in a query window and forms in a form window. The window is usually as illustrated here, with two columns, **Action** and **Comment**, and an **Action Arguments** area beneath.

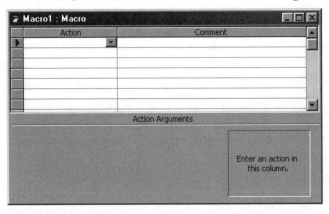

In the **Action** column the action for the macro is selected from a drop-down list. In the **Comments** column you can add comments to act as a reminder of the function of the macro. Even with simple macros, it is good practice to add brief comments to this column so that the workings of the macro are clear to other users – or to yourself when you revisit the macro a few months after writing it! The **Action Arguments** are properties of the action which qualify its function.

Task 1: A macro to open a form

This macro is easy to create and one which is frequently used.

1   Click on the **Macros** button in the Database window and click **New** to display the Macro window.

2   Click in the first **Action** cell and open the list box. Choose **OpenForm** from the list of available actions.

When you do this you will see that an argument section appears in the lower left of the macro window. Most actions have arguments which need to be defined; some require more than others – we will come back to this in 'Understanding actions and arguments' later in this unit.

4   Open the **Form Name** list in the **Action Arguments** section and select *Membership*. Leave the other arguments as their default values.

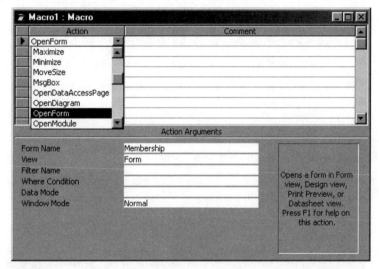

5   The **View** argument is set to **Form**, which opens the form in run mode. The **Where Condition** can be used like a query to determine which records to display (we will use this in Unit 43). Leave this argument blank to open the form displaying the first of all records.

6   Key into the **Comment** column a description such as *"**This opens the Membership form.**"*

7   Save the macro with the name *Chelmer*.

i   *Note: a macro must be saved before it can be run or executed. Choose **File-Save** or press F12 to save the macro.*

8   Test the macro by running it. If the Macro window is still open, click on the **Run** button. If you have closed the macro, the **Run** button is in the Database window.

9   When the macro is run, the *Membership* form is displayed, open at the first record.

10   Close the form and the macro.

Modifying a macro

A macro may need to be edited to change its actions or correct an error. All or part of a macro may be copied from one macro window to another to save having to repeat work when you are creating new macros which are similar to existing ones. Macros may also be copied from one database to another.

Select the macro that you wish to modify and click the Design button in the database window. The macro window opens and you can make your changes.

Task 2: Editing a macro

In this task the macro created in the last task will be opened and edited so that when it opens the *Membership* form, it displays the form ready to accept a new record. This is useful when a new member's details are to be entered.

1   Open the *Chelmer* macro in Design view.

2   Add a second action to the macro: select **GoToRecord** from the list.

3   To define which record to go to, open the **Record** list box and select *New*.

4   Save the macro and run it. This time the *Membership* form should be displayed ready to accept a new record.

5   Close the form and the macro.

Task 3: Sizing and positioning the form

To add a further refinement to the form-opening macro, you can set the size and position of the form on the screen. Sizing and positioning a form using a macro gives consistency to your database application.

1   Open the *Chelmer* macro in Design view.

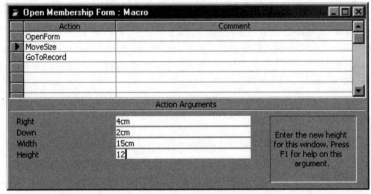

2   Highlight the second row and use **Insert-Rows** to insert a blank row in the macro sheet between the **OpenForm** and the **GoToRecord** actions.

3　In the new row select the action **MoveSize**. Set the arguments as shown in the illustration on page 206. The **Right** and **Down** arguments determine the distance between the upper left-hand corner of the form window and the edges of the Access window which contains it.

4　Save the macro and run it.

5　You may need to adjust the numbers in the MoveSize arguments to suit your form and screen size. To do this, close the Membership form and edit the macro.

6　Save the changes and run the macro.

7　Close the form and the macro.

Understanding actions and arguments

The macro actions available in Access can perform any menu commands, and the arguments are often the selections that you would make from a dialog box. Macro actions can also control processes such as synchronising the records in a form. There are many actions available, but there is only room to consider a few here along with their associated arguments.

Action	Argument	Function
FindRecord	Find What	Searches through a table, form, or dynaset and finds the next record matching the specified criteria
	Match	
	Match Case	
	Search	
	Search As Formatted	
	Only Current Field	
	Find First	
OpenForm	Form Name	Opens or activates a form in one of its views.
	View	
	Filter Name	
	Where Condition	
	Data Mode	
	Window Mode	
PrintOut	Print Range	Prints the current database object according to the settings specified.
	Page From	
	Page To	
	Print Quality	
	Copies	
	Collate Copies	

Executing macros

You can run a macro in many ways. If you are creating quick macros for immediate use, you may want to run them by choosing them from the Database window. To create a system that is more automated or one that is easier to use, you can run a macro in a variety of ways which are outlined briefly below and are discussed in more detail later.

Running from the Macro window

A macro can be run from its window. This is useful for testing a macro. To run it, click on the **Run** button on the toolbar or choose **Run-Run**. If the active macro window contains a group of macros (see Unit 40), only the first in the window runs.

From any window

Choose **Tools-Macro-Run Macro** and select the macro from the list in the **Run Macro** dialog box. Click **OK**.

From another macro

A macro can be run from another macro using the **RunMacro** action. The argument for this action is the name of the macro to be called. When the called macro has run, Access moves on to the next action in the calling macro. The macro may run repeatedly if either the **Repeat Count** or **Repeat Expression** is set.

From an event

The running of a macro can be 'triggered' by an event. An event can be the opening or closing of a form or report, or it can be the selection of a control. For example, a macro which opens a form can be run when a field is selected. A macro that validates an entry can be run when a field is exited. These kind of macro events make your database application much more professional in operation.

From a button

This is another way to make your database application more professional. Command buttons are a very easy addition to a form. By clicking on a button a macro can be run to open another form, for example.

From a shortcut key

It is a good idea to assign frequently used macros to a shortcut key, for example *Ctrl+M* could be assigned to the *Chelmer* macro.

Creating macro groups

What you will learn in this unit

It is useful to keep related macros together – partly so that you can keep track of them more easily, and also because grouped macros can be displayed together in one macro window. This means you can work on several macros without having to open and close lots of windows, each with only a few actions in it.

A macro can be assigned to a command button so that when the button is clicked the macro runs. Buttons may be added to existing forms that are based on tables or they can be added to blank forms. A blank form which does not have an associated table is known as an 'unbound form'. By adding buttons to it, you can create a menu form used to access other database objects.

By the end of this unit you will be able to:

❑ create a simple macro group

❑ add buttons to a form

❑ assign macros to the buttons.

Creating macro groups

To distinguish macros in one window each has its own name. The macro name is entered in the **Macro Name** column of the window, which is displayed by clicking on the **Macro Names** button ▦ in the toolbar or by choosing **View-Macro Names**. This column is displayed to the left of the **Action** column.

Each macro in the window begins with the action to the right of its name. The macro ends when it reaches the beginning of the next macro or it runs out of actions. There is no need for a specific end action before the next one.

When a macro window contains several macros then to refer to a specific one within the group use the following syntax: *macrowindowname.macroname*, where a full stop separates the macro window name from that of the macro, e.g. *Chelmer.NewBooking*. To run a particular macro in a group choose **Tools-Macro** and select the macro from the drop-down list; macro names are listed using the syntax described above.

i   *Note: if the macro name is omitted then the first macro in the group will run.*

Task 1: Creating a macro group

In this task another macro will be added to the *Chelmer* macro. This macro will open the booking form ready to take a new booking.

1 Display the *Chelmer* macro window.

2 Click on the **Macro Names** button in the toolbar.

3 Leave a couple of blank rows below the existing macro and in the **Macro Name** column put **NewBooking**.

4 In the **Action** column select the action **OpenForm**. Set the **Form Name** argument to *Bookings*.

5 The second action is **GoToRecord**, with the argument of **Record** set to *New*.

6 Save the macro. The Chelmer macro is now a macro group, containing two macros in one window.

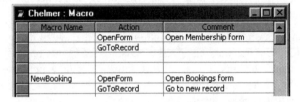

7 To run this part of the macro group select **Tools-Macro-Run Macro**.

8 In the **Run Macro** dialog box select *Chelmer.NewBooking* from the drop-down list box and click **OK**.

9 Close the form and the macro.

Adding command buttons to a form

A macro can be made convenient to run by assigning it to a button on a form, either existing or blank. The button can then be clicked to run the macro.

1 Open a form in Design view and display it by the side of the Database window.

2 Click the **Macros** button in the database window.

3 Click and drag the name of the macro on to the form where you want the button.

4 The button will have the name of the macro on it by default, but it can be changed.

5 Display the form in View mode and click on the button to run the macro.

Task 2: Creating a blank form and adding buttons to it

In this task you will create an unbound blank form that will only contain two command buttons. The first will be one which when clicked on will open the Membership form ready to accept a new member's details. The second button will open the *Bookings* form ready to accept a new booking.

To create a blank unbound form:

1 Click on the **Forms** button in the Database window and click **New**. Leave the **Choose the table or query...** box empty, as this form is not bound to a table or query. Choose Design view.

2   To add a command button, display the blank form and the Database window side by side.

3   Click on the **Macros** button in the database window and select *Chelmer*.

4   Drag the macro onto the Detail section of the form. A button appears with the name *Chelmer* on it.

5   The name on the button can be changed by editing the **Caption** property. Open the button's **Property sheet** and edit its name to read **New Member**. If you scroll through the properties you should find that the **On Click** property is set to *Chelmer*, i.e. the first macro in the macro group will run when the button is clicked.

6   Use **Edit-Select Form** to select the form and set the properties of the form as follows (leave the others as their defaults):

Property	Setting
Caption	Form Menu (the name that will appear title in the bar of the form)
Default View	Single Form
Scroll Bars	Neither
Record Selectors	No
Navigation Buttons	No

7   Save the form as *Form Menu*. Run the form and click on the **New Member** button you have just created. Close the *Membership* form.

8   Return to Design view of the *Form Menu* form.

9   Drag the *Chelmer* macro onto the form again. A button appears with the name *Chelmer* on it.

10   Edit the Caption property to change the button's label to *Make Booking*.

11   Change the **On Click** property (currently *Chelmer*), to *Chelmer.NewBooking* so that the *NewBooking* macro will run when this button is clicked.

12   Add a title and adjust fonts as illustrated below.

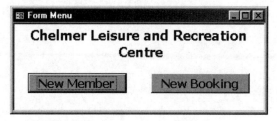

13   Save the form and try the new button.

Task 3: Adding a close button to a form

This will be a very simple macro to close the open object, which might be a form or report. In the preceding task, closing the form after adding a new member or taking a new booking would be simple if a button labelled **Close** was added to both the *Membership* and *Bookings* forms.

The macro to close an object is one of a stock set of procedures, and does not need to be added to the macro window. Instead, it is created in the form's Design view:

1 Display the *Membership* form in Design view. Check that the **Control Wizards** button in the Toolbox is depressed.

2 Select the **Command Button** tool from the Toolbox and click at the bottom of the form. The Command Button Wizard starts.

3 Select **Form Operations** from the **Categories** list and **Close Form** from the **Actions** list. Click Next > .

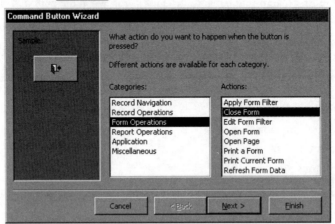

4 Choose a picture or text for the button (check the **Show all pictures** box to show more choices). Click Next > .

5 Give the button the name **Close Membership Form** and click Finish .

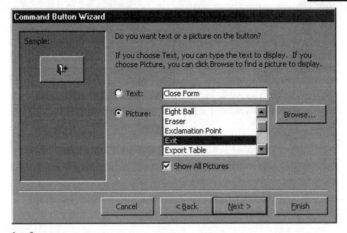

6 Save the form.

7 Test the macro by clicking on the **Close** button.

8 Add a **Close** button to both the *Bookings* form and the *Form Menu* form. Notice that the button's **OnClick** property is set to **Event Procedure**. Save the forms and test your macros.

Assigning macros to keys

What you will learn in this unit

It is useful to be able to assign a frequently used macro to a keystroke as this gives the operator more choice when using the database. The example we shall consider is that of *Ctrl+M* to display the *Membership* form ready to accept a new member's record and *Ctrl+B* to display the *Booking* form. Examples of other shortcut keys that could be used are *Ctrl+Q* to quit or *Ctrl+P* to print.

By the end of this unit you will be able to:

❏ assign macros to keys

Assigning a macro to a key

All key assignments must be created in a separate macro, which must be called **AutoKeys** so that Access knows it is a key assignment macro. In the AutoKeys macro each key combination has a name and this name must follow the naming convention shown in the table below.

Key Combination	Macro Name
Ctrl-letter	^letter
Ctrl-number	^number
Function key	{F1} and so on
Ctrl-Function key	^{F1} and so on
Shift-Function key	+{F1} and so on
Insert	{Insert}
Ctrl-Insert	^{Insert}
Shift-Insert	+{Insert}
Delete	{Delete} or {Del}
Ctrl-Delete	^{Delete} or ^{Del}
Shift-Delete	+{Delete} or +{Del}

To assign a macro to a shortcut key

1   Create and save the macros and/or macro groups to which you wish to assign shortcut keys.

2   Open a new macro window and display the Macro Name column. This macro will become a macro group in which all shortcut keys are defined.

3   In the macro name column put the macro name, for example, **^p**.

4   The action for this macro will be a **RunMacro** action which will call one of the macros you have already created. See below for more on the RunMacro action.

5   Select the macro name that you are calling from the **Macro Name** argument list.

6   Use the **Comment** column to note which macro is being called.

7   Save the shortcut key macro as *AutoKeys*.

8   Any shortcut keys you wish to set up later must be added to this macro.

The RunMacro action

A macro can be run from within another by using the **RunMacro** action. The arguments for this action are the name of the macro to be run, and the number of times it is to repeat. The macro may be set to repeat a set number of times or an expression can be used to test whether it has been performed the required number.

When the main (or calling) macro is run it performs its list of actions. When the RunMacro action is reached the specified macro runs the required number of times. When that has finished Access returns control to the next action in the calling macro.

Task 1: Assigning shortcut keys

In this task the shortcut key *Ctrl+M* (^m) is to be assigned to the macro that opens the *Membership* form ready to accept a new member's record and *Ctrl+B* (^b) to open the *Bookings* form.

To create an AutoKeys macro:

1   Open a new macro sheet. Display the **Macro Name** column.

2   Put *^m* in the **Macro Name** column.

3   In the **Action** column select the **RunMacro** action and set the **Macro Name** argument to *Chelmer* (this is the first of the Chelmer group of macros, which opens the *Membership* form).

4   In the **Comment** column type *"Open Membership form at new record"*.

5   In the next row of the **Macro Name** column put *^b*.

6   In the **Action** column select the **RunMacro** action and set the **Macro Name** argument to *Chelmer.NewBooking* (this is the *NewBooking* macro of the Chelmer group).

7   In the **Comments** column put *"Open Bookings form at new record"*.

8   Save the macro as *AutoKeys*.

9   Open the *Chelmer* menu and try using the shortcut key.

You may have noticed that in many Windows applications the shortcut letter in a menu or on a button is underlined. You can do this, by displaying the form or report containing the button in Design view and editing the Caption so that an ampersand (&) precedes the letter to be underlined. For example, *Make Booking* would be typed as *Make &Booking* so that it appeared as *Make Booking* on the button.

Assigning macros to events

What you will learn in this unit

Specific events in forms and reports can be used to 'trigger' the running of a macro. Examples are the opening of a form, the user selecting or exiting from a field control or double-clicking on a field.

By assigning macros to events the database system becomes more professional as set procedures within the system become automated. Event-driven macros can be used to open multiple forms together, print reports using specific queries, or create error checks that are more extensive than those available through control properties. There are more form events than report events.

By the end of this unit, you will be able to:

❑ assign a macro to an event

❑ use conditions to determine how a macro will run

❑ use control reference correctly

❑ appreciate that more complex procedures can be achieved using small programs or modules

The events for a form or report can be found under the Events tab of the Properties sheet. Forms, controls and reports have different events associated with them. The following tables illustrate some of the events to which macros can be assigned.

Events in a form or record

Form property	Event	Example of use
On Open	Runs the macro when the form opens but before displaying a record.	To open or close other forms when the form opens.
Before Insert	Runs when the user begins to enter data into a new record.	To display extra information or a warning message.
Before Update	Runs after the user has finished changing or entering the record but before it is updated in the database.	To display a dialog box asking the user to confirm that the record be updated.
After Update	Runs after the user has edited or entered the record and after it has been updated in the database.	To update other forms using the data in the new record.
On Delete	Runs when the user deletes a record but before it is actually deleted.	To ask for confirmation as to whether the record should be deleted.
On Close	Runs as the form is about to close but has not disappeared from the screen.	To ask if data may be transferred when the form is closed.

Events in a form control

Property	Event description	Example of use
On Enter	Runs the macro when a control is clicked i.e. as it receives the focus.	To ask for a password before allowing data entry.
On Click	Runs when a button is clicked.	To print the form.
Before Update	Runs after the user leaves a control but before the control is changed.	To validate newly entered data and ask for it to be corrected.
On Dbl Click	Runs when the user double clicks on a control or its label.	To display a form with information regarding data entry.
On Exit	Runs when the user attempts to move to another control but before the focus moves away.	To define the next control using the GoToControl action.

Events in a report

Report Event	Event Description	Example of use
On Open	Runs the macro when the report opens but before printing.	To display a form in which to enter criteria.

Assigning macros to a form or report

To assign a macro to an event, first create and save the macro.

To assign a macro to the required form, report or control:

1 Open the form or report in Design view.

2 Select the form, report or control to which the macro is to be assigned.

   To select a control, just click on it;

   To select a section, click on the section header.

   To select the whole form or report, use **Edit-Select Form** or **Edit-Select Report**.

3 Display the Properties Sheet by clicking on the **Properties** button in the toolbar.

4 Select the required event in the properties table.

5 Open the combo box and select the macro name to be assigned to this event.

6 Save the changes made and test the macro.

Using conditions

Your macros can have the capability to make decisions about how they operate. Macros can test whether a condition is true and if so they can run actions you specify. Click on the **Conditions** button in the macro window toolbar to display the **Condition** column.

In this column you enter expressions that can be evaluated as true or false. If it evaluates as true, the macro action on its right runs; if false the action doesn't run.

Expressions test the values of control names, for example:

[Surname]="Smith"   True, when *Surname* control contains the text "Smith".

[Membership Fee]<20   True, when the *Membership Fee* control is less than 20.

Task 1: Using conditions to control the focus in a form

In this task you will assign a macro to the *Member/Class* control in the *Bookings* form which will control whether the focus moves to the *Membership No* control or to the *Class No* control.

1   Create a new macro group called *Booking*. Display the **Condition** column by clicking on the **Conditions** button in the toolbar. There will be two macros in the group, named after the controls to which they will be assigned.

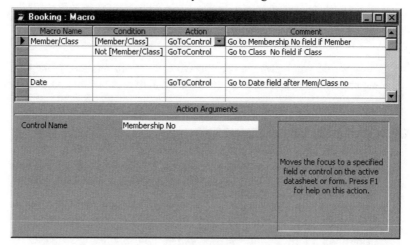

2   The *Member/Class* macro has two conditions, one if the *Member/Class* control is true and the other if it is false. If the control is true then the **GoToControl** action specifies *Membership No* (as illustrated). If the control is false then the **GoToControl** action specifies *Class No*.

3   To move the focus to *Date* after either a Membership or Class number has been entered, the macro *Date* is used. This macro uses a **GoToControl** action with the Control Name argument *Date*.

4   Save the macro group as ***Booking***.

5   Display the *Bookings* form in Design view.

6   Click on the *Member/Class* control and set the **On Exit** property to *Booking.Member/Class*.

7   Set the **On Exit** control of *Membership No* to *Booking.Date*. Repeat for the *Class No* control.

8   Save the form and test the macro group by entering some data.

Using Tab Order and GoToControl together

Beware! If your **Tab Order** *and* **GoToControl** *macros do not work in harmony, form navigation will be difficult! Consider the case below: the tab order is shown by the arrows on the left, and the effect of the macros is shown on the right. A user navigating between fields using the* <u>Tab</u> *key will get stuck in a tab cycle on the form which never reaches the* Room/Hall/Court, Booking No *or* Time *fields:*

Member/Class -> Membership No *or* Class No -> Date -> Membership No -> Date -> Membership No -> Date... *etc!*

How would you rearrange the Tab Order to avoid this loop? Sketch a schema on paper first, using arrows as in the diagram above, then test it on the *Bookings* form.

Control reference syntax

To be able to refer to a control name from within a macro the correct syntax must be used. If the way in which the control is referred to does not follow the rules of syntax then the macro will not work.

The syntax for referring to controls is as follows.

Control on a form: *Forms!formname!controlname*

Control on a report: *Reports!reportname!controlname*

Control on a subform: *Forms!mainformname!subformname.Form!controlname*

If the name of the form, report or control contains spaces then it must be enclosed in square brackets, for example:

Forms![Membership Category]![Membership Fee]

If the macro is run from the form or report containing the control then the control can be referred to by the control name alone. This is known as the short syntax, for example: *[Membership Fee]*

For the **GoToControl** action used in the task above, the control is referred to by its name only, since you can only go to a control on the same form or report which the macro is run from. When creating more advanced macros you may need to use the full syntax described above, as in the later stages of the next task.

Task 2: Using a form to enter report criteria

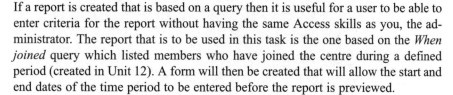

If a report is created that is based on a query then it is useful for a user to be able to enter criteria for the report without having the same Access skills as you, the administrator. The report that is to be used in this task is the one based on the *When joined* query which listed members who have joined the centre during a defined period (created in Unit 12). A form will then be created that will allow the start and end dates of the time period to be entered before the report is previewed.

To begin with, use the Report Wizard to create a single-column report from this query. Save the report with the name *When joined*.

The rest of the task involves creating an unbound form, a macro group, a module and editing the underlying query and report. This is a long task, so follow the steps carefully.

Step 1: create an unbound form

1   Click on the **Forms** button in the database window and click **New**. Leave the **Choose the table or query...** box empty as this form is not bound to a table or query.

2   Select Design View and click **OK**.

3   In Design view set the properties for the form as shown below:

Property	Setting
Caption	Period under investigation (the name that will appear in the title bar of the form)
Default View	Single Form
Views Allowed	Form
Scroll Bars	Neither
Record Selectors	No
Navigation Buttons	No
Dividing Lines	No

4   Add two unbound text boxes for the start and end date criteria

5   Set the properties for the text boxes as follows:

Property	Setting
Name	Start Date (first text box)
	End Date (second text box)
Format	Short Date (both text boxes)

6   Edit the label of the first text box to read *Period beginning* and the second text box to read *Period ending*.

7   Add text to indicate the purpose of the form, as illustrated below (Your form will not look like this yet; the *Search* and *Cancel* command buttons will be added to the form after you create macros for them).

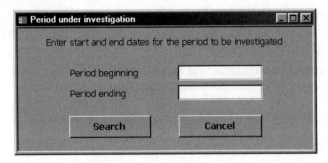

8   Save the form and give it the name *When joined*.

Step 2: create a module that is used by one of the macros

Modules have not been introduced as they involve programming which is beyond the scope of this book. However, for this task you can copy the code below to create a simple module. This is a function which will return either 'true' or 'false' depending whether a specified form is loaded. Modules may be classed as 'standard' (available globally), or they may be attached to a form or report. In this case the function will be attached to the *When joined* report.

1   From the Database window open the *When joined* report in Design view. Click on the Code button 🔲 in the toolbar to display a module window.

2   Type the line ***Function IsLoaded(MyFormName) As Boolean*** and press *Enter*. You'll notice that when you type *As B...* a list box opens up with various code options, and you can just choose **Boolean** instead of typing it all. This will happen with other parts of the code as you type, too.

3   Key in the rest of the module exactly as shown. The line **End Function** is preset and you just add the lines in between. The lines beginning with a single quote (') are comment lines which are not active parts of the code; they are ther to help explain what is going on.

```
Chelmer Leisure - Report_When joined (Code)
(General)                                isloaded

  Option Compare Database

  Function isloaded(MyFormName) As Boolean
  'Accepts: a form name
  'Purpose: determines if the specified form has been loaded
  'Returns: True if form is loaded, False if not
  Dim i As Integer
      isloaded = False
      For i = 0 To Forms.Count - 1
          If Forms(i).Name = MyFormName Then
              isloaded = True
              Exit Function 'Quit function once form has been found
          End If
      Next
  End Function
```

If you are familiar with Basic you will notice that a *For...Next* loop and an *If* statement are used to test the names of open forms against the name specified, and to set the function to true if a match is found.

4   Save and close the Visual Basic Editor window. The function will be saved as part of the report when the report design is saved.

Step 3: create the macros for the form

The four macros used by the form will be kept in one macro group as illustrated at the end of this step.

1   In the Database window, click the **Macros** button, and then **New**.

2   Create a macro that opens the unbound *When joined* form. Display the **Macro Names** column. Give the macro the name *Open Dialog*, and select the **OpenForm** action.

3   Set the action arguments for **OpenForm** as follows.

Argument	Setting
Form Name	When joined
View	Form
Data Mode	Edit
Window Mode	Dialog

4   Add a second action that cancels previewing or printing the report. This action will only take place if the form doesn't load for some reason. Click the **Conditions** button, and type the following expression in the **Condition** column:

> *Not IsLoaded('When joined')*

Select *CancelEvent* as the action for this condition being true. The function *IsLoaded* checks whether the named form is loaded.

5   Add a macro to the group that closes the form. Give the macro a name such as *Close Dialog*. Select the **Close** action. Set the action arguments as follows.

Argument	Setting
Object Type	Form
Object Name	When joined

6   Create a macro for the *Search* button. This macro hides the form so that the report becomes visible. Give the macro a name such as *Search*, and select the **SetValue** action. Then set its action arguments as follows.

Argument	Setting
Item	[Visible]
Expression	No

7.   Create a macro for the *Cancel* button. This macro closes the form. Give the macro a name such as *Cancel*, and select the **Close** action. Then set its action arguments as follows.

Argument	Setting
Object Type	Form
Object Name	When joined
Save	No

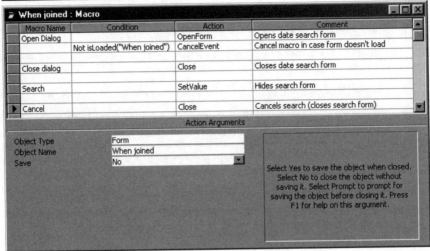

8   Save and close the macro group. Give the macro group a name that reflects the general purpose of the group, such as **When joined**.

Step 4: add OK and Cancel command buttons to the form

1   Re-open the unbound form *When joined* in Design view.

2   Using the Toolbox, add a command button for **OK** (without using the Wizard), and set its properties as follows.

Property	Setting
Caption	Search
On Click	When joined.Search
	(macrogroup.macroname)

3   Add a command button for **Cancel** (without using the Wizard), and set its properties as follows.

Property	Setting
Caption	Cancel
On Click	When joined.Cancel

4   Save and close the form.

Step 5: edit the criteria in the underlying query When joined

Here we will replace the static criteria in the *Date of Joining* field with an expression which picks up the values entered into the *When joined* form.

1   Open the *When joined* query in Design view.

2   Replace the criteria for the *Date of Joining* field. Enter this replacement expression to refer to controls named *Start Date* and *End Date* on the *When joined* form:

Between [Forms]![When joined]![Start Date] And [Forms]![When joined]![End Date]

3   Save the changes and close the query.

Step 6: attach the macros to the When joined report

1   Open the *When joined* report in Design view, and set the following properties for the report.

Property	Setting
OnOpen	When joined.Open Dialog (Name of the macro that opens the *When joined* search form)
OnClose	When joined.Close Dialog (the macro that closes the search form)

2   Save the report, close it and open it in View mode. The search form should pop up, asking you for dates; enter some dates which you know will return a few member records, and click **Search**.

3   Try adding two unbound text boxes into the report header so that the title reads List of members that joined between *Start Date* and *End Date*, where the dates entered into the search form appear in the title.

Unit 43

Macros for data validation

What you will learn in this unit

When a table is defined it is possible to set **Validation Rules** on a field to check that valid data is entered. One rule prevented a *Category No* greater than 6 from being entered as there are only six categories of membership. Validation rules are limited in what they can do, and macros can take validation one stage further. This unit demonstrates the use of macros for data validation.

By the end of this unit you will be able to:

❑   use macros for data validation

❑   run a start-up macro

❑   use macros to select records.

Using macros for data validation

The kind of validation that a macro can perform is to check whether a member signing for a class is the right sex for that class. This will be considered in the following task. Another example is checking that a room is available at a certain day and time before a booking is accepted.

Task 1: Validating bookings for classes

This task uses a macro that will check whether a person booking a class is of the right sex. It will prevent a female member booking into a male class and vice versa.

When a booking is made the *Class Lists* main/subform is used. The membership number is entered into the subform (*Class Member List*). To check whether the member is male or female the membership data must be accessed. We will open the *Membership* form, go to the record of the entered number and check the member's sex.

We don't actually want to see the *Membership* form though, so we will open it as a hidden window. The validation macro which does this will be assigned to the **Before Update** event of the *Class Member List* form. The **BeforeUpdate** event runs the macro *after* data has been entered by the user, but *before* it is actually stored in the database.

To create this validation macro:

1   In the Database window, click the **Macros** button, and then **New**.

2   Select the **OpenForm** action and set the action arguments as follows:

Argument	Setting
Argument	Setting
Form Name	Membership
View	Form
Where	[Membership No]=Forms![Class List]![Class Member List].Form![Membership No]
Data Mode	Read Only
Window Mode	Hidden

3 Add a second action that displays a message box. This action will only take place if the member is male and the class is female only. Click the **Conditions** button, and type the following expression (in one line) in the **Condition** column:

Forms![Membership]![Sex] And Forms![Class List]![Male/Female/Mixed]="Female"

4 Select **MsgBox** as the action for this condition being true. Set the properties for the message box as follows.

Argument	Setting
Message	This is a female only class
Beep	Yes
Type	None
Title	Classes Validation

5 Add a third action that cancels the event, so the data will not be stored in the database. This action is dependent upon the same condition as the row above, and to indicate this put an ellipsis (three dots in a row: ...) in the **Condition** column. Select the **CancelEvent** action.

6 The fourth action undoes the current record. Put an ellipsis (...) in the **Condition** column, and select **RunCommand** as the action and set its property.

Argument	Setting
Command	Undo

7 Add a fifth action that displays a message box. This action will only take place if the member is female and the class is male only. Click the **Conditions** button, and type the following expression in the **Condition** column:

Not Forms![Membership]![Sex] And Forms![Class List]![Male/Female/Mixed]="Male"

8 Select **MsgBox** as the action for this condition being true. Set the properties for the message box as follows.

Argument	Setting
Message	This is a male only class
Beep	Yes
Type	None
Title	Classes Validation

9   Add a sixth action that cancels the event. This action is also dependent upon the condition in the row above, and to indicate this an ellipsis is put in the **Condition** column. Select the **CancelEvent** action.

10 Add a seventh action that undoes the current record (same as the fourth action). Put an ellipsis in its **Condition** column.

11 The final action is to **Close** the Membership form. Set its arguments as follows.

Argument	Setting
Object Type	Form
Object Name	Membership

12 Save the macro using the name *Male Female Validation*.

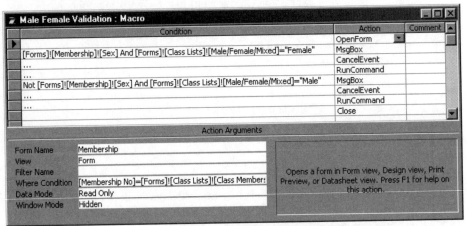

13 Open the *Class Member List* form in Design view. Display the form property sheet, open the **Before Update** property of the form (under the **Event** tab) and select **Male Female Validation**. Save and close the form.

14 Select the *Class Lists* main/sub form and open it. Try entering a female member into a male class and vice versa to test your macro.

If the system doesn't work it is likely that a name has been mistyped – open the macro in Design view and check it carefully. If it all appears to be correct, it is possible that you have used Autoform instead of the Form Wizard to create one or more of the forms used in this task. As mentioned in earlier units, the version of Access available at the time of writing appears to retain a hidden, internal name for a form created with Autoform, which you cannot change after it has been created.

Regardless of what you decide to call your Autoform form when prompted to save it, Access remembers the default name it chose for the form, and if you do not use this one when writing macros, it gets confused and doesn't know which form you're referring to!

I hope that the version of Access you are using now has had this bug ironed out, but if not, the only sure-fire workaround is to delete the Autoform form and create a new one using the more reliable Form Wizard instead.

Running a macro at start-up time

To give a database application a professional look a macro can be written which will run when the database is opened. This macro can open required forms and set any defaults. Typically a start-up macro would open a form which displayed a main menu for database functions. This might have various buttons that the user can click depending on what they want to do with the database.

The macro to perform the start-up tasks is written as for any other macro, but it is saved with the name *Autoexec*. Whenever a database is opened, Access looks for a macro called *Autoexec*, and if it finds one then it will be run. If you need to do development work on the database, you can stop the *Autoexec* macro running by holding down *Shift* when you click **OK** or *Enter* to open the database.

Using macros to create a record amendment form

Once a table has been created, such as the *Membership* table, it must be maintained. In this activity we consider the amendment of records. A member might change their address or category of membership, or supply information not previously given. Records can be edited by viewing the table, using the **Find** facility to locate the record and making the changes. This is not a friendly interface. A more sophisti-cated method is to use a form through which records can be found and edited.

The next task creates an amendment form for the *Membership* table (shown be-low), which uses a list box to display membership numbers. Users will be able to select the number from the list to go to the record they need to update.

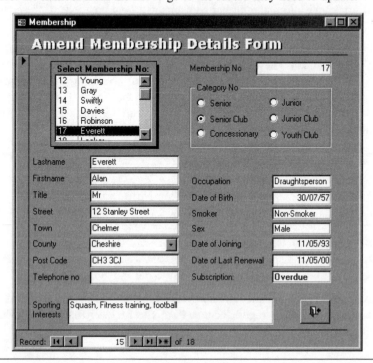

Task 2: Membership record amendment form

In this task a form and several small macros will be created.

1   Use the **Forms Wizard to** create a single column form based on the *Membership* table. Give the form the title *Amend Membership Details Form*. Display the form in design view and adjust the positions of the controls to allow room for the addition of the list box.

2   With the **Control Wizard** button in the Toolbox depressed, choose the **List Box** button and click on the form where you want the list box. In the **List Box Wizard** dialog box select the **I want the list box to look up the values in a table or query** option. Click [Next >].

3   Select the *Membership* table and click [Next >]. Select *Membership No* and *Lastname* as columns in the list box by clicking on [>], then click [Next >]. Remove the tick from the **Hide key column** check box as we are using the key to search for members. Adjust the widths of the columns in the list box as necessary.

4   Click [Next >], then [Next >] again to accept that *Membership No* is the field to be used by the form.

5   Leave the **Remember the value for later use** option selected and click [Next >].

6   Edit the label of the list box to read *Select Membership No:* and click [Finish].

7   Display the property sheet for the list box control and give it the name *Select Membership No*.

8   You may wish to make further adjustments to the positions of the controls on the form. When finished, save the form as *Amend Membership Details*. Close the form.

9   Open the macro **Chelmer** in Design View. Scroll down to the end of the existing macros and add a new one with the name **Find Record**. This macro will be used whenever a selection is made in the list box, to give focus to the **Membership No** control, search for the appropriate number and then return focus to the **Select Membership No** field in case the user wants to search again. Give it the following actions:

Action	Argument
GoToControl	Membership No
Find Record	=[Select Membership No]
GoToControl	Select Membership No

10   Save the macro. Open the *Amend Membership Details* form in Design view. Click on the list box, display its property sheet and assign the macro *Chelmer.FindRecord* to the list box's **After Update** property. Save and close the form.

11   Add another macro called *AmendOnLoad* to the *Chelmer* macro group. This macro has just one action, to give focus to the *Select Membership No* field when the form is opened.

Action	Argument
GoToControl	Select Membership No

12　Close and save the macro group. Reopen the *Amend Membership Details* form in Design view. Use **Edit-Select Form** and display the form's property sheet. Assign the macro *Chelmer.AmendOnLoad* to the **On Load** property of the form.

13　Click on the *Membership No* control and set its **Tab Stop** property to **No**. Also set its **Locked** property to **Yes**, to stop it being accidentally changed.

14　Save the form. Try using it to search for a member's records and make some changes. As a finishing touch you could add a **Close** button to this form.

You should find this form useful to search for records based on the member's membership number. You could design a similar form to search by members' names instead, but for it to be any use you would first have to create a query to extract the names and sort them alphabetically.

Integrative tasks

These tasks draw on this and the last four units concerning the use of macros.

Task 3: A report menu

This task creates a form containing several buttons which when clicked will preview a certain report. The underlying macro for each button opens a report, an action similar to that for opening a form.

1　Display the *Chelmer* macro window.

2　In the next convenient row put **Membership Report** as the name of this macro.

3　Select the **OpenReport** action. Set the arguments for this action as follows.

Argument	Setting
Report Name	Members2
View	Print Preview

4　In the **Comment** column, type the description **Preview Membership Report**.

5　Save the macro group.

6　In a similar fashion create macros to open the *Labels New Members*, *Classes4*, and *Bookings* reports.

7　Create a blank unbound form. Add to it a title, e.g. **Reports Menu** and add four buttons, one for each macro just created.

8　Label each button and assign the appropriate macro to it. Remember to use the correct syntax, e.g. **Chelmer.Mailing**, for the **On Click** property. Save the form as **Reports Menu** and run it.

Task 4: A query menu

This task creates a form containing several buttons which when clicked will run a certain query. The underlying macro for each button opens a report, an action similar to that for opening a form.

1   Display the *Chelmer* macro window.

2   In the next convenient row put **Membership Report** as the name of this macro.

3   Select the **OpenQuery** action. Set the argument for this action as follows (leave the others at their default settings):

Argument	Setting
Query Name	Members' Sporting Interests

4   Key into the **Comment** column the description **Sporting Interests Query**.

5   Save the macro group.

6   In a similar fashion create macros to open the *Member Ages*, *Fitness Suite Bookings* and *When joined* queries.

7   Create a blank unbound form. Add to it a title, e.g. **Queries Menu** and add four buttons, one for each macro just created.

8   Label each button and assign the appropriate macro to it. Remember to use the correct syntax, e.g. **Chelmer.Sporting Interests**, for the **On Click** property. Save the form as **Query Menu** and run it.

A database application

What you will learn in this unit

In the earlier units we have explored the creation and use of tables, queries, reports, forms and macros. In order to create a fully operational database system – known as an *application* – it is necessary to link all of these components together. In this unit we explore some of the issues associated with creating a working application.

By the end of this unit you will be able to:

❑   understand the issues and stages in the design of an application

❑   use forms and macros to create a series of linked menus

❑   create a simple application for the use and maintenance of a database

❑   appreciate the complexity of relational database design

The aim of this unit is to begin to draw the various components of the Chelmer database that you have created in this book into the beginnings of an application. We will not seek to explore the wide range of features that can be used in the design of applications, such as drop-down menus, menu bars and pop-up forms, but will instead concentrate on using the basic features to tie the database together.

Understanding applications

Why do we need applications? Earlier units have introduced you to the creation of the component parts of applications: tables, forms, reports, queries and macros. (Code Modules might also be included in an application but we have not attempted these in this book.) Through the database window you are able to select tables, call up a form, edit data in tables, perform queries on tables and produce reports. This is perfectly adequate for a small database used only by its creator, but real applications are often tailored for specific environments and non-skilled users.

Chelmer's leisure management system would not access the database components through the database window. Users would start the system up and view a main menu which offers them a number of options, such as 'add a new member' or 'make a booking'. We would not expect the leisure centre staff to have to remember the name of the table which needs to be accessed in order to perform these actions. They should be able to click on a button or choose a menu option and move straight into the form that allows them to carry out the right function. So for example, an opening or main menu screen might appear as illustrated in Figure 44.1.

When the user clicks on the first option a form, such as **Membership**, would be displayed. When the user clicked on **System Maintenance**, a second menu would

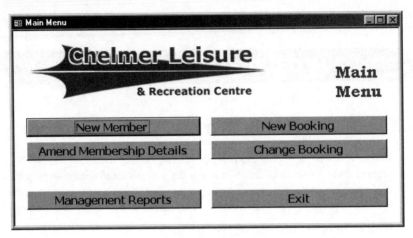

Figure 44.1

be displayed which would offer further options, perhaps to open the various tables in Design view, or to generate management reports.

Clicking on one of the **Management Reports** button could lead to a third menu asking which report the user wants to produce, as illustrated below.

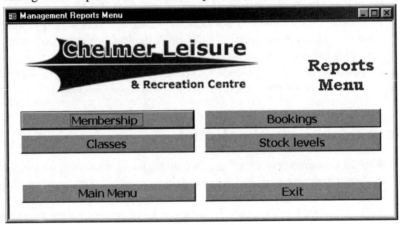

Figure 44.2

What then is a database application? The *Access User's Guide* offers this succinct definition.

'A Database Application is a set of related Microsoft Access database objects that you can use to accomplish a particular database task. For example, if you use a certain set of forms and reports frequently, you can create an application that gives you easy access to these forms and reports and displays them conveniently in the Microsoft Access window.'

↔ In Units 39 to 43 you developed some simple macros that could be used with forms and reports. You can use other macros to create a customised application with more advanced features. For example, you can create custom menu bars for forms, assign common actions to menu commands or key combinations, and automate various tasks such as printing daily reports or backing up your database.

Designing applications

In this book, we have created the database components first and are now proceeding to integrate them into one application. This is not the way these things should be done! Now that you have the skills to create the component parts of a database, you would sit down to design your next database application in a different way.

A thorough analysis of what data is to be stored and how it relates to each other would be undertaken, and then a similar analysis of who is going to use the database and for what purpose. This should determine which forms, reports, queries, macros and modules are necessary and the function of each of them.

Task 1: Understanding applications

The Management Reports Menu illustration above shows a menu for generating reports. Draw on paper a similar menu for adding and updating data in the Membership table. Indicate which of the forms and reports that you have already created might be accessed via this menu.

Creating a simple application

The sample application illustrated so far in this unit is very simplistic. For example, only forms are used for the display of menus; windows, pull-down menus, menu bars and pop-up forms are not used. Yet even these simple menus start to illustrate some important features of good application design.

Design must depend upon the application. In particular the sequencing of the screen should make it easy to run through a normal task sequence, and it should be easy to move between related but distinct tasks (notice that in Figure 44.2 there is a button for returning to the main menu).

Most systems have three types of users: systems managers (who have responsibility for maintaining the system, managers (seeking management reports and summary data), and operators (on the front desk, taking bookings, meeting members and answering enquiries). These users need to perform different operations using the system. Menus and menu options must be grouped in such a way that different users find their applications easily accessible.

So for example, in Figure 44.1 it is easy to go straight from the main Chelmer menu to desk functions such as making a booking, but functions that might be more useful to managers are tucked away under System Maintenance. Ideally, workstations on the bookings desk would not display the maintenance options, or would have them password-protected. This is beyond the scope of this book, however.

A real system based on multiple tables is very complex to create and would involve much more input than we can pursue in this book. In Task 2 we create a small application based solely on the Membership and Bookings tables, using some of the forms and reports that we have already created, as well as some new forms which will hold the application menus.

Task 2: Creating a mini-application

In this task we will start by creating the *Main Menu* form, then move on to creating and linking macros to them. Where possible we use macros already created in Units 39 to 43.

1   Open a new form and add a form header.

2   Open the form header and insert a logo as in Figure 44.1. Add the title *Main Menu*.

3   Open the detail section and insert the buttons as in Figure 44.1.

4   Save the form as *Main Menu*.

↔ 5   Review and create appropriate macros similar to those already created in Units 39-43. We need the following functions (in this task we'll skip the System Maintenance menu and go straight to the Management Reports menu):

Button	Macro
New Member	Opens the *Membership* form at a new record.
Amend Membership Details	Opens the *Amend Membership Details* form.
New Booking	Opens the *Bookings* form at a new record.
Check a Booking	Opens the *Bookings* form at the first record, ready for the user to search using **Edit-Find**.
Management Reports	Opens the *Management Reports Menu* form.
Exit	Closes the *Main Menu* form.

6   When you have created all the macros listed above, open the form again in Design view.

7   Add the macros to the buttons in turn, by clicking on the button and inserting the macro name as the **OnClick** property on the properties sheet.

Task 3: Creating the System Maintenance menu

Use a similar aproach to that in Task 2 and create the System Maintenance menu shown in Figure 44.2.

Task 4: Creating the Management Reports menu

The *Management Reports Menu* can be created using similar principles to those outlined in Task 3 Unit 43. Try modifying the menu that you created in that task to look like Figure 44.3.

By using conditions in your macro you can either print, print preview or edit the report design, depending on the value of the option group control.

8   Add the option group with **Print**, **Print Preview** and **Edit report** options.

9   Edit its properties to give it the name *ReportOptions*.

10   Set the default of this option group to **Print Preview**.

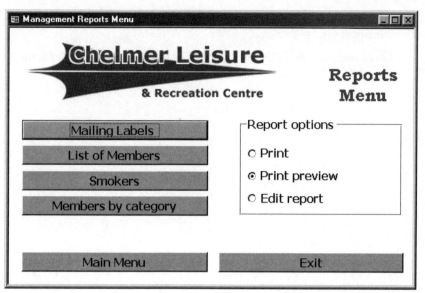

Figure 44.3

11   Add new conditional actions to your macros for previewing reports:

Condition	Action	View argument	Comment
[Frame0]=1	OpenReport	Print	Print report
[Frame0]=2	OpenReport	Print Preview	Open report in Print Preview
[Frame0]=3	OpenReport	Design	Open report in Design view

Integrative tasks

The following tasks call upon application design skills introduced in this unit.

Task 5: Creating the queries menu

Design a **Membership Queries Menu** which is consistent with the other menus that you have designed, to display the following data:

Membership Queries Menu

New Query

Existing Query

Task 6: Designing a bookings table main menu

1   Design a *Bookings Main Menu* for the *Bookings* table which is similar to that for the *Membership* table.

2   What's wrong with this menu for the person on the bookings desk? Think about the functions that this person would need to perform. Think about the questions that customers might ask, for which they would need to provide an answer.

3   Which if any of these functions might require the user to have access to data in other tables in the database?

4   Could customers make their own bookings through a system with the main menu in Figure 44.1 ? What additional security might be advisable?

Quick reference 1

Data for tables

Membership table data

Note that the Membership number is allocated automatically and cannot be edited. If you delete a record, you will lose that number, but this doesn't matter. If your numbers are different from those shown here, just make a note of the differences for reference with any tasks that use the numbers.

Membership no	Category	Lastname	Firstname	Title	Street
1	2	Walker	Andrew J	Mr	16 Dovecot Close
2	1	Cartwright	Denise	Mrs	27 Bowling Green Rd
3	6	Perry	Jason R	Mr	59 Church Street
4	2	Forsythe	Ann M	Miss	2 Ferndale Close
5	1	Jameson	Donna	Mrs	25 Alder Drive
6	3	Robinson	Petra	Miss	16 Lowton Lane
7	5	Harris	David J	Mr	55 Coven Road
8	2	Shangali	Imran	Mr	47 High Street
9	1	Barrett	Martha A	Mrs	7 Oldcott Way
10	1	Weiner	George W F	Mr	6 Church Street
11	6	Ali	David	Mr	33 Meriton Road
12	2	Young	Aileen	Ms	78 Highgate Street
13	5	Gray	Ivor P	Mr	4 The Parade
14	5	Swift	Freda	Miss	23 Ferndale Close
15	1	Davies	Sandra M	Mrs	61 Hallfield Road
16	1	Robinson	Rebecca	Mrs	9 Moss Street
17	2	Everett	Alan	Mr	12 Stanley Street
18	4	Locker	Liam	Mr	2 Beech Close
19	4	Locker	Alison	Miss	2 Beech Close
20	1	Jones	Edward R	Mr	17 Mayfield Avenue

	Town	County	Post code	Telephone no	Occupation	Date of birth
1	Chelmer	Cheshire	CH2 6TR	01777569236	Builder	12/3/52
2	Meriton	Cheshire	CH9 2EV	01777552099	Housewife	29/11/60
3	Chelmer	Cheshire	CH1 8YU			3/6/82
4	Chelmer	Cheshire		01777 569945	Receptionist	5/8/73
5	Chelmer	Cheshire	CH2 7FN		Housewife	4/12/70

	Town	County	Post code	Telephone no	Occupation	Date of birth
6	Bradford	Staffs	ST10 2DZ	01778890523		7/7/84
7	Chelmer	Cheshire	CH3 8PS	01777569311	Retired	22/5/28
8	Chelmer	Cheshire	CH1 7JH	01777561553	Accountant	15/3/55
9	Meriton	Cheshire	CH9 3DR	01777557822	Teacher	25/11/60
10	Chelmer	Cheshire	CH1 8YV		Electrician	10/2/58
11	Chelmer	Cheshire	CH4 5KD	01777569066		14/7/81
12	Branford	Staffs	ST10 4RT	01778894471	Civil Servant	25/10/51
13	Chelmer	Cheshire	CH1 7ER	01777565715	Unemployed	12/4/47
14	Chelmer	Cheshire	CH2 8PN	01777567351	Retired	14/9/27
15	Meriton	Cheshire	CH9 1YJ	01778891441	Clerk	1/2/65
16	Chelmer	Cheshire	CH2 8SE	01777568812	Housewife	18/5/68
17	Chelmer	Cheshire	CH3 3CJ		Draughtsperson	30/7/57
18	Chelmer	Cheshire	CH3 8UH			30/12/83
19	Chelmer	Cheshire	CH3 8UH			30/12/83
20	Chelmer	Cheshire	CH2 90L	01777 567333	Bus Driver	22/12/58

	Date of joining	Date of last renewal	Sporting interests	Smoker	Sex
1	3/2/92	3/2/97	Tennis, squash	Yes	Yes
2	16/7/91	16/7/96	Aerobics, swimming, running, squash	No	No
3	12/12/96	12/12/96	Judo, Karate	No	Yes
4	16/9/91	16/9/96		No	No
5	15/6/92	15/6/96	Aerobics, squash Yes	No	
6	3/1/95	3/1/97	Swimming, Judo	No	No
7	1/2/94	1/2/97	Badminton, cricket Yes	Yes	
8	6/4/92	6/4/96	Weight training, squash	No	Yes
9	4/10/93	4/10/96	Keep fit, swimming	No	No
10	15/7/92	15/7/96	Weight training, squash	No	Yes
11	2/10/94	2/10/96	Judo, swimming, football	No	Yes
12	9/8/92	9/8/96	Keep fit, Aerobics, squash	Yes	No
13	5/1/95	5/1/97		Yes	Yes
14	16/9/93	16/9/96		No	No
15	5/4/92	5/4/97	Aerobics, squash, swimming Yes	No	
16	6/12/91	6/12/96	Tennis, Aerobics	No	No
17	5/11/93	5/11/96	Squash, Fitness training, football	No	Yes
18	13/6/92	13/6/97		No	Yes
19	13/6/92	13/6/97		No	No
20	17/5/91	17/5/96	Weight training	Yes	Yes

Membership category table data

Category no	Category type	Membership fee
1	Senior	£25.00
2	Senior Club	£30.00
3	Junior	£10.00
4	Junior Club	£15.00
5	Concessionary	£18.00
6	Youth Club	£20.00

Classes table data

Class no	Class day	Class time	Class tutor	Class activity	Male/female/mixed
1	Monday	10:00	Evans	Ladies' Aerobics	Female
2	Monday	11:00	Franks	Weight Training	Male
3	Monday	15:00	Latham	Body Conditioning	Mixed
4	Monday	19:00	Wheildon	Step Aerobics	Mixed
5	Tuesday	10:00	Jackson	Men's Multi-gym	Male
6	Tuesday	14:00	Adams	Ladies' Multi-gym	Female
7	Tuesday	19:00	Jackson	Family Multi-gym	Mixed
8	Wednesday	10:00	Evans	Ladies' Aerobics	Female
9	Wednesday	14:00	Latham	Body Conditioning	Mixed
10	Wednesday	15:00	Franks	Weight training	Female
11	Wednesday	19:00	Franks	Weight training	Mixed
12	Thursday	11:00	Latham	Weight training	Male
13	Thursday	14:00	Wheildon	Step Aerobics	Mixed
14	Thursday	15:00	Adams	Multi-gym	Mixed
15	Thursday	19:00	Latham	Body Conditioning	Mixed
16	Friday	10:00	Latham	Body Conditioning	Female
17	Friday	11:00	Wheildon	Step Aerobics	Mixed
18	Friday	14:00	Jackson	Men's Multi-gym	Male

Class list table data

Class No	Membership No
1	2
1	5
1	16
4	4
4	6
5	7
5	10
5	1

Bookings table data

Booking no.	Room/Hall/Court	Member/ Class	Membership/ Class no	Date	Time
1	Fitness Suite	Class	1	13/5/96	10:00
2	Fitness Suite	Class	2	13/5/96	11:00
3	Sports hall 2	Class	3	13/5/96	15:00
4	Sports hall 1	Class	4	13/5/96	19:00
5	Fitness Suite	Class	5	14/5/96	10:00
6	Fitness Suite	Class	6	14/5/96	14:00
7	Fitness Suite	Class	7	14/5/96	19:00
8	Fitness Suite	Class	8	15/5/96	10:00
9	Sports hall 2	Class	9	15/5/96	14:00
10	Sports hall 2	Class	10	15/5/96	15:00
11	Sports hall 2	Class	11	15/5/96	19:00
12	Sports hall 2	Class	12	16/5/96	11:00
13	Sports hall 2	Class	13	16/5/96	14:00
14	Fitness Suite	Class	14	16/5/96	15:00
15	Sports hall 2	Class	15	16/5/96	19:00
16	Sports hall 2	Class	16	17/5/96	10:00
17	Sports hall 2	Class	17	17/5/96	11:00
18	Fitness Suite	Class	18	17/5/96	14:00
19	Court 1	Member	2	13/5/96	18:00
20	Court 2	Member	17	16/5/96	14:00
21	Court 3	Member	15	14/5/96	11:00
22	Court!	Member	12	15/5/96	19:00

Stock Levels table data

Item Code	Item	Stock	Re-order level
1	Sports towel	52	25
2	T-shirt (small)	72	20
3	T-shirt (medium)	17	20
4	T-shirt (large)	42	20
5	Skipping rope	13	10
6	Knee support	7	5
7	Ankle support	3	5
8	"Buns of Steel" video	66	30

Data definitions

Bookings table

Name		Type	Size
Booking No		Auto Number	4
Room/Hall/Court	*Index*: Primary key	Text	20
Member/Class	*Required*: True		
	Index: Ascending	Yes/No	1
	Required: True		
Membership No		Number (Long)	4
Class No		Number (Long)	4
Date	*Required*: True	Date/Time	8
	Format: d/m/yy		
	Index: Date+Time		
Time	*Required*: True	Date/Time	8
	Format hh:mm		
	ShortIndex: Date+Time	Time	

Classes table

Name		Type	Size
Class No	*Index*: Primary key	AutoNumber	4
Class Day	*Required*: True	Text	10
Class Time	*Required*: True	Date/Time	8
	Format: hh:mm	Short time	
Class Tutor	*Index*: Ascending	Text	30
Class Activity	*Required*: True	Text	20
	Index: Ascending		
Male/Female/Mixed	*Validation Rule*: "Male" or "Female" or "Mixed"	Text	
	Validation Text: Please enter Male, Female or Mixed		

Membership table

Name		Type	Size
Membership No	*Description*: Automatic membership numbering *Index*: Primary key	AutoNumber	4
Category No	*Description*: Categories are 1-Senior, 2-Senior Club, 3-Junior, 4-Junior Club, 5-Concessionary, 6-Youth Club *Validation Rule*: <=6 *Validation Text*: Please enter a category between 1 and 6 *Required*: True	Number (Byte)	1
Lastname	*Required*: True *Index*: Lastname+Firstname	Text	25
Firstname	*Index*: Lastname+Firstname	Text	30
Title		Text	10
Street	*Required*: True	Text	30
Town	*Default value*: Chelmer *Required*: True	Text	25
County	*Default value*: Cheshire *Required*: True	Text	20
Post Code	*Format*:>	Text	20
Telephone No		Text	12
Occupation		Text	50
Date of Birth	*Format*: Short Date	Date/Time	8
Date of Joining	*Format*: Short Date	Date/Time	8
Date of Last Renewal	*Format*: Short Date	Date/Time	8
Sporting Interests		Memo	0
Smoker	*Format*: ;"Smoker";"Non-Smoker"	Yes/No	1
Sex	*Format*: ;"Male";"Female"	Yes/No	1

Membership category table

Name		Type	Size
Category No	*Index*: Primary Key	Byte	1
Category Type	*Required*: True	Text	15
Membership Fee	*Required*: True	Currency	8

Tutor table

Name		Type	Size
Lastname	*Index*: Primary Key	Text	25
Initials		Text	3
Title		Text	10
Street	*Required*: True	Text	30
Town	*Default value*: Chelmer	Text	25
	Required: True		
County	*Default value*: Cheshire	Text	20
	Required: True		
Post Code	*Format:*>	Text	20
Telephone No		Text	12
National Insurance No		Text	10
Date of Birth	*Format*: d/m/yy	Date/Time	8
Qualifications		Memo	0

Class list table

Name		Type
Class No	*Index*: Primary Key	Number (Long)
Membership No	*Index*: Primary Key	Number (Long)

Stock Levels table

Name		Type
Item code	*Index*: Primary Key	Number (Integer)
Item		Text
Stock		Number (Integer)
Re-order level		Number (Integer)

Quick reference 2

Basic Windows operations

If you have not previously used Windows, you are strongly recommended to run through the tutorial that is supplied as part of the Windows package to introduce new users to Windows. Though Windows comes in many varieties, the key operations are the same in the 97, 2000, Millenium and NT editions.

This appendix briefly summarises some of the key operations and should act as a ready reference to some of the terminology that is used elsewhere in the book.

Mouse pointer shapes

When the mouse is pointed at different parts of the screen, the pointer shape changes to show it is ready to perform different tasks. Some commands also change the pointer shape.

This table lists some common pointer shapes as encountered in Access.

Pointer	Meaning
I	The pointer is over a text area. Click to position an insertion point where text may be typed.
▷	The pointer appears over menus, non-text areas of windows, inactive windows, scroll bars or toolbars. You can choose from a menu or click a button. You can use the pointer to drag (hold down the left mouse button while you draw an area on-screen, then release the button) to make a selection.
✛	The pointer is over the edge of a cell. You can select the cell now.
⧗	Access is performing a task that will take a few seconds.
↔	Appears along the borders between window sections or columns
↨	Drag to resize the section or row.
▷?	The Help pointer appears after you press _Shift+F1_. You can now point to any item on the screen and click to view specific Help.
✛	This pointer appears when you have selected **Move** or **Size** from the **Control** menu. You can move the window to a new position or drag the window border.
↓	This pointer appears over the grey bar at the top of a column in a table, query or filter. Click to select the column.

➡ This pointer appears in the record selection bar. Click to select the record.

↖ This is the drag and drop pointer, which appears when you make a selection. Drag the selection to its new location and release the mouse button to drop or insert the selection.

🔍 This is the zoom pointer which appears in print preview, allowing you to magnify and reduce the size of the on-screen preview.

↔↕↖↗ The pointer is on the sizing handle of a window or a control. The shape varies according to the handle. Drag to resize the object.

☝ In form or report design this pointer is used to move an individual label or control.

✋ In form or report design this pointer is used to move a label and control pair, or a selected group of controls.

+ This pointer appears next to a Toolbox icon and indicates the position of the control on the form or report design. Click to position the control.

Basics of Windows: a Quick Review

The Windows screen has the following features.

Menu bar

The menu bar shows the titles of the various pull-down menus that are available with a given application. To select a menu option, first select the menu by placing the mouse pointer over the name of the menu on the menu bar and click the left mouse button. The menu will appear. Move the mouse pointer to the menu option you require and click the left mouse button again. Note that any menu options displayed in light grey are not currently available. Menus can also be accessed via the keyboard: press the *Alt* key together with the underlined letter of the menu option, e.g. to select the **File** menu press *Alt+F*.

Control menu

The Control menu is found on all application and document windows. To access it, click on the Control Menu icon in the far left of the title bar, or press *Alt+Spacebar*. The exact contents are different for different windows, but typically include such basic window operations as Restore, Move, Size, Minimize, Maximize and Close.

Maximize, minimize and restore buttons

Clicking on the Maximize button 🔲 enlarges a window to its maximum size, so that it fills the whole desktop.

Clicking on the Minimize button ⬛ reduces the window to an icon on the Taskbar. When you shrink an application window to an icon, the application is still running in memory, but its window is not taking up space on your desktop.

Clicking on the **Restore** button ⬒ will restore a minimized or maximized window to its previous size.

Clicking on the **Close** button ☒ closes the window.

Title bar

The title bar tells you which window is displayed. You can move a window by dragging on its title bar (as long as the window is not maximized, i.e. not taking up the whole screen).

Taskbar

At the bottom of your screen is the Taskbar. It contains the **Start** button, which you use to quickly start a program, find a file, or get Help. Beside the Start button you will probably see some small icons which are used to get to common applications quickly.

When you start an application, a button appears on the task bar with the name of the application and current document name (if a document is open). You can use this button to switch between the application windows you have open.

Dialog boxes

Windows uses dialog boxes to request information from you, and to provide information to you. Most dialog boxes include options, with each option asking for a different kind of information.

After all the requested information has been supplied, you choose a command button to carry out the command. Two that feature on every dialog box are **OK** and **Cancel**. **OK** causes the command to be executed, **Cancel** cancels the operation and removes the dialog box from the screen. These buttons represent the two means of quitting from a dialog box. To choose a command button, click on it, or if the button is currently active (highlighted by a thickened border), press the _Enter_ key.

There are a number of different kinds of controls found in dialog boxes.

❑ Text boxes are where you can type in text, such as a filename. The presence of a flashing vertical bar, or the insertion point, indicates that the text box is active and that you may enter text. If the text box is not active, place the mouse pointer on the box and click. The insertion point will then appear in the box.

❑ List boxes show a column of available choices. Items can usually be selected from a list box by clicking on the item; in some situations you may need to double-click.

❑ Check boxes are used to control options that you can switch on and off. You can select as many or as few check box options as are applicable. When an option in a check box is selected it contains a ✓ ; otherwise the box is empty. To select a check box, click on the empty box.

❑ Radio buttons appear as a set of mutually exclusive options – you can select only one at a time, though this can be changed by selecting a different button. The selected button contains a black dot. To select a radio button, click on it.

❏ Scroll bars appear at the side of windows and list boxes. They appear when the information contained in a window cannot be displayed wholly within that window. Both vertical and horizontal scroll bars may be present, depending on whether the contents of the window are too long or too wide to fit inside it.

The small block in the middle of the bar represents the position of the currently displayed portion of the whole object. You can move to a different position in the object by moving this block. You can move it either by clicking on the scroll bar arrow boxes, clicking on the scroll bar itself, or by dragging the block.

Quick reference 3

Access Toolbars

Access window

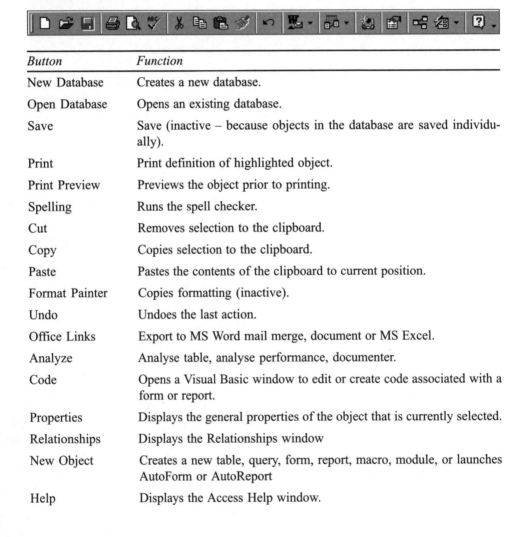

Button	Function
New Database	Creates a new database.
Open Database	Opens an existing database.
Save	Save (inactive – because objects in the database are saved individually).
Print	Print definition of highlighted object.
Print Preview	Previews the object prior to printing.
Spelling	Runs the spell checker.
Cut	Removes selection to the clipboard.
Copy	Copies selection to the clipboard.
Paste	Pastes the contents of the clipboard to current position.
Format Painter	Copies formatting (inactive).
Undo	Undoes the last action.
Office Links	Export to MS Word mail merge, document or MS Excel.
Analyze	Analyse table, analyse performance, documenter.
Code	Opens a Visual Basic window to edit or create code associated with a form or report.
Properties	Displays the general properties of the object that is currently selected.
Relationships	Displays the Relationships window
New Object	Creates a new table, query, form, report, macro, module, or launches AutoForm or AutoReport
Help	Displays the Access Help window.

Database window

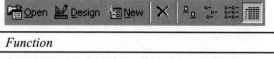

Button	Function
Open	Opens or runs the selected database object.
Design	Opens the selected object in Design view.
New	New form, report, table, etc.
Delete	Delete selected database object.
Large icons	Displays database objects in large icons. Icons can be dragged anywhere in the window, like icons on a desktop.
Small icons	Displays database objects in small icons.
List	Displays database objects with small icons in columns (layout cannot be changed).
Details	Lists database objects with details such as file size and creation date.

Table design view

Button	Function
View	Displays the data in the table in the form of a datasheet.
Save	Saves the table.
Print	Print (inactive).
Print Preview	Print preview (inactive).
Spelling	Spell check (inactive).
Cut	Removes selection to the clipboard.
Copy	Copies selection to the clipboard.
Paste	Pastes the contents of the clipboard to current position.
Format Painter	Copies formatting (inactive).
Undo	Undoes the last action.
Primary Key	Sets primary key for selected field(s).
Indexes	Displays the Indexes dialog box.
Insert Rows	Inserts a row above the current row.
Delete Rows	Deletes the current row(s).
Properties	Displays properties of table.
Build	Displays a tool for defining the selected item or property, often as an expression (only enabled if builder available).
Database window	Displays the Database window.
New Object	Creates a new table, query, form, report, macro, module, or launches AutoForm or AutoReport.
Help	Displays the Access Help window.

Query design view

Button	Function
View mode	Displays the data in the query in the form of a datasheet.
Save	Saves the query.
Print	Print (inactive).
Print Preview	Print preview (inactive).
Spelling	Spell check (inactive).
Cut	Removes selection to the clipboard.
Copy	Copies selection to the clipboard.
Paste	Pastes the contents of the clipboard to current position.
Format Painter	Copies formatting (inactive).
Undo	Undoes the last action.
Query Type	Drop-down list for the type of query: Select Query (default type), Crosstab query for summarising data, Make Table query, Update query, Append query or Delete query.
Run	Runs the query.
Show Table	Displays the Show Table dialog box for adding tables to a query.
Totals	Displays total row in QBE grid for statistical summary.
Top Values	Finds the top values in the active query based on a percentage or number of rows.
Properties	Displays the properties of the query.
Build	Displays the Expression builder.
Database window	Displays the Database window.
New Object	Creates a new table, query, form, report, macro, module, or launches AutoForm or AutoReport.
Help	Displays the Access Help window.

Datasheet and form view

Button	Function
Design view	Displays table in Design view for modification.
Save	Saves the table layout.
Print	Prints the datasheet.
Print Preview	Displays a print preview.
Spelling	Spell check.
Cut	Removes selection to the clipboard.

Copy	Copies selection to the clipboard.
Paste	Pastes from the clipboard to current position.
Format Painter	Copies formatting (inactive).
Undo	Undoes the last action.
Insert Hyperlink	Inserts or modifies a hyperlink address.
Sort Ascending	Displays records in ascending order of current field.
Sort Descending	Displays records in descending order of current field.
Filter by Selection	Filters records based on selected data.
Filter by Form	Displays a form for the entry of filter criteria.
Apply Filter	Displays filtered records.
Find	Search for selected data.
New Record	Go to new record.
Delete Record	Removes record.
Database window	Displays the Database window.
New Object	Creates a new table, query, form, report, macro, module, or launches AutoForm or AutoReport.
Help	Displays the Access Help window.

Form design view

Top row

Button	Function
View	Runs the form.
Save	Saves the form.
Print	Prints the form.
Print Preview	Displays the print preview.
Spelling	Spell check (inactive).
Cut	Removes selection to the clipboard.
Copy	Copies selection to the clipboard.
Paste	Pastes from the clipboard to current position.
Format Painter	Copies formatting from one control to another; double-click to copy to several controls, *Esc* to finish.
Undo	Undoes the last action.
Insert Hyperlink	Inserts or modifies a hyperlink address.
Field List	Displays the field list window.
Toolbox	Displays the Toolbox as a window or toolbar.

AutoFormat	Applies your choice of predefined formats to the form.
Code	Displays an Access Basic form module in the Module window.
Properties	Displays the properties sheet.
Build	Displays a builder for the selected item or property (only enabled if builder available).
Database window	Displays Database window.
New Object	Creates a new table, query, form, report, macro, module, or launches AutoForm or AutoReport.
Help	Displays the Access Help window.

Bottom row

Button	Function
Object	Select a section of a form, a control, or the entire form.
Font	Drop-down list of fonts.
Font Size	Drop-down list of font sizes.
Bold	Applies bold typeface.
Italic	Applies italic typeface.
Underline	Applies underlining.
Align Left	Aligns contents of label or control to the left.
Center	Centres contents of label or control.
Align Right	Aligns contents of label or control to the right.
Fill/Back Color	Drop-down background colour selection.
Font/Fore Color	Drop-down foreground colour selection.
Line/Border Color	Drop-down border colour selection.
Line/Border Width	Drop-down border width selection.
Special Effect	Drop-down special effect (raised, sunken, etc.) selection.

Report design view

Top row

Button	Function
View	Previews report.
Save	Saves the report.
Print	Prints report.
Print Preview	Displays a print preview.
Spelling	Spell check (inactive).

Cut	Removes selection to the clipboard.
Copy	Copies selection to the clipboard.
Paste	Pastes from the clipboard to current position.
Format Painter	Copies formatting from one control to another; double-click to copy to several controls, _Esc_ to finish.
Undo	Undoes the last action.
Insert Hyperlink	Inserts or modifies a hyperlink address.
Field List	Displays the Field list window.
Toolbox	Displays the Toolbox window.
Sorting and grouping	Displays the Sorting and Grouping dialog box.
AutoFormat	Applies your choice of predefined formats to the report.
Code	Displays an Access Basic report module in the Module window.
Properties	Displays the properties sheet.
Build	Displays a builder for the selected item or property (only enabled if builder available).
Database window	Displays Database window.
New Object	Creates a new table, query, form, report, macro, module, or launches AutoForm or AutoReport.
Help	Displays the Access Help window.

Bottom row

Button	Function
Object	Select a section of a report, a control, or the entire report.
Font Name	Drop-down list of fonts.
Font Size	Drop-down list of font sizes.
Bold	Applies bold typeface.
Italic	Applies italic typeface.
Underline	Applies underlining.
Align Left	Aligns contents of label or control to the left.
Center	Centres contents of label or control.
Align Right	Aligns contents of label or control to the right.
Fill/Back Color	Drop-down background colour selection.
Font/Fore Color	Drop-down foreground colour selection.
Line/Border Color	Drop-down border colour selection.
Line/Border Width	Drop-down border width selection.
Special Effect	Drop-down special effect (raised, sunken, etc.) selection.

Report and form print preview

Button	Function
View	Displays report or form in Design view for modification.
Print	Print.
Zoom	Zoom in or out.
One Page	Displays print preview one-page format.
Two Pages	Displays print preview two-page format.
Multiple pages	Displays print preview multiple-page format.
Zoom	Controls the amount of magnification.
Close	Closes preview and returns to design.
OfficeLinks	**Merge It with MS Word**: Merges the output of a table, query, form, report or module with a Word document – to insert names and addresses into a form letter, for instance.
	Publish It with MS Word: Displays the output of a table, query, form, report or module as a Word document.
	Analyze It with MS Excel: Displays the output of a table, query, form, report or module as a n Excel spreadsheet.
Database window	Displays the Database window.
New Object	Creates a new table, query, form, report, macro, module, or launches AutoForm or AutoReport.
Help	Displays the Access Help window.

Glossary

Access	A relational database product.
Alignment	When applied to a group of controls, this refers to their position relative to each other. When applied to a single control, it refers to the position of text within the control frame.
Case sensitive	Distinguishing between upper and lower case text.
Check boxes	Boxes offering a list of options which you can switch on or off.
Control	An individual design element of a report or form.
Control menu	The menu found on all windows accessed by clicking on the Control Menu icon in the far left of the title bar.
Data type	The type of data allowed in a particular field.
Database	A collection of related data.
DataBase Management System (DBMS)	Software used to manipulate and present data held in a computer.
Database window	The principal window of a database, giving you access to all the tables, queries and other database objects within it.
Datasheet view	The view in which you can view and enter data in tables.
Default value	A value entered automatically by Access in a field in a new record.
Design view	The view in which you can create and modify tables, forms, reports and queries.
Detail	The detail section of a form or report, i.e. the actual data from records in a database.
Dialog box	A box used to request or provide information.
Dynaset	A temporary table produced as the result of a query.
Field	A piece of data within a record.
Field description	The description of a field. It may be up to 255 characters long.
Field list	A list of fields that a form was based upon.
Field name	The name of a field. Field names can be up to 64 characters including spaces. Full stops (.), exclamation marks (!) and square brackets ([ ]) are not allowed.
Field properties	Detailed definitions of a data type.

Filter	A means of displaying selected records.
Font	The style of text, like a typeface in printing.
Form	An on-screen method of collecting information for a database.
Group footer	A section marking the end of a group in a report.
Group header	A section marking the beginning of a group in a report.
Grouped report	A report with selected fields placed in a row. Records are grouped according to the value of a field in the table or query.
Inner-join	A kind of relationship between tables. It displays all the records in one table that have corresponding records in another table.
List boxes	Boxes showing a column of available choices.
Macro	Series of keystrokes or steps that can be set to run automatically or when a user performs a certain action.
Mailing label reports	Reports for creating mailing labels.
Make table query	A kind of query which selects data from a table (or more than one) and creates a new table from that data.
Maximize button	The button that enlarges a window to its maximum size.
Menu bar	The bar showing titles of various pull-down menus that are available in an application.
Minimize button	The button that reduces a window to a small icon at the bottom of the screen.
Module	Programs or sets of instructions designed to perform a specific task or series of tasks.
Null value	An empty field.
One-to-one relationship	Relationship between tables where for a particular field in one table there is only one matching record in the other.
One-to-many relationship	Relationship between tables where for one field in one table there are many matching records in the other.
Option buttons	A list of mutually exclusive items on a form, only one of which can be selected by a user.
Page footer	A section that appears at the bottom of every page of a report.
Page header	A section that appears at the top of each page of a report such as a running title and page number.
Preview	An on-screen preview of how a page will look when printed.
Primary key	A field or combination of fields that uniquely identifies a record.
Properties sheet	A list of properties of a component of a form or report, which determine its appearance, behaviour and the data it holds.

Queries	A method of asking questions of a database.
Query By Example (QBE)	A method of querying by which you give the database an example of what you are looking for, and instruct it to find similar records.
Query criteria	The method of framing questions to allow specific records to be retrieved from the database.
Query Design window	The window from which you design a query.
Record	A set of details about an individual item. Each item has a separate record in the table.
Report	Collection of data, usually the result of a query, designed and formatted for printing.
Report footer	A section that appears at the very end of a report.
Report header	A section that appears at the very beginning of a report.
Restore button	The button that restores a minimized or maximized window to its previous size.
Row selector symbols	Symbols at the edge of a table row, which you click on to select a row of information.
Screen form	Interfaces which give access to the tables and queries in a database in a user-friendly way, instead of directly in Datasheet view.
Scroll bars	Bars which appear at the side of windows and list boxes when all the information cannot be displayed within the window. They allow you to scroll through the information.
Single-column form	A form which allows the user to input one record at a time.
Single-column report	A report with all selected fields in a single column.
String	A collection of characters (letters, numbers, and punctuation marks) that make up the data in a field.
Table Design window	The interface that allows you to define the structure of your table.
Tables	The primary building block of a database – a table holds data in a grid, where each column holds a particular kind of information about an item, and each row holds a different item.
Tabular form	A form which displays more than one record on the screen.
Task bar	The bar at the bottom of the screen containing the Windows Start button and buttons for active windows.
Text boxes	Boxes which allow you to type in text.
Title bar	Top section of a window containing the name of the window. Changes colour to indicate whether the window is active or inactive.

Toolbox   A selection of tools with which controls and text are added to a form or report.

Unbound form   A blank form which does not draw data from an associated table or query.

Update query   A kind of query which selects records from a table and changes the data in them.

Validation rules   Tests used to detect mistakes in data entry.

Wizards   Series of dialog boxes which help you create forms, reports, etc. using preset values.

Zero length string   "" empty quotes, used to indicate that there is no data for the field in that record.

Index